SACRED
STRATEGIES

• • •

SACRED
STRATEGIES

Transforming Synagogues from Functional to Visionary

• • •

ISA ARON
STEVEN M. COHEN
LAWRENCE A. HOFFMAN
ARI Y. KELMAN

THE
ALBAN
INSTITUTE
Herndon, Virginia
www.alban.org

The Alban Institute
2121 Cooperative Way, Suite 100
Herndon, VA 20171

Peah 1:1 in chapter 4 is from *Gates of Prayer*, translation copyright © 1985 Central Conference of American Rabbis.

Cover design by Spark Design.

Library of Congress Cataloging-in-Publication Data

Aron, Isa.

  Sacred strategies : transforming synagogues from functional to visionary / Isa Aron, Steven M. Cohen, Lawrence A. Hoffman, and Ari Y. Kelman.

    p. cm.

  Includes bibliographical references.

  ISBN 978-1-56699-401-9

  1. Synagogues--United States--History--21st century. 2. Jewish leadership--United States--History--21st century. 3. Judaism--United States--History--21st century. I. Cohen, Steven Martin. II. Hoffman, Lawrence A., 1942- III. Kelman, Ari Y., 1971- IV. Title.

  BM653.A755 2010

  296.6'50973--dc22

                        2010005514

10   11   12   13   14   VG   5   4   3   2

*To the wonderful lay and professional leaders
at eight inspiring congregations:*

*Beth Jacob Congregation, Mendota Heights, Minnesota
Congregation Agudath Israel, Caldwell, New Jersey
Congregation Beth Am, Los Altos Hills, California
Congregation Beth Shalom, Overland Park, Kansas
Temple Beth Elohim, Wellesley, Massachusetts
Temple Israel, Boston, Massachusetts
Temple Micah, Washington, D.C.
Westchester Reform Temple, Scarsdale, New York*

Contents

◆ ◆ ◆

Acknowledgments

• • •

For the four authors, this project has been both an incredible learning experience and a rewarding partnership. Each time we would gather together to discuss our research or writing, we would remark at how enjoyable it was to work together. We have been blessed with this opportunity to learn from one another, and from everyone who gave of their time, energy, and support.

We owe a great debt of gratitude to everyone who took valuable time to speak with us about their lives and their congregations. We conducted most of our interviews between 2005 and 2006, studying eight congregations: Congregation Agudath Israel (Caldwell, NJ), Congregation Beth Am (Los Altos Hills, CA), Beth Jacob Congregation (Mendota Heights, MN), Congregation Beth Elohim (Wellesley, MA), Congregation Beth Shalom (Overland Park, KS), Temple Israel (Boston, MA), Temple Micah (Washington, DC), Westchester Reform Temple (Scarsdale, NY). We spoke with more than 175 people, each of whom generously shared his or her experience, observations, and insight with us. (Please see their names listed in appendix A). We would also like to thank the members and leaders of the eight congregations who agreed to participate in this work anonymously. To everyone who lent their voices to this work, and to their congregations: Thank you—for your hospitality, your wisdom, and your generosity of spirit. Your voices have made this book what it is.

This project was funded through the generosity of several foundations and individuals:

- The Commission on Jewish Identity and Renewal of UJA-Federation of New York. In particular, we would like to thank Rabbi Deborah Joselow and Dru Greenwood for their continued guidance and support.
- The Nathan Cummings Foundation, and Rabbi Jennie Rosenn, in particular.
- The Combined Jewish Philanthropies of Boston, and Barry Shrage, in particular.
- Arthur Winn of Boston
- Synagogue 2000
- The Esther F. and William J. Bushman Beth Shalom Endowment Fund of the Jewish Community Foundation of Greater Kansas City
- An anonymous donor

We thank them for believing in us, and in this project.

Ari Y. Kelman conducted most of the interviews at the eight synagogues that are featured in this study. Rabbi Adam Allenberg and Rabbi Karen Sherman, both of whom were students at the time, conducted interviews at eight additional congregations that also participated in Experiment in Congregational Education (ECE) and Synagogue 2000 (S2K). They were diligent and effective interviewers, and helpful to us in conceptualizing the study. We also thank Rabbi Rachel Kort and Rachel Margolis for their work in coding these interviews.

Two consultants discussed our findings and offered valuable critique of our writing at critical junctures. We thank Professors Barbara Kirschenblatt-Gimblett and Riv-Ellen Prell for their expertise and their insight, but, even more, for their ability to prod us to think (and to write) more deeply.

Before being sent to the publishers, our manuscript was pruned by Rabbi Suzanne Singer and Lynn Flanzbaum. At the Alban Institute, the manuscript benefited greatly from the discerning eye of Acquisition Editor Beth Gaede as well as the editorial suggestions and copyediting of Andrea Lee. We are deeply grateful to all four for their painstaking work in making the manuscript more readable.

We owe a debt of gratitude to Richard Bass, director of publishing at Alban, for accepting the manuscript for publication. We also thank Andrew Grant, John Merriman, Joy Merriman, and Amy Blumenthal for their assistance at various stages of the project.

Finally, we thank the friends, colleagues, relatives, and students who read portions of the manuscript (sometimes two or three times) with red pencils in their hands. They are: Dr. Bill Aron, Amy Asin, Rabbi Laura Geller, Dru Greenwood, Dr. Tali Hyman, Rabbi Marion Lev-Cohen, Dr. Michelle Lynn-Sachs, Professor Sara Lee, Richard Siegel, Rabbi Rachel Timoner, Dr. Rob Weinberg, and Cyd Weissman.

CHAPTER I

Snapshots of Visionary:
The Congregations We Studied

Had Marty Prosky and his family not moved to a new neighborhood, they might never have experienced the joys of Shabbat. Their old synagogue was "comfortable" but not "spiritually uplifting." After their move, Marty and his wife went synagogue shopping and ended up at Temple Micah in Washington, D.C.

> What's wonderful about [the Micah "family minyan"] is that they will actually go through a Shabbat service and . . . you'll learn the Hebrew, you'll learn the tune and you'll learn the English, and you'll learn why you're saying it, and talk about it. And it's exactly what I needed thirty years ago to make the Shabbat service meaningful. . . .
>
> We have gone to services more in the last year than probably any ten or fifteen years. . . . On the average, it's probably one or two times a month, which is a lot more than we would ever have gone to our [previous synagogue]. And we're always happy when we have. . . . Every Friday night that we said, "We really want to go to temple," and we do it, we were always very happy and the kids are always happy. I can't really say that that's a synagogue experience that I have had anywhere.

Nancy Michaels's oldest daughter had attended the typical Sunday morning "drop-off" religious school program at Westchester

Reform Temple in Scarsdale, New York. By the time their younger children reached the religious-school age, the synagogue had introduced "Sharing Shabbat," an alternative family experience that parents attended along with their children.

> It sounded really good, to do something with your child. . . . We loved it. . . . Whenever I went to services I always felt good. . . . Being there with your kid was just so special. . . . I don't think I had ever done Torah study before. I can't say I was an active participant, but I always liked listening and learning, and it was new to me. . . . I liked being with the people and having a community. It was like a home away from home, in a way.

What enabled Marty Prosky and Nancy Michaels to experience synagogue life in a new way? What inspired them to become active, enthusiastic participants, rather than nominal members who paid their dues but rarely took part in the congregation's activities? They were fortunate to have found congregations that were entrepreneurial, experimental, and committed to engaging their members. In these synagogues, even congregants who join with minimal expectations find themselves drawn to the spirituality of worship, the intellectual challenge of Torah study, and the warmth and obligations of a Jewish community. This book is about eight synagogues that reached out to people like Marty Prosky and Nancy Michaels and helped them connect to Jewish life in a new way.

Ordinary and Extraordinary Synagogues

To most American Jews, the synagogue is a vehicle for temporary Jewish affiliation, while married and with children living at home. From 60 to 70 percent of all Jews join synagogues at some point in their lives, but only 40 percent are members at any given time; and only a fraction of that 40 percent is actively engaged in what the synagogue does—most synagogues see no more than 20 percent of that 40 percent on a regular basis. The other 80 percent join just for High Holiday seats, a bar or bat mitzvah for their children, and a rabbi on call for life-cycle events and hospital visits—in other words, a place to acquire Jewish "goods and services."

The parking lot may be full every Shabbat but the cars vary from week to week, depending on the bar or bat mitzvah family and guests who have taken over the sanctuary. In the words of one rabbi, "It's the facade of success. The sanctuary is full, but no one is becoming very Jewish." Similarly, despite a flurry of classroom activity on school days, the vast majority of students are under thirteen. While the terms *family* and *community* are repeated often, congregants don't form deep or abiding friendships; they feel as isolated when they leave as when they arrived. And while hundreds may turn out for an annual "mitzvah day," social justice is barely mentioned during the remaining 364 days of the year.

To be sure, not all synagogues and not all congregants fit this description. Members of Orthodox congregations, for example, attend more regularly on Shabbat and holidays, particularly since the 1980s.[1] And among non-Orthodox Jews as well,[2] a number of synagogues can boast of strong, organic communities.[3] Every synagogue, moreover, has at least some loyalists who attend regularly and participate actively. Many readers of this book are likely to fall into this category.

But the large percentage of marginal synagogue members raises some important questions: Given the annual cost, why do so many Jews pay so much but attend so little? What is the difference between the marginals and the loyalists? How can some congregants describe their synagogue as "warm, welcoming, and stimulating" while others find it cold, foreboding, and uninspiring? Most important, why do some synagogues have a culture of active participation while others don't?

Despite differences among movements, all American synagogues are beset by such social forces as endemic secularity and rampant individualism. This book provides an in-depth look at eight synagogues that have bucked these trends to create cultures of wide participation and deep engagement. Their sanctuaries are filled with synagogue "regulars"; adult learning opportunities are numerous and well attended; congregants care for one another in tangible ways; and social justice is an abiding concern for more than just a social action committee. To cite a few examples:

- Shabbat morning at Congregation Agudath Israel in Caldwell, New Jersey, highlights a congregation that values sacred purpose, and accents the building of community while respecting membership diversity. On any given Shabbat, more than three hundred congregants fill the sanctuary for a lively, participatory service. For congregants seeking other avenues of engagement, the congregation hosts a weekly Torah study and a biweekly Shabbat meditation, or "Shalom Yoga." The synagogue has also developed a full roster of age-appropriate youth programs that balance worship, learning, and socializing. From "Torah for Tots" to the "Mini Minyan," "Mini Congo," and "Teen Schmooze," the halls and classrooms of the synagogue are alive with action throughout the Shabbat service. When services are over, everyone gathers for an extended kiddush, seen by the congregation's leaders as integral to the Shabbat experience because it fosters a sense of community. Rabbi Alan Silverstein explains, "My model of a good shul [is] multiple gateways to engagement."
- Carol Clingan of Temple Beth Elohim, in Wellesley, Massachusetts, knew that her congregation had changed dramatically when she compared the relative isolation she felt after her father died in 1998 to the outpouring of community support she received when her mother died in 2001. "When my father died, . . . there was no synagogue tradition of communal shiva and no involvement of the congregants in comforting mourners." By contrast, "When my mother died . . . we had people calling, people cooking, coming over,

comforting . . . the congregation changed [so much] in that short amount of time, in terms of community."

- Twice a month Congregation Beth Shalom, in Overland Park, Kansas, offers its Tefillah 2000 service, led by a group of congregant musicians and assisted by one of the rabbis, who weaves teaching and discussion into the service. Kay Grossman, a relatively new member of the congregation, explains how this service draws her in. "There is a flow to it, yes . . . the music is a huge part, but the cognitive piece is a part for me, too. . . . All in all, what happens is I just feel more spiritual." Devra Lerner, one of the musicians, appreciates the "commitment to keep the experimental openness to growth. . . . There's a sense of, 'Let's see where this leads. How can we improve and how can we touch more people?'"

The synagogues profiled in this book did not start out with cultures of engagement. Though each had successful programs, even the most loyal supporters were cognizant of ways their synagogue was failing. A parent at Beth Elohim recalls, "When my now third grader was in kindergarten, I was horrified. . . . The things that she brought home—the stupidest worksheets. They were so boring." A long-time congregant at Congregation Beth Shalom observes, "The services were routine and the words didn't have any meaning, particularly. You went because you wanted to be there and because it was a connection and a community, but the services were really not grabbing in any particular way." Most congregants assumed they would be "High Holiday Jews," drop their children off for religious education, and, maybe, attend the occasional lecture or service.

Many congregants are still bemused to find themselves attending their own Sunday morning classes as well. They did not think of themselves as having spiritual needs until they discovered unexpected comfort and inspiration at Shabbat services. They didn't realize that Torah study could be both intellectually challenging and personally moving. They didn't appreciate the value of community until they experienced it firsthand. And they were not aware that their concerns about social justice could be joined to those of others, and that, as a group, they could wield considerable political clout in their local communities.

The stories of these individuals offer powerful examples of how synagogues can help their congregants discover and fulfill previously unknown needs. Here are but three examples:

- Steven Goldman and his non-Jewish wife joined Temple Israel of Boston, looking for a place to raise their children Jewishly but hoping themselves to remain "more or less anonymous." Steven chuckles at this recollection, because ever since he discovered the Temple's social justice project, *Ohel Tzedek*, which involves people through one-on-one encounters called *mifgashim*, "I keep getting involved in more and more things. . . . It was my first experience of Jews doing social action in a very real, serious way. And it makes Judaism something that I can feel like I am a part of, because that's a real part of my understanding of what it means to be part of a community, what it means to be Jewish."

- Amy Asin, of Congregation Beth Am in Los Altos Hills, California, recalls the meeting she and her husband had with Rabbi Rick Block, when they first joined the congregation: "Rick asked us why we were joining a congregation. Barry [my husband] said, 'Because I want to build a Jewish community.' I said, 'Because I wanted a place to worship.' Rick said to us, 'That's not the point—the point is to become Jewishly educated adults.' He knew from the start it would be about learning, but we didn't."

- Darlene (a pseudonym) had just come out as a lesbian when she and her partner showed up at Rosh Hashanah services at Beth Jacob Congregation in Saint Paul, Minnesota. The elderly *gabba'i* "came over to us, and immediately offered us to come and open the ark. The two of us, together. . . . Nobody knew us from Adam. I'm not sure he even got it, what our relationship was, but that was how welcoming it was, and how welcome we felt. Wow. Here we are, and we've never been here before and we're up on the bimah and nobody seems to be blinking. And you walk in there, people are welcoming, they shake your hand, they say hello."

Behind these testimonials lies the larger story, the story of how the synagogues themselves were transformed, from "limited liability" institutions[4] to sacred communities; from shuls with schools to congregations of learners;[5] from having clergy who made hospital visits to having congregants who visit one another; from having a small and somewhat beleaguered social action committee (or no social action committee at all) to joining a citywide social justice coalition that engages a broad range of congregants.

By making such changes, these synagogues have joined a national trend in churches too. The news is filled with stories featuring evangelical megachurches transforming the face of American religious consciousness. But quietly and with much less fanfare, mainline churches too are starting to move into the twenty-first century with a new sense of intellectual, spiritual, and prophetic excitement, reaching far beyond the small band of regulars and into the very heart of the church's membership rolls.[6] If religion in America has a future beyond just its conservative right wing, it will depend on this kind of transformation of church—and synagogue—culture.

Two Decades of Concerted Change

What enabled these synagogues to embrace a larger, more ambitious vision of congregational life? And once having that vision, what enabled them to enact it? Clearly the time was ripe. In 1998, a study identified no fewer than forty local and national initiatives devoted to improving congregational life, the earliest one emerging only eight years prior.[7] By now, some of those have ended, while others have begun, so that estimating just how many exist today is difficult. But one thing is clear: interest in revitalizing synagogue life has not abated. Among leaders of the organized Jewish community, there has emerged a broad consensus affirming the centrality of renewed synagogues for a vital Jewish communal life.

As the founding directors of the oldest and largest synagogue change projects, projects that were national in scope (Isa, of the Experiment in Congregational Education, and Larry, along with Ron Wolfson, of Synagogue 2000), we knew that of the synagogues that participated, some succeeded beyond all expectations, some achieved more modest successes, and some remained largely unchanged. We also knew that a short-term evaluation did not tell the whole story. Some congregations that had impressive starts were unable to sustain momentum over time; they didn't fully understand that the goal was not simply to introduce new programs but to create a culture of change. Conversely, some congregations that seemed, at first, to be trapped by inertia surprised us by their ability to regenerate themselves.

By 2005, with the synagogue transformation movement fifteen years old, Isa and Larry joined forces with Steven Cohen to investigate the factors that went into significant and lasting change by studying eight synagogues that demonstrated success. We were fortunate to be able to hire Ari Y. Kelman as our research assistant; he conducted most of the interviews over a two-and-a-half-year period (2004–2006). Later, Ari joined us as a fourth investigator. In all, 175 synagogue leaders (rabbis, cantors, educators, and board members, past and present) and a selection of congregants, ranging from intensely committed to largely inactive, were interviewed. Our sample also included places that experienced only modest change or no change at all. (Details relating to the data collection can be found in appendix A; our interview protocol can be found in appendix B.)

As we designed this book and debated our findings, we informally referred to this as our "good to great" study—a reference to *Good to Great*, a 2001 bestseller that probed the factors that underlay exceptional corporations. We were interested in congregations that had gone from commonplace to extraordinary. We hoped to identify readiness factors and understand organizational dynamics that enabled "revolving door" synagogues delivering goods and services to become vibrant communities that inculcate intense and active Jewish living.

The authors of *Good to Great* had it relatively easy; a corporation's profit is its bottom line—an obvious measure of "good-ness" and "great-ness."[8] But what is a synagogue's bottom line? Increased attendance at services? More adult learning? More involvement in social justice? On the face of it, these seem obvious signs of progress, but the issue is more complex than one might imagine.

There are actually two indices of success, one *quantitative*—the number of participants in congregational activities; the other *qualitative*—the degree to which congregants engage in these activities and the impact these activities have on them. Of the two, the *quantitative* is harder to document. Churches see worship as so central that they count worshipers from week to week as a measure of success. Synagogues, however, see worship as but one of many ways to identify as Jews. How could we possibly count every study group, mitzvah project, and lecture series? However, ample *qualitative* evidence could be gathered by asking congregants about their experiences. Though we can't reduce synagogue greatness to a set of numbers, we can paint a convincing picture of it through the interviews we conducted and the stories people shared.

As we sifted through our data, certain patterns became clear. The synagogues in our study successfully challenged their congregants to be life-long, year-round, thoroughly committed and practicing Jews.[9] We call these synagogues "visionary." Visionary synagogues have six characteristics in common:

- *Sacred purpose*: a pervasive and shared vision infuses all aspects of the synagogue.
- *Holistic ethos*: the parts are related to each other, such that the whole is greater than the sum of its parts. *Torah, avodah*, and *g'milut chasadim* are intertwined throughout synagogue life.
- *Participatory culture*, on all levels: congregants, lay leaders, professionals, and family members of all ages engage in the work of creating sacred community.
- *Meaningful engagement* is achieved through repeated inspirational experiences that infuse people's lives with meaning.
- *Innovation disposition* is marked by a search for diversity and alternatives and a high tolerance for possible failure.
- *Reflective leadership and governance* are marked by careful examination of alternatives, a commitment to overarching purpose, attention to relationships, mastery of both big picture and detail, and a planful approach to change.

Part 1 of this book demonstrates how these characteristics are exemplified in practice. Chapter 2 gives a more detailed picture of the six characteristics of visionary congregations, illustrating them with the reflections of those we interviewed. In chapters 3 through 5, we focus more closely on what being visionary means for the four central aspects of synagogue life: worship, learning, community building, and social justice.[10] These chapters paint a picture of what greatness looks like in each core area, as seen at a number of the congregations in our study. Having painted a composite portrait of excellence in congregational life, we turn, in part 2, to the questions with which we began: What enabled some congregations to become visionary? What hindered others from doing so? What theories of organizational life are helpful in understanding synagogue change? What advice might we give to congregational leaders who would like to transform their congregations, and to federations and foundations that seek to support this transformation?

Our hope is that this book will help a variety of audiences: synagogue leaders looking for ways to transform their congregations; federations and foundations interested in encouraging and supporting this transformation; and researchers in the field of congregational studies who, we hope, will find many questions and issues they would like to explore further.

PART I

Exploring
Congregational Vision

• • •

CHAPTER 2

A Portrait of "Visionary":
The Characteristics We Saw

Congregational leaders who embark upon change efforts develop contrasting images of the qualities they seek in their congregation and of the characteristics they hope to shed, transcend, or avoid.[1] They aspire to become what we call *visionary congregations*, those that most effectively develop, nurture, and apply powerful, widely shared, and widely understood visions of the sacred community. In contrast, they distinguish their communities from what we call *functional congregations*, those that may excel at performing discrete functions that satisfy their consumer-members but tend to fall short of genuinely achieving an integrated sense of sacred community.

The composite images we draw here emerge clearly from our interviews with the lay and professional leaders of eight transformed congregations. Not only can they point to their currently held view of their congregation's ideal features, some can also point to the time when their dreams began to take shape and when their dissatisfactions came into sharper focus.

A critique of the present is essential for a vision of a better future to emerge and is intrinsic to the synagogue change effort. All engaged congregational leaders had to face their congregations' shortcomings and envision the ideal state to which they could realistically aspire. The transformation of Temple Beth Elohim in Wellesley, Massachusetts, provides one example of how congregational leaders become dissatisfied with the current state of affairs and develop a vision of a far more compelling alternative. Leaders of this congregation trace the start of their intentional change efforts to a provocative intervention by the local federation head, Barry Shrage. In 1995 this gutsy and highly regarded Jewish communal professional publicly took the congregational leaders to task for failing to make the most of their community.

Shrage's challenge was aimed not only at the congregation but also at individuals, asking them to reflect on the discrepancy between their knowledge of Western civilization and their ignorance of their Jewish heritage. He challenged them to take a more thoughtful approach to their Jewish choices. For Terri Rosenberg these remarks really hit home:

> It is sad that, in general, we are not embarrassed about being Jewishly ignorant. Moreover, I didn't even think about my ignorance—it was a blind spot and therefore quite an aha moment when I saw the contrast between how I approached the Jewish education of my children and how I approached everything else. Barry sounded the alarm and woke me up to my passivity and lack of responsibility for a legacy of 3,500 years that I was willing to abandon by default. He forced me to ask myself the question, "Is Judaism meaningful enough to me to want to pass it on to my children, and if the answer is yes, how will I do that if I am illiterate myself?" I realized that at the very least, I needed to make an informed choice, which for me meant learning Jewish texts. Once I experienced the beauty and meaning of Torah, my life changed.

Congregational transformation, then, began with the leaders' coming to grips with the inadequacy of their own Jewish lives and that of their congregation. Dissatisfaction with the seemingly adequate, functional present was a necessary prelude to envisioning the extraordinary congregation they wanted to become.

Through the course of our interviews, our key informants provided contrasts between "the congregation we once were" and the
"congregation we have now become." Some spoke of *them* (other,
more typical congregations) versus *us* (a very special congregation), distinguishing the ordinary and mediocre congregation
from the extraordinary and vital congregation.

The Functional Congregation

The eight synagogues we studied varied in many ways: size, denomination, region of the country, surrounding population density, Jewish population size, leadership style, resources, and more.
These variations notwithstanding, a synthesis of their remarks
points to two distinct types of congregations, functional and visionary. Plainly evident in this portrait are some of the key ingredients of the functional congregation: consumerist purpose,
segmentation, passivity, meaninglessness, resistance to change,
and lack of reflectiveness.

CONSUMERIST PURPOSE

Most contemporary American synagogues outside of Orthodoxy
appeal to their congregants largely through the services and programs they offer. Among the services most widely sought after are
a fitting venue to celebrate a bar or bat mitzvah, the requisite religious school education to prepare the child for this widely celebrated life-cycle event, worship services on Rosh Hashanah and
Yom Kippur, and the availability of the rabbi to attend to weddings, funerals, and hospital visits. Larry Hoffman terms these
"limited liability communities," defined as "a particular class of
market community, offering specialized services for a fee."[2]

Congregations that provide their congregants with discrete
services may indeed give the appearance of succeeding. They
may attract large numbers of members, albeit with a high rate of

turnover. They may provide well-administered services, be they for worship or education. And they may produce balanced budgets and financial stability. Isa Aron describes the functional congregation as follows:

> The atmosphere . . . is quiet and businesslike. Its schedule is regular and predictable. In the mornings the nursery school children arrive; in midafternoon . . . the religious school students begin streaming in. . . . On most evenings small clusters of adults come in. . . . They sort themselves quickly, and rarely linger in the hallways. On Friday nights and Saturday mornings hushed murmurs can be heard in the sanctuary. . . . A problem lurks beneath the surface: Most of the adult activities are run by the same small group of people, week in and week out. These . . . synagogue "regulars" . . . are proud of the congregation, but in truth they feel a bit beleaguered. They wonder why most of their fellow congregants don't participate more often, and why these others don't seem to value the institution in which they have invested so much of themselves.[3]

At its heart, the notion of consumerist purpose is about the relationship between the congregation and its members, and their relationships with one another. In the absence of a commanding and inspiring vision for itself as a sacred community of caring members, the functional congregation focuses on the provision of sought-after services to paying customers, who are seen—and see themselves—as consumers of services rather than members of a sacred community.

SEGMENTATION

Functional congregations are distinguished not only by the nature of the services they provide their consumer-members, but also in the manner in which they are structured to provide and deliver these services. In functional congregations, services are produced and delivered discretely, in segments, with little relationship to one another. Worship, the religious school, adult programs, and administration all function independently, without synergy.

Segmentation of functions can take a number of forms. One is spatial; many congregations are architecturally constructed to segregate such functions as worship, children's education, adult education, and social action. Another is programmatic. For example, board meetings are devoted exclusively to administrative matters with little attention to personal meaning and engagement, and little reference to overall purpose. Worship often lacks opportunities for learning or for putting worship into action through acts of caring or social justice.

Still another manifestation of segmentation can be seen in the relations between the various members of the synagogue and the several subcommunities of which they are a part. Parents are not involved with their children's studies; children are often unwelcome at adult-oriented services; board members have little to do with the liturgical life of the congregation; regular attendees at one worship service have little interaction with those who regularly attend a service meeting at a different hour.

Segmentation can also apply to institutional mission. Functional congregations understand their mandate narrowly, as existing separate and apart from the other local Jewish communities and the larger society. They view their paying members as their sole constituency. Hoffman's formulation of "congregational atomism" denotes "the assumption that synagogues, like atoms, are autonomous entities, rather than parts of a larger whole, the community."[4] In contrast with the atomistic or segmented approach, a more holistic approach sees the spirit and practice of torah not just in the classroom, *avodah* not just in the sanctuary, and *g'milut chasadim* not just the province of the caring or social action committee. Rather, the visionary congregation sees the classroom, the sanctuary, and the variety of committees as all suffused with commitment to learning, piety, and loving-kindness.

PASSIVITY

In functional congregations' highly rationalized (that is, clean and efficient) service delivery system, the expert professionals—clergy, educators, and administrators—produce, manage, market, and deliver the sought-after services. (This observation is more applicable to larger congregations than to smaller ones where the congregation relies on a small core of volunteers to do much of this work.) But the excessive reliance on highly skilled professionals comes with a price: passivity, a condition marked by congregants' lack of participation and engagement in congregational activity. Worshipers sit quietly watching the performance of the clerics on the bimah. Parents drop off their children at religious school, handing over full educational responsibility to professional school directors. Board members focus on managerial issues rather than tackling core challenges of sacred mission and strategic action. They leave real decision making to the rabbi, other professionals, and a small inner circle of donors and volunteers.

The struggle to encourage participation can persist despite repeated efforts to counteract a culture of passivity. For years Congregation Beth Shalom, a conservative congregation in suburban Kansas City, has sought to make worship services more participatory. In 1998 the rabbis and key lay leaders instituted an innovative worship service, known as Tefillah 2000, as an alternative to the traditional service in the main sanctuary. This service introduced musical instruments and a more participatory style of worship, where more of the service is chanted aloud and in unison by the worshipers. Some congregational leaders consider this effort largely successful, though some are still dissatisfied, noting how difficult it is to reverse an ingrained culture. A congregant remarks, "You go into the sanctuary and the Tefillah band is up in front, and I call it a band because they have become a performance. They have not become part of enhancing the participation in services. It's the same people still sitting and watching."[5] Even with the introduction of contemporary music into the worship, the congregants are "still sitting and watching."

Passivity operates both quantitatively and qualitatively. Quantitatively, it results in low rates of attendance and engagement in congregational events, programs, and activities. Qualitatively, it means little genuine enthusiasm at the events, even among the few who do attend.

MEANINGLESSNESS

Closely related to passivity is the meaninglessness experienced in worship, learning, and other congregational activities. (To be precise, "less than deeply meaningful" would be a more apt, albeit wordier, description.) This characterizes communities that generally fail to excite, provoke, mobilize, or inspire congregants. The experience in such congregations may be pleasant, comforting, and familiar, but it lacks a sense of transcendence, awe, reverence, and sacredness.

Our informants at transformed synagogues spoke of an earlier time when congregants failed to derive much meaning from worship and learning, experiencing them as largely routine activities. It is commonplace to hear in the precincts of American congregations, "Services are boring." By the same token, with respect to religious school, one can frequently hear the refrain, "My children hate Hebrew school, just like I did." Congregants who participate in these kinds of activities may do so out of a sense of obligation to a decreasingly compelling tradition or by dint of intrafamilial obligation: "I go because my spouse wants me to go." "I go to set a good example for my children."

Through the 1960s or so, synagogue involvement provided meaning for many. In terms advanced by social theorist Peter Berger, congregational life then was "plausible." It made sense. It was undergirded by the ideology of ethnic survivalism, the persistence of the Jews' outsider status, and nostalgic sentimentality.[6]

Congregational participation connoted successful adaptation to American middle-class life and social acceptability, as Judaism became one of the three recognizably American religious faiths.[7] Through their largely Conservative congregations, called "ethnic church[es]" by sociologist Marshall Sklare, Jews could perpetuate their traditions, accommodate to the America that still kept them socially and geographically apart, and give expression to the essentially ethnic construction of Judaism that prevailed at the time.

The very act of coming together in synagogues on the High Holidays, and for weddings and bar mitzvah celebrations, accommodated two conflicting dimensions of midcentury Jewish identity[8]: American Jews at the time sought both to assure group survival and to achieve full integration into the larger society. The postwar years were a time when middle-class white Americans were building churches, attending them in large numbers, and sending their children to Sunday schools. Jews who were intent upon achieving middle-class respectability could find meaning in attending their own prayer services and in sending their own children to Hebrew schools. They were acting proudly as Jews, and at the same time integrating into middle-class, suburban America. The very same behaviors that can often seem meaningless today— attending High Holiday services or sending one's children to religious school—were meaningful because of their social context and, more specifically, because they allowed for the pursuit of two goals: to remain a Jew and to become an American.

Between the 1960s and the 1980s, what social theorists call this "plausibility structure" (the symbolic system that makes everything seem legitimate and sensible) collapsed. As one congregant in Congregation Beth Shalom put matters, "A lot of people of the previous generation didn't know how to daven, but were prepared to come out of nostalgia's sake, to sit through something, even if they didn't know what to do with it. They were prepared to be part of it. This is a different generation."

In more recent times, for the thoroughly Americanized and highly educated baby boomers, ethnic nostalgia has come to feel kitschy.[9] The decades-long drive for acceptance in America[10] largely achieved its goal. Because they occupy some of the most prestigious, influential, and affluent strata in American society, Jews no longer feel the same need to demonstrate their suitability for social integration.[11] In the wake of these changes, congregations in general, and worship in particular, have needed to develop new compelling rationales, to justify themselves as providers of meaningful experience in what some have called the "spiritual marketplace"[12] or "experience economy."[13]

RESISTANCE TO CHANGE

The rapid shifts in the societal position and cultural orientation of American Jews has induced a cultural lag to which many congregational leaders have been slow to react. Congregational leaders often fail to fully appreciate the extent to which Jewish engagement has become increasingly a matter of choice rather than a matter of necessity. American Jews today are not only freer to choose whether to be Jewish, they are also freer to choose how, when, where, and why to be Jewish.[14] Even when older Jews are keenly aware of the rapidly changing world in which they live and lead, they may react (as have many middle-aged or elderly people since time immemorial) with a degree of bafflement and resentment at the views and practices of the younger generation.

Most find change especially difficult and unsettling, if not unnecessary, given their years of success in following well-established patterns and practices. Leaders may be attached to an aspect of the service, even if others find this element to be desultory. The same may be said for the ingrained pattern of delegating *bikkur cholim* (visiting the sick) to the clergy or for routinized patterns of governance. The cause of this attachment might be nostalgia or comfort. Long-standing leaders are skilled in the old ways, unable to easily learn new approaches and unlikely to abandon practices that have served them well for decades. Their commitment to routine and their resistance to change is the fifth major characteristic of the functional congregation.

Certainly, the reasons to resist change are numerous and varied, powerful and deep-seated, explicable and, we hasten to add, even at times legitimate.[15]

UNREFLECTIVE LEADERSHIP

Resistance to change is due, in part, perhaps in large part, to leaders' resistance to reflection. Congregations, like other organizations, can perceive, learn, reflect, internalize, and adapt—or not. When they do, they effectively learn from changing environments, they critically assess their performance, they develop and adopt new insights and behaviors, and they do all of this on a continuing basis. Rabbi Rick Jacobs at Westchester Reform Temple, Scarsdale, New York, provides a pertinent and instructive anecdote about how his synagogue used to operate: "Right after Rabin was murdered, we had the opportunity to bring [famed Israeli author] Amos Oz to speak. Well, somebody was looking at the calendar saying, 'We have a meeting that night.' . . . Committees were defining synagogue life. People were doing perfectly nice things, but the synagogue was being defined by the business of administration, and not by . . . learning, prayer, healing, all those core things of Judaism."

Drawing upon the work of Peter Senge and other learning organization theorists, Isa Aron observes, "Synagogues require the capacity to think clearly about their goals, conduct rigorous and scrupulous self-assessments, and brainstorm creative initiatives. . . . To truly serve its current members and appeal to its future ones, every synagogue needs to become a learning congregation."[16] Of course, relatively few congregations meet these expectations.

Rather, many congregations, and certainly the purely functional congregations, resist reflection and ultimate learning, growth, adaptation, and vision.

CHARACTERISTICS OF THE FUNCTIONAL CONGREGATION

The foregoing description of the functional congregation may be summarized as follows:

Consumerism: the fee-for-service arrangements provide consumers with discrete services, in particular, education of children for ceremonial celebration of bar or bat mitzvah and clergy officiation at life-cycle ceremonies.

Segmentation: programs stand on their own, with little integration of worship, learning, caring, social action, or community building.

Passivity: professionals exercise firm control over congregational functioning; worshipers sit passively; parents drop off children for religious schooling; boards deal with marginalia.

Meaninglessness: rote performance of scripted interactions, with little genuine significance or feelings of transcendent connection with Jews and Judaism.

Resistance to change: the routine is supreme, preventing diversification and serious consideration of alternative modes and structures.

Nonreflective leadership: focuses on program and institutional arrangements rather than purpose and vision.

The Visionary Congregation

Six key features characterize the functional congregation; an equal number of contrasting features characterize the opposite ideal type, the visionary congregation: Sacred purpose, holistic ethos, participatory culture, meaningful engagement, innovative disposition, and reflective leadership.

SACRED PURPOSE, SACRED COMMUNITY

At the heart of the visionary congregation is an overarching commitment to sacred purpose, a commitment that suffuses all aspects of the community. Where the functional congregation delivers specified services to consumer-clients, its visionary counterpart provides sacred experiences to members of a holy community (recalling the traditional Hebrew terminology for a congregation, *k'hillah k'doshah* [sacred community]). References to a sacred community or to a sense of sacred purpose emerged repeatedly in our interviews.

As befitting the notion of sacred purpose, the work of the congregation is intimately connected with godly pursuits. Josh Seidman, a midthirties congregant at Temple Micah in Washington, D.C., found sacred meaning in Micah House, a social service run by the congregation: "However we conceive of God, Micah House is God's work. So, I bring that spiritual mindset to my board meeting. We started off . . . every session with some sort of prayer, or poem, or song." Note how the sense of sacredness infuses his view not only of the homeless shelter but also of the board meetings.

Charles Goldberg of Congregation Agudath Israel, a Conservative congregation in Caldwell, New Jersey, locates the drive toward holiness in the wider sense of community. "What you would see is Jews who are participatory, who are a community, who interact with all the best of what Judaism has to offer in terms of loving thy neighbor and being a mensch. And all, old and young, wealthy and not wealthy, all together. We are learning from each other and helping each other get closer to God."

Charles's sensibility echoed other interviewees who saw sacredness as inextricably connected to how congregants interact with one another. While at Temple Israel of Boston, Rabbi Jonah Pesner was instrumental in advancing a faith-based congregational organizing effort that advocated affordable housing legislation. Jonah speaks of the method he used as "a theology of organizing," thus clearly linking his efforts to the Divine: "Martin Buber once said, "The reason we need the heavenly voice from above is that without the divine voice from above, it becomes the simple self-assertion of the group. So for me, *Ohel Tzedek* [the congregation's social justice initiative] is about creating the divine in human space. There is sanctity in it. That's why we always start with a blessing, or a piece of text, and end with a blessing."

When sacred purpose comes to be thoroughly infused throughout the culture of the congregation and is widely embraced by the congregants, members develop a powerful sense of obligation to Judaism and the congregation and mutual responsibility toward one another. Sociologist Nancy Ammerman writes that "people are more committed to an organization when they have meaningful work to do, when they feel a sense of attachment to others in the group, and when they see the group as representing a moral good that allows them to transcend merely personal interest."[17] Some communities produce a public good, or, in the case of congregations, what we may call a sacred good. Such congregations are more able to elicit loyalty and generate commitment among their members, both to the larger community and to each other. Peter Wang, an active lay leader at Westchester Reform Temple remarked, "One of the things we talk a lot about now is the sense of covenant, the idea that people should understand that being a member has obligations as well as benefits."

Despite differences across communities and individuals, synagogue leaders are remarkably consistent in citing the same three to four anchors of their communities, echoing those of Jewish tradition as well as that of other American religious denominations. One major study of Christian congregations finds that American churches are heavily committed to the "production" of three sacred goods: worship, education, and social justice activities, with the latter generally coming in a distant third.[18] The parallels with Judaism are striking. Classic rabbinic sources refer to synagogues by three names: *Beit Knesset*, *Beit Midrash*, and *Beit T'fillah* referring to the three functions of community, learning, and prayer.

Ric Rudman, lay leader at Congregation Beth Am, a Reform temple in northern California, puts matters simply, "Beth Am has four pillars—education, community, worship, and social action."

At Congregation Agudath Israel, across the continent in New Jersey, Rabbi Alan Silverstein uses the same concepts:

> My model of a good shul is multiple gateways into engagement along three basic patterns: *torah, avodah, g'milut chasadim.* Torah is the learning mode—these are people I call "head Jews." They are best going to connect through learning. So that's one piece. Second piece is *avodah shebalev,* which is the spirituality part—prayer, meditation. And the third is *g'milut chasadim,* which is the caring committee stuff, the *tikkun olam* stuff, the committees that build communities stuff, friendship networks. The synagogue is kind of the Rosenzweigian "ladder of commitment" that everyone is somewhere on those three quotients. Our goal is to help you ascend on those three ladders. Different folks will ascend at a different pace in a different way.

Rabbi Rick Jacobs of Westchester Reform Temple provides a summary of his congregation's mission along very similar lines, adding *chavurah* (creating sacred community) and being a part of *Klal Yisrael* (the worldwide Jewish community) to the pillars talmud torah, avodah, and tikkun olam. "We try to see ourselves in a different light and then . . . use [these pillars to] look at what we do."

Connecting the synagogue with sacred purpose requires both ongoing attention and intentionality; it does not come naturally, organically, or easily to most American Jews. Sacred purpose is tied to a concept of the Divine and to a sense of what God wants of us. It is embodied and expressed in concrete actions that reinforce the connection between seemingly mundane congregational activities (such as committee meetings) and the sacred purpose to which the community is dedicated. Thus, it makes more sense to speak of a continuum of sacredness, with consumerism and sacredness representing opposite ends of the spectrum. Those congregations we regard as visionary generally succeed at building sacred community, even as they struggle to avoid slipping into the pattern of providing discretely produced and delivered services to congregants-as-consumers.

The line between functional, consumerist communities and visionary, sacred communities is often blurred and occasionally crossed. But the consumerist-sacred distinction is genuine nonetheless, and it underlies several other major distinctions between functional and visionary congregations.

HOLISTIC ETHOS

Visionary communities maintain a holistic ethos where the parts are integrally related to the whole. This ethos attempts to minimize boundaries between people, programs, institutions, groups, and space and to promote cooperation between and among the various domains of the congregation. It rejects dualisms such as particularism versus universalism, education versus entertainment, and study versus action. It rejects the segmentation of functions common in most congregations, such as compartmentalizing worship, learning, caring, and social action. It also rejects an atomistic view of the congregation as separate from everyday life, the larger Jewish community, and the larger society.

Peter Wang at Westchester Reform Temple reflects a holistic view of Jewish education, which he credits to his involvement with the Experiment in Congregational Education (ECE):

> The ECE initiative here had a lifelong learning approach that every opportunity, every encounter with the synagogue is an encounter for learning, and to do that not just as a supplemental school environment but as part of the whole fabric of the synagogue life. For example, we never used to have *d'var torah* before meetings, and now it has actually become a very significant part of virtually every meeting at the temple.

Several dimensions to the holistic approach emerge in the fore-going passage. One feature is that education is seen as a lifelong process, instead of something intended strictly for the childhood years, as it is in most congregations. Another feature is that op-portunities for Jewish learning extend beyond the confines of the classroom: Jewish learning occurs anywhere, and can be applied anywhere. In a general sense, a consciousness of Jewish learning is present in all arenas of synagogue activity. In the same way, con-sciousness of the sacred, social justice, and the building of com-munity can touch all aspects of congregational life.

In holistic communities the worship services, children's re-ligious education, caring for others, adult education, and social justice initiatives all serve as portals into increased congregational engagement. Indeed, such imagery is at the heart of Randi Brok-man's narrative of her growing involvement with Congregation Agudath Israel, the Conservative synagogue in New Jersey, begin-ning with its nursery school:

> Our chavurah has been together since our first children were four. We
> basically went through life together—through sending our children
> off to school, through growing up, through the bar mitzvah cycle. We
> went through illnesses, job changes, and unemployment. Then we went
> through sending the kids off to college and the loss of parents. This had
> a connecting effect—a strong sense of community.

A holistic approach to community building and congregational functioning also serves to diminish many of the social barriers within the congregation as well as those separating the congrega-tional community from the larger population. The more holisti-cally inclined communities strive (in word and in deed) for their congregants to feel a sense of inclusion. Of particular concern to the congregation are those congregants who believe that they may be considered marginal. A member of Beth Jacob Congrega-tion in Mendota Heights, Minnesota, is a lesbian living with her non-Jewish partner. She certainly has reason to feel uneasy about being accepted in conventional Jewish communities. She remarks about the welcoming and inclusive Conservative community to which she has belonged quite happily for many years: "There's so much diversity there. Families are obviously drawn there—families who are converts, families who are mixed, families who are drawn there because there are other people like them. They learn it's a comfortable place."

Inclusiveness, welcoming, diversity, and comfort (as in making people feel comfortable with their Judaism or with the congregation) have become watchwords in the rhetoric and practice of contemporary Jewish congregational life. Critical observers have expressed concern that these tendencies serve to blur boundaries between Jews and others, undermining commitment to Jewish peoplehood. The issue is far from resolved and beyond the immediate scope of this work. That said, visionary congregations are committed in principle to minimizing instances in which congregants, or prospective congregants, feel excluded, unwelcome, or uncomfortable.

The commitment to inclusivity is evident in the treatment of major donors in visionary congregations as well. The ongoing need for donations poses a dilemma for congregations, especially those committed to minimizing social class differences and other barriers among the members. For centuries, Jewish congregations have inscribed the names of major donors onto highly visible places in their edifices; as a rule, they also publicly express gratitude, offering recognition to the bigger donors at dinners, worship services, and other gatherings. In striking contrast with this long-standing practice, the eight transformed congregations we studied have all developed ways of limiting donor recognition, to avoid calling attention to economic differences. In the midst of a major capital drive, Temple Micah, for example, adhered to a policy of strict nonrecognition even for the largest donors, including those who had pledged six figures. At Temple Beth Elohim, whose members are reputed to contribute as much as one quarter of the local federation's total annual campaign, congregational leaders have struggled with questions of limiting donor recognition.

Westchester Reform Temple (WRT) is located in one of the wealthiest suburbs in North America, Scarsdale, New York. Yet here too, a lay leader testifies to the deep-seated commitment to inclusiveness that militated against the usual practices of privileging capable and generous donors: "A contribution of one million dollars might not automatically assure the naming of a building. . . . At WRT you cannot have seats up front because you give more money. Whoever gets there first can sit wherever they like. This is the culture of our temple."

Holistic thinking, then, demands attention to the integrity of the whole. A holistic approach to congregational life is one that diminishes social boundaries and one that takes a systemic view of synagogue functioning, including in its purview the various factors that affect worship, learning, and acts of loving-kindness.

PARTICIPATORY CULTURE, PARTICIPATING CONGREGANTS

In a community dedicated to sacred ends and operating in a rich and holistic fashion, one would not be surprised to find member-congregants fully participating in the affairs of their communities, devoting time, energy, and passion to one another and the community as a whole. Of course, such instances in contemporary times are relatively rare occurrences. In premodern Jewish congregations and many Orthodox services today, prayer services are marked by chanting and singing in approximate unison, with worshipers proceeding at their own pace in individual prayer. With the advent of modernity, Jews came to see the traditional style of communal prayer as disorganized, indecorous, and contrary to the Western spiritual aesthetic they had internalized.[19] Particularly in Reform temples in Germany and the United States, the late-nineteenth and early- to mid-twentieth centuries saw the adoption of more scripted, more organized, more decorous, and seemingly more reverential worship experiences. As for rabbis and cantors, congregants expected them to maintain an aura of aloofness and distance from the laity.

This hierarchical relationship was given physical expression in the spatial arrangements of most congregations' sanctuaries. Rabbis and cantors performed on raised platforms in front of well-dressed "audiences" of orderly and respectful worshipers seated (and occasionally standing at predetermined times) in the pews.

The Chavurah movement of the late 1960s and 1970s challenged this ethos, which movement leaders saw as passive, disempowering, and inauthentic for congregants. They constructed small, intimate communities where worshipers sat in the round and often on the floor, and where liturgical leadership rested upon the laity. The very title of the movement's best known and most widely read publication, *The Jewish Catalog: A Do-It-Yourself Kit*, speaks to the goal of liberating the laity from dependence on rabbis and other professional Jews.

The sweeping changes inaugurated by the Chavurah movement not only came to influence American Judaism in general but also reflected shifts in the wider religious culture. In their work on generational shifts in American religion, Jackson Carroll and Wade Clark Roof trace the evolution of four congregational models in American history, with the participatory model constituting the fourth and most recent.[20] Their description of this model bears striking resemblance to the ideals of the transformed Jewish congregations in this inquiry:

> This [participatory] congregation designs its programs to meet the needs of an increasingly diverse and well-educated laity—different "audiences"—who are self-conscious about their participation and choose to be involved on their own terms and not necessarily those set by a leadership elite. Lay initiative and participation in all aspects of

congregational life, including decision making and corporate worship, are emphasized. Church architecture, especially worship space, also bears witness to the shift to participation, away from earlier practice where worship was a performance before passive observers.[21]

The desire for greater participation in worship has meant that conflicts have emerged between generations with differing attitudes and cultural backgrounds. This conflict has been played out in recent years through controversy over music and the role of the cantor. All of the extraordinary synagogues in this study have addressed this question; some have seriously revamped their services. In particular, Reform congregations, with their greater liturgical flexibility and the availability of musical instruments, have moved to make worship services more musically accessible and engaging. In response, some veteran cantors see the new melodies as belonging at summer camp, not in a formal worship service. Rabbi Danny Zemel, of Temple Micah, responds, "They'll use the word *camp music* as if I'm supposed to be embarrassed by the sound of *camp*. So my standard response . . . is to say that 'my favorite sound in the sanctuary is the sound of everybody singing together.'" Congregant David Wentworth agrees, "It's very participatory, musically. We're not exactly a gospel group, but the point is there's real involvement of the members of the congregation."

In Conservative congregations as well, participation is held up as an important value. Cantor Joel Caplan, of Congregation Agudath Israel, explains how he contains the role of the choir to maximize congregational singing: "Some of our members say, 'With a choir, I feel like I'm getting sung at. I want to daven. I want to sing along with them.' So now, even as our choir has improved greatly, almost all the things that our choir sings during services are harmonizations of melodies the congregation already knows how to sing. The congregation is singing the melody, and the choir's providing harmony."

A participatory approach in the educational realm is often evident in the religious school. In contrast with their predecessors and many of their counterparts, educational directors at the visionary congregations we studied have made parental engagement a key objective. Sharon Halper, former educational director at Westchester Reform Temple, recalls one initiative: "We empowered parents to become their children's Jewish educators. An essential piece for me was the family activity in the first year it occurred in place, in the congregation, and after that, they became take-homes. The goal was that students and parents were learning separately, but were on a similar track because the curriculum was always focused around Torah."

Joel Sisenwine, rabbi of Temple Beth Elohim, argues that participation is key in synagogue governance as well: "You have to allow lay leaders a place to fail and to succeed. It is necessary for them to grow Jewishly. There's a tendency for synagogues to hire professionals to ensure that they don't fail, but that is the death knell of a strong community."

If greater participation by the laity in the life of congregations is so empowering, why doesn't more of it take place? What keeps congregations from expanding the roles of congregants—in worship, in education, or in governance? Rick Jacobs believes that most of his rabbinic colleagues are reluctant to share power with the laity. In his view, they are, at best, prepared to humor the laity, to give the appearance of lay empowerment. He sees genuine involvement of lay leadership as essential to his own effectiveness and the success of his congregation:

> I can say over and over again, "We need to empower lay people because first of all, it will be key to having people lead meaningful Jewish lives." And the fear you might have as a rabbi is that when they get empowered, you're going to get a little bit of a marginal role in the synagogue. If it's going to happen, it hasn't happened yet. There's enough stuff to

do. People still need a rabbi here, and I love when people are learning
and teaching; it is not like it takes away my role. I still have plenty to do,
but I have partners.

For leaders, clerical or otherwise, of visionary congregations,
a highly participatory culture signifies not loss of control but
success in leadership. Congregants' participation, initiative,
and leadership are not seen as impinging upon the preroga-
tives of leadership; they are signs of its effectiveness and success
in making engagement with the congregation truly inspiring
and meaningful.

MEANINGFUL ENGAGEMENT

A major theme in American religion over the last twenty years or
more has been the rise of meaning seeking on the part of Americans of all faiths. Among its causes: the decline in the power of
received doctrine, the pluralization of meaning systems (be they
religious faiths or others), the expansion of freedom of individual
choice, and the loosening of institutional ties. As a result, authority has moved from received tradition and its interpreters (clergy, parents, educators) to the realm of the individual. In Robert
Wuthnow's terms, religious adherents have increasingly shifted
from the mode of "dwellers," where extant religious structures are
sufficient, to that of "seekers," where the journey is an end in itself.

Sociologist Charles Liebman was among the first to explicitly
note the shift among Jews. Writing in the late 1980s, and drawing
upon the earlier work of Marshall Sklare he noted the rise of personalism.[22] "Personalism is the tendency to transform and evaluate the [Jewish] tradition in terms of its utility of significance to
the individual."[23] He contrasts the new personalism with the traditional Jewish approach to religious obligation: "Personal choice
is endowed with spiritual sanctity, and contrary to past tradition
it is always considered more virtuous than performing an act out
of a sense of obedience to God."[24] Subsequent research provided

additional evidence of the extent to which a search for personal meaning and personalized religious experience had come to characterize American Jews in the last third of the twentieth century.[25] Theologically and ideologically, leaders in the Reform and Reconstructionist movements have relatively little hesitancy in revising practice to supply a greater sense of meaning or, to be more precise, experiences and contexts where congregants find, derive, and create meaning for themselves. But even the more tradition-minded and halakhically oriented Conservative and Orthodox movements have responded and adjusted to Jews' increasing demand for meaning in their lives.

Visionary congregations are purposeful about the delivery of Jewish meaning, or opportunities for meaning making, to their congregants. Leaders and congregants actually think hard about such matters. A participant in a discussion about prayer at Congregation Beth Shalom remarked, "How do we engage people more? People want to learn. How can we help them learn about their own religion and services? How can they connect to the service, to God, how can they feel spiritual?"

Clearly, the delivery of meaning is a challenge to capable and well-intentioned rabbis as well as the cantors with whom they serve. As noted earlier, the issue of liturgical music is one of the many areas of ongoing concerns to the clergy. Teddy Klaus, music director of Temple Micah, discusses how music can make the service more meaningful, combining familiar and cherished elements with those that are innovative and stimulating: "We've become a little bit stagnant—and this is age-old in worship—there's a tension between familiar and fresh. If we have any fault, we rely on the familiar too much. I always look for something fresh even within the same music. For example, we do the same *k'dushah* [a section of the *Amidah*, the standing prayer] every Shabbat morning, and if I played it exactly the same way, I would go crazy."

In other words, Klaus is aware—as are meaning-oriented cantors everywhere—that music can either aid or inhibit the congregants' experiences of meaningfulness in the service. Music and melodies that are familiar link one with tradition, real or imagined, but at the risk of being experienced as routine and uninspiring. Music and melodies that are innovative and contemporary evoke other reactions, such as stimulation, excitement, curiosity, or discomfort. The choice of how best to balance these and other musical options varies with time, place, congregants, and context.

In Jewish education as well, both teachers and learners have come to value how the learning experience can contribute to the opportunities to find meaning. In their study of the Florence Melton Adult Mini-School, a worldwide network of several dozen adult Jewish learning programs, Grant et al. conclude "that the core impact of the Mini-School upon learners' Jewish identities centers on 'meaning-making,' the enhanced ability to derive sense and purpose from one's everyday Jewish activities."[26] Nancy Belsky, lay leader at Temple Beth Elohim, echoes these findings (note how often the word *meaning* and its variant appear in her comments):

> Rabbi [Alan] Ullman is a Reform rabbi who basically teaches Torah study with a very contemporary approach. In other words, "Let's read this. Now, what does it mean in 2006?" For example, this week's parashah [Torah portion] talks about the eternal light. God says, "Have an eternal light in the shul and the garb of the people." What he might do with that is say, "Okay, let's look at all of the clothing that the priesthood's supposed to wear and analyze why." So what does that mean today? When you wear priestly clothes, what does that mean? It means you have a certain role in the community, which means there are certain expectations from you. If you wear a Chanel suit, what does that mean? It means you can afford it. Well, that means you need to give more to *tz'dakah* [charity]. So he looks for the "What does that mean today? What are the responsibilities?" I found that meaningful and I found that relevant. I would say what Rabbi Ullman did was he created meaning. He created relevance.

Current and potential congregants choose to affiliate and to become more or less involved in congregational life based in part upon the extent to which such involvement provides them with genuine meaning, such that Judaism speaks to people's most keenly felt moral questions and personal issues. With the growing diversity of American Jewry, congregations are challenged now more than ever to provide environments and experiences where meaning making can happen. As people and culture continue to diversify and evolve, the objective requires ongoing innovation. As Alan Wolfe observes, "All of America's religions face the same imperative: Personalize or die."[27]

INNOVATIVE DISPOSITION

Throughout Jewish history proponents of radical change have generally argued that failure to change will leave a Judaism incapable of attracting a more acculturated, integrated, and modernized younger generation. Their opponents have argued that large-scale changes are inconsistent with the time-honored values of Judaism; minor adjustments, rather than wholesale revamping of established patterns, can succeed in bridging the gaps between the past and the future. Moreover, proponents and opponents of change have advanced different readings of Jewish history. Proponents of innovation see historic changes in Judaism as necessary, desirable, and largely faithful to true Jewish values, citing numerous examples in Talmudic and rabbinic writings that attest to an ongoing pattern of change. Opponents see historic changes as minimal, unavoidable, and problematic, arguing that the changes that have been documented and authorized were undertaken carefully, slowly, and by authorities well versed in and faithful to Jewish tradition.

The leaders of the visionary congregations with whom we spoke cast themselves as change agents who promote innovation but carefully pace and monitor change. Rabbi Alan Silverstein of Congregation Agudath Israel is a leading Conservative rabbi thought by many to hold a relatively traditional place on the movement's ideological spectrum:

We're a can-do type of place. We didn't have a lot of change management issues, because people here are accustomed to trying things. Those
things that don't work, don't work. Some things have to be tweaked.
Other things just fit right in. I use my rabbi's fund as an entrepreneurial
fund—investing in interesting concepts that we can try out for a couple
of years. Then if they work, the lay leadership talk about institutional-
izing them in the budget. If they don't work, then they fall by the way-
side. So, the idea of synagogue transformation is an ongoing ideological
commitment for us.

Ric Rudman, a former president of both Congregation Beth Am in
Los Altos Hills, California, and Stanford University's Hillel board,
is the former chief operating officer of a large nonprofit research
and development firm. He can readily see connections between
the corporate culture and his congregation:

Beth Am is an entrepreneurial community—it reflects the broader
community in Silicon Valley. So the congregation is willing to try new
things, often without knowing exactly where they will lead. This is really exciting, because it opens the culture up to experimentation. We've
been able to attract a group of members who always push the envelope,
which leads to continuous improvement in every aspect of congregational life. Every ten years or so you should take all the things you really
cherish and zero base them. What do we know now? What's the current
reality? Where do [we] want to be in five years? And what changes do
we have to make in the current model to get there? That will lead to new
insights and improvements in the system.

As might be expected, Conservative and Reform communities approach innovation quite differently. The Conservative movement
adheres to more traditional notions of what constitutes authentic Judaism; the Reform movement prides itself on its agility and
readiness to adapt and respond to the shifting needs and demands
of its congregants. With all the talk of nondenominationalism and

the blurring of denominational boundaries, the constituencies of the two movements differ considerably.[28] Compared with Reform Jews, Conservative Jews report higher levels of Jewish education and ritual observance, making for differences in aesthetic and stylistic sensibilities.

Reflecting these distinctions, Cantor Joel Caplan of Congregation Agudath Israel is more cautious about changing the worship service: "I'll introduce maybe four or five congregational melodies in the course of a year. Not more than that that's new because otherwise I get people who come up to me and say, 'You changed the whole service. You ruined the whole thing for me, I couldn't sing along with anything.'"

Congregations and leaders, then, differ over the locus, extent, scope, and pace of desired innovation. Denominational and congregational ideology, lay and professional personnel, financial and other resources, and shul politics come into play at various times to determine the nature and depth of innovation. In all instances where leaders recount a period of transformation, they mention significant changes in clerical and other professional personnel— a new rabbi, often followed by a new cantor, educator, assistant rabbi, or others.

Part and parcel of the spirit of innovation is the understanding that not all changes will succeed, as Susan Wolfe, former board member of Congregation Beth Am explains, "When you attempt change you have to be willing to fail. It doesn't all work. At Congregation Beth Am we've had failures—big failures. Then we step back and regroup and revamp and then try to do it better the next time. But if you don't make any mistakes, you don't learn anything."

Given the complexity of instituting and monitoring innovation, a visionary congregation requires a leadership and an organizational culture not merely predisposed to innovate but also committed and capable of engaging in genuine reflection.

REFLECTIVE LEADERSHIP

For years social scientists have been tracking the ever-quickening pace of change in technology, culture, and society. Management experts have been nearly unanimous in proclaiming that corporations and the people who lead them need to develop the tools to make sense of the changing world around them, to recognize emerging obstacles and opportunities, to manage adaptation and innovation, to assess their successes and failures, and to adjust their responses in light of these assessments. Innovation demands ongoing reflection and attention, as Rabbi Rick Jacobs of Westchester Reform Temple makes clear: "We came to believe strongly that learning informs change, whatever change we want. If we want to change our tikkun olam program, if we want to change worship, we don't just ask the rabbis and the cantors to make the changes. Instead we gather a wide cross section of laypeople and professionals to learn, think, experiment, and refine."

At Congregation Beth Am, leaders discovered that the commitment to the ongoing feedback, reflection, and adaptation had to be kept in front of the congregation. In the case of one program, they found themselves saying repeatedly, "*It is an experiment.* It's going to keep changing. We need your input; this is why we're evaluating."

Rabbi Jonah Pesner of Temple Israel in Boston points to how reflection, even in a functional congregation, requires constant attention and reinforcement. This theme recurs repeatedly. Congregations can strive for transformation and excellence, but retaining a reflective stance is absolutely crucial. He described meetings where the initial tendency was to plug regular programs into the congregation's calendar, but the staff would question the rationale, asking, "Shouldn't we consider where people are?" and so they would gather lay leaders to talk about what adult learning on Israel, for example, should look like, what they want "to own" and what "they want to create out of that." They would ask, "'Why are we putting that on the calendar? Just because we've always done it? Shouldn't we consider where people are?' What we kept coming to was: let's get together a group of lay leaders and have them talk to us about what should adult learning on Israel look like. Let's see what they want to own. What do they want to create out of that?" A genuinely reflective leadership team really listens to the rank and file.

Finally, Rick Jacobs recalls how the congregation engaged in a sophisticated discourse on revising congregational worship: "People would say, 'I didn't like Joan Baez in the '60s, and I like her less in my temple.' And then people say, 'I came from a Conservative temple, and for me an organ is goyish.' So we started to have these tools to think about our worship. The discussion wasn't 'What do you love or what do you hate?' But, 'Can you identify the meeting, the meditative, and the majestic?'"

These remarks point to a number of elements in reflective leadership and decision making. Among them are the introduction of conceptual thinking, critical examination of current practice, exploration of successful alternatives, and deliberative application of lessons learned.

CHARACTERISTICS OF THE VISIONARY CONGREGATION

We summarize our description of the visionary congregation as follows:

Sacred purpose: a pervasive, shared vision that infuses all aspects of the synagogue

Holistic ethos: the parts are related to each other and to the whole; ritual, learning, caring, social action, and community appear in several areas of functioning; lay and professional leadership function cooperatively; boundaries within and around the community are more porous and fluid

Participatory culture on all levels; congregants, students, lay leaders, professionals, and parents engage in the work of the sacred community

Meaningful engagement: achieved through repeated inspirational experiences that provide genuine meaning to people's lives

Innovation disposition: marked by a search for diversity and alternatives, a tolerance of failure, ability to address and overcome resistance to change, and a willingness to abandon less functional ways of doing things

Reflective leadership and governance: marked by careful examination of alternatives, a commitment to overarching purpose, attention to relationships, mastery of detail, and a planful approach to change

These six characteristics, broadly considered, underpin much of the work that follows in this book. No congregation performs perfectly as a visionary congregation in all aspects. Rather, we envision these six characteristics as continual, in which the core distinction of a visionary congregation is that it is always in pursuit of sacredness over consumerism, holism over segmentation, participation over passivity, innovation over routine, and so on. The chapters that follow illustrate how these characteristics are exemplified in the areas of torah, avodah, and g'milut chasadim.

CHAPTER 3

Visionary Worship: *T'fillah* that Engages

The synagogues we studied care deeply about congregational prayer. It went by different names: *t'fillah*, among Conservative Jews, who did it in shul; *worship*, for Reform congregations who found it in synagogues or temples. But it was the same thing in different cultural clothing: a renewal of public prayer by a generation whose parents and grandparents had pretty much taken it for granted.

Everyone we talked to was either proud of or troubled over what was happening in their sanctuaries. All five Reform synagogues had decided worship wasn't working and were radically overhauling it. Two of the Conservative congregations had made Shabbat t'fillah the high point in their week. The third one had named its entire project Tefillah 2000 and was somewhere in the middle: unhappy with its t'fillah, desirous of changing it, but conscious of traditional constraints. All eight places thought synagogue prayer mattered.

This kind of intense concern for prayer is new to American Jews who, historically, have cared relatively little about it. People "went to services" or not—more usually, not—but, either way, treated prayer like a snowy day in winter: some like it, some don't; but no one thinks it something that they can or should do anything about.

Why this sudden interest in prayer, even in ECE (Experiment in Congregational Education) synagogues that were focused on learning and could have ignored prayer altogether?

Why Prayer? Why Now?

Premodern Judaism valued prayer no less than the rest of God's commandments, but its hallmark was study: its ideal was the *talmid chakham*, the Torah sage, not the spiritual ascetic seeking God through meditation and prayer. Worship was more fundamental to churches than to synagogues.

As nineteenth-century Jews in Western Europe encountered modernity, however, their appreciation of prayer increased. They modernized services and built synagogues where beautiful sanctuaries dominated. Largely Reform, but also modern Orthodox, they brought their respect for beautiful worship to America. Eastern European Jews who arrived between 1881 and 1924 differed. They had not encountered Western aesthetics; they related to Judaism culturally and ethnically rather than religiously. But they too built synagogues here—giving us Conservative and Reconstructionist Judaism. During the Eisenhower years, Jews of all denominations moved to the suburbs and established synagogues there.

Suburban synagogues, however, were usually constructed with tiny sanctuaries compared to their massive social halls and school wings. One look at them demonstrates how little these Jews accepted worship as central to their Judaism. A Gallup poll begun in the wake of World War II, and posed annually ever since, asks Americans how frequently they attend services. Remarkably, some 40 to 44 percent of Americans said then—*and still say today*—that they attend weekly. The Jewish sample is too small to know for sure, but, unofficially, Gallup estimates that Jews attend about half as often as the overall population. That would set average Jewish attendance at about 20 percent, a figure that anyone familiar with synagogue life would likely question. Without some special reason to bring them there, what congregation sees 20 percent of its membership at weekly services?

In 1993, rather than *ask* people if they attend, some social scientists actually *counted* them as they walked through the door, and they discovered that Americans overreport attendance by a whopping 100 percent![1] That would place average church attendance at about 20 percent and the Jewish equivalent closer to 10 percent—a more likely figure, certainly. In most of North America, regular synagogue visitors would regard 10 percent attendance of our adult population rather good, even unusual.

Given all this, the focus on worship renewal that we observed in our study is nothing short of revolutionary. It began by the late 1970s when baby boomers started joining synagogues for their children and seeking spirituality for themselves. It picked up steam in the 1980s and was fully under way by the 1990s, when synagogue transformation became the rage.

REFORM PRACTICE: MUSIC, MUSIC, MUSIC

Especially in Reform synagogues, music would be the key to transforming the service. Baby boomers grew up in the 1960s with the guitar, and by the 1980s, the national biennial of the Reform movement was highlighting its own folk stars in late-night concerts, first and foremost, Debbie Friedman, whose music turns up everywhere in our study. At one point, the disconnect between the official Friday night biennial service and the unofficial after-service concert became patent enough for some observers to say that the real liturgy began only after the final kaddish had ended. People sat passively through the worship but came alive for the concert afterward.

This synagogue folk music was responding to the mood of the times. But it was also informed by Jewish text and spirituality. Eventually, more sophisticated melodies emerged, replete with small orchestral accompaniment. Sound was becoming the most important symbolic marker of generational identity.[2] At the 1983 biennial, for the first time, as far as anyone can recall, an entire congregation of some five thousand finished the night swaying back and forth, their arms around each other, in what could not be farther removed from the old and dying style that had relegated worshipers to passive listeners who never moved their bodies, except as directed by the service leader.

By 1995 when an initial cohort of synagogues intent on worship change gathered in Synagogue 2000's (S2K) first conference, many more composers had joined the revolution, and not just composers affiliated with the Reform movement. Common Conservative options included the neo-Hasidic sound of Shlomo Carlebach, Craig Taubman's guitar and band service, and the modified Argentinean tradition of New York's BJ (B'nai Jeshurun Synagogue). Jews were also listening to Israel's annual music festivals, which provided new liturgical staples like *Yerushalayim Shel Zahav* and *Y'did Nefesh*. Debbie Friedman, meanwhile, had shaped what were being called "healing services," part of a new sensitivity to people in pain—physical, psychic, or spiritual. The service resembled a folk concert where the audience sang along to music that replaced fear and pain with hope and empowerment.

The singing mirrored larger trends of the time: greater traditionalism, individualism, and emotionality—what we call here "a culture of experience"[3] and "a new romanticism" (see below). Its communal sound broke down arbitrary barriers separating clergy from congregants and congregants from each other. Its worship responded to baby boomers, now widely called a generation of seekers[4], and, soon to follow, their children, who would differ in many respects but who would be no less alienated from worship styles of the past.

CONSERVATIVE JUDAISM:
COMPETENCE, COMPETENCE, COMPETENCE

The story of Conservative Jews has its own trajectory, divisible into three distinctive periods: pre-World War II, a postwar era, and a renaissance that began somewhere in the 1980s.

Until World War II

Unlike Reform Judaism (a transplant from Central Europe), Conservative Judaism in America was born among Eastern European immigrants who came of age in the 1940s. Its synagogues had been around since 1913, but with no overall movement consciousness and no liturgy of its own until 1946, when what became known as the Silverman prayer book was published, using as its prototype the siddur of Rabbi Morris Silverman of West Hartford, Connecticut. Until then, Conservative synagogues had developed no singularly distinctive worship style: some synagogues featured a late Friday night service with organ music; English prayers were not uncommon; the original Silverman siddur had contained transliteration of important Hebrew passages.

Post-World War II

As the preferred movement for Eastern European Jews, Conservative Judaism set the pace for postwar suburbanization. Its synagogues served densely packed Jewish settlements, especially on the East Coast. Billed by its first prayer book editors as "modern" but "traditional," Conservative worship differed from Reform by being more friendly toward tradition and more attune to halakhic precedent.[5] Hebrew became a sine qua non to the point where the new *Siddur Sim Shalom* came out in 1985 with little concern for sexisms in the English, since Conservative Jews were expected not to need the English anyway. Nonetheless, for those confined to prayer in English, the editor hoped that "a new and felicitous translation [would allow] an emotionally satisfying experience to the greatest degree possible." It would provide "at least part of what it is to pray in the manner that we call davening in Hebrew."[6]

From the 1980s On

The Conservative movement's youth congregations, summer camps, and day schools produced laypeople, not just rabbis and cantors, able to lead traditional services. By the 1980s, graduates of these institutions were looking for their own brand of spiritual fulfillment.

As time wore on, a certain style set in: the yarmulke was refashioned as a small and stylish *kippah*; with the admission of women to the minyan, the *tallit* blossomed with pastel designs. Congregants sought upbeat *ruach* (spirit), not just music in the traditional cantorial modes called *nusach*, or in what was pejoratively labeled "mumble davening." Musical options like Carlebach, Taubman, Israeli folk, and BJ abounded. *Kavvanah* became the Conservative word for what Reform Jews called spirituality; it was characterized as "good davening," which defied easy description, although one knew it when one saw it. It required competence.

THE 1990S: THE NEW ROMANTICISM

Entering the 1990s, Reform and Conservative synagogues sought similar goals, informed by their own distinctive spiritual inheritance, and by what their leaders had experienced in their respective denominational youth cultures. But a deeper trend lay behind them both, a *new romanticism*.

Romanticism was a literary, artistic, and philosophical movement that became dominant following the Napoleonic wars. The *Encyclopedia of Literature* defines it as a reaction against the Enlightenment and the Enlightenment's stress on "reason, order, balance, harmony, rationality and intellect." Romanticism, by contrast, "emphasized the individual, the subjective, the irrational, the imaginative, the personal, the spontaneous, the emotional, the visionary, and the transcendental."

Romanticism served political ends as well. The French Revolution had fought monarchy, church, and privilege with the Enlightenment agenda of "liberty, equality, fraternity." When the revolution finally ended with the defeat of Napoleon, romanticism provided reactionary nationalist regimes with an intellectual rationale for a return to their past. A cadre of scholars, especially in Germany, studied their nation's culture with an eye toward revealing its historical genius.

For Jews seeking civil rights, romanticism was a double-edged sword. The Romantic era gave them room too to demonstrate themselves as an evolving people with a proud and noble history; but simultaneously, it marked them off as inherently different from the cultures where they were demanding inclusion. European Judaism arrived in America, therefore, with all the benefits of romanticism but with a heavy corrective also—a desire to retain the old Enlightenment values (reason, order, balance, harmony, rationality, and intellect), for only these could justify Jewish inclusion in the body politic of another nation. Enlightenment inclusivity as established by men like Thomas Jefferson and James Madison was precisely what had made America so welcoming of Jews in the first place.

So until the cultural revolution of the 1960s, Jewish worship was governed by reason, order, balance, harmony, rationality, and intellect. Jews preferred the model of New England Episcopalians and Unitarians to the more Romantic varieties of Baptists and Methodists. That is why Classical Reform lasted so long and why neo-Hasidism did not catch on so quickly. Classical Reform was the Episcopalian model of "worship by the mind"; neo-Hasidism followed the Methodist model of "worship by the heart."[7] When baby boomers reached maturity and synagogue leadership in the 1980s, however, they established the Romantic preference for emotionality, religious catharsis, and inner experience—what has aptly been labeled "expressive individualism"[8] and "post-modern primitivism."[9] Staid, rational, and orderly prayer was out; neo-Hasidic mysticism and emotionality were in.

Theologically, rabbis turned from the rationalism of Mordecai Kaplan to the poetry of Abraham Joshua Heschel. Musically speaking, Reform synagogues replaced the organ with the guitar; in Conservative shuls, where instruments were banned, Carlebach threatened nusach. Reform sought spirituality; Conservative wanted good davening.

The good davening option characterized the two Conservative congregations in our study that were so proud of their t'fillah. But in most congregations, good davening grew up in the margins, usually in opposition to the normative cantor-led sanctuary service. Its advocates were what pioneer sociologist Max Weber called "religious virtuosi"—Conservative camp and day-school graduates, capable of leading services on their own. It became a mark of pride, for example, to have "a full kri'ah"—a reading of the entire weekly parashah instead of just the third that the Conservative movement has officially established as a valid option. Some Conservative synagogues sought to reign in such separatism by establishing good davening in the sanctuary and expanding a cohort of learned Jews who can read Torah and appreciate a full kri'ah there. They were trying to lock out the erosion of tradition by locking in an appreciation of prayer competence.

OLD GUARDS, NEW GATHERINGS

Both Reform and Conservative had to fight their own respective old guards, and both were stymied by what had become bar and bat mitzvah "factories." Synagogues were faced with weekly Shabbat gatherings dominated by extended family and friends of at least one—and up to three—candidates for bar or bat mitzvah. Not all the attendees were even Jewish, much less Jewishly literate. In reaction, congregation regulars sometimes chose alternatives elsewhere in the synagogue, thereby exacerbating the problem by abandoning the central sanctuary to the weekly visitors. Reform synagogues reemphasized Friday night as the congregational option and offered just a small alternative study minyan (with or without services) in the morning. Conservative synagogues had largely given up late Friday night services and had to fight the bar and bat mitzvah syndrome by insisting that the Shabbat morning service be retained for communal, not just the bar or bat mitzvah family, worship. But given the bar and bat mitzvah numbers, that was hard to accomplish—hence the break-off of traditionalist minyanim seeking kavvanah outside the sanctuary. Rabbis were then faced with an issue of community: does a synagogue need a single Shabbat worship focus, or can it be balkanized into two or more services?

Given the importance of music, it is no surprise to see that cantors, especially, struggled with the "worship wars" that came to the fore in the transformation efforts of the 1990s. The battle had begun a decade earlier, an index of the cultural conflict between cantors trained in the music of high art and tradition and a generation of worshipers demanding congregational singing.[10] Sanctuary services featured the former; break-off minyanim insisted on the latter.

Reform cantors were experts in Jewish art music and traditional nusach but untrained in the techniques of congregational engagement. For both reasons, they felt put upon by rabbinic colleagues who demanded folk music that the cantors thought any song leader could perform. When these cantors fought back or faltered, they were sometimes forced to leave—or allowed to stay, but in fear that what they were asked to do and what they had been trained to do were two altogether different things.

Conservative cantors—more likely to go by the Hebrew, *chazanim*—were equally troubled, in their case by the loss of nusach specifically, which they identified as their authentic art. Nusach is a complex tradition of cantorial interpretation rooted in different musical modes—sets of sliding sounds, unlike the Western musical octave built on individual notes. Modes change with the service and the calendrical occasion. Great cantors master artistic interpretation of these modes. They learn also a musical repertoire of great prayers—Kol Nidre, for example. By the 1990s, Conservative Jews still wanted Kol Nidre; it was not so clear that they wanted much else. And inside the break-off minyanim, leaders of davening with no cantorial training readily substituted their own brand of musical kavvanah, sometimes based on nusach but usually not. At Conservative cantorial conventions, some members advertised their fear for the future of the cantorate by wearing buttons saying "Chazanasaurus."

Important to note is that in both cases, worship change was driven by internal movement elites. A small percentage of Reform and Conservative Jewish youth had attended camps and day schools where prayer had intrigued them through its emotionality: Reform camps taught singing and Conservative camps taught davening, but they were functional equivalents—prayer in the Romantic mode. It was those educated camp or day school graduates who found the pre-Romantic sanctuary services particularly unengaging. The challenge to worship, therefore, was as much a sign of denominational educational success as it was a symptom of worship failure.

Our interviews exposed all this being played out politically: among congregants old and young and between cantors on one hand and rabbis on the other. It took considerable leadership to insist on the urgency of worship, to remain open to what it might be, and to negotiate the conflict that ritual change inevitably occasions.

Measuring Worship:
Drama, Components, and Strategy

Worship is best likened to an art—a performative art, akin to drama[11]—and has several components:

- *Script*—a prayer book
- *Choreography*—the way the script is played out (egalitarian prayer roles, announcements from the pulpit, and so forth)
- *Music*—part of both script and choreography, but set apart here as a separate component because it is so central
- *Space to stage the performance*—usually a sanctuary

- *Props*—sacred ones like the Torah scrolls and the Ark that houses them, but ordinary items, too, like the reader's desk
- *Scheduled performances*—morning, afternoon, or evening; arranged around calendrical events relevant to the script (Shabbat morning, Sukkot eve, and so forth)
- *Actors*—usually a rabbi, a cantor, and others called to the bimah

The congregation attends in several roles: as *audience*, its members observe the drama going on about them; as *actors*, they perform their roles within the play; and as *critics*, they return home, applauding or panning the performance in which they have just participated. Change amounts to fiddling with an age-old drama in the presence of audience and actors who are familiar with a single classical performance and are not likely to take kindly to someone who challenges it. The worship leader or planner is cast in the role of *director*, who hopes they will appreciate the performance (as audience), adapt to new roles (as actors), and write positive reviews when it is over.

In determining the course of worship change, rabbis must decide which of the above worship *components* to alter. Of them all, the seventh, the actors, will prove most challenging, since the actors are actual people who can refuse to go along with their instructions. In addition, they must determine a *strategy* that goes beyond the choice of components. Strategically, they have three options:

Strategy 1: *Insist on moderate to maximal change* and hope the other actors and congregation will go along; accompany the change with a campaign of classes, sermons, and meetings to explain why the changes are necessary.

Strategy 2: *Institute alternative worship performances*, parallel services to satisfy critics who want something other than what is happening in the main sanctuary.

Strategy 3: *Make only minimal or moderate change*, choosing those components that are least likely to evoke resistance.

The Reform synagogues we studied differed from the Conservative ones—they used different strategies and emphasized different components. This observation runs counter to the common wisdom that sees American Judaism entering a stage of postdenominationalism, at least on the non-Orthodox end of the spectrum. Since worship is the ritualized marker of identity, even if congregants in both movements were to adopt the same positions on halakhic issues (kashrut, for instance), their worship style would still distinguish them as distinctive denominational preferences.

Another way to look at it is to differentiate belief from experience. Except among the Orthodox, denominations have come to matter less for the beliefs they espouse than for their capacity to facilitate experience that people consider satisfying and authentic.[12] Worship transformation ranks high today because it is supremely experiential. Conservative and Reform Judaism differ in the nature of the experience they offer. When it comes to prayer, Reform Jews we studied felt relatively little allegiance to inherited performance and were willing, even anxious, to adopt strategy 1, making wholesale change. Conservative Jews, by contrast, insisted on maintaining allegiance to old forms. They preferred strategies 2 and 3, arranging alternative services and making only minimal to moderate changes in the worship components. Given the difference of perspective, looking at the two movements separately is useful. First, how did our Conservative congregations respond to worship challenges?

Conservative Patterns

Our research revealed few Conservative rabbis (and even fewer cantors) opting to change t'fillah. They much preferred addressing learning. In part, that is because study has been the hallmark of Conservative Judaism, which has emphasized day schools and Hebrew competence, for example. Enhancing congregational learning continued longstanding Conservative policy. But in part also, it reflected a rabbinic uneasiness with opening issues of public prayer to a fully democratic discussion. There were exceptions of course, but overall that fear characterized Conservative congregations throughout our experience in the field. A rabbi who declined to work with S2K put it well: "Why would I join a process where people will ask me to do what halakhically I cannot? What if, for example, they want musical instruments on Shabbat? Then what will I do?"

When change did occur, Conservative congregations treated the Hebrew script of prayer as sacrosanct. Music was an area of conflict, the rabbi preferring congregational melodies and the cantor (where there was one) holding out for nusach. An easy component choice was worship space, where halakhic concerns are minimal. Also, rabbi and cantor can more easily agree on altering the configuration of the sanctuary to facilitate congregational engagement, while leaving the traditional prayer service intact. Two of our congregations, unwilling to make large changes in the major *inanimate* performance components (script, choreography, and music), changed the *human* components (the congregants) by setting up impressive training programs to provide congregants with the skills required to negotiate the service knowledgably. Rather than change the worship, that is, they changed the worshipers.

CONGREGATION AGUDATH ISRAEL

We have seen that, unwilling to change the service, Conservative congregations commonly opted for service alternatives (strategy 2). A good example is the Shabbat *N'shamah* (Shabbat of the soul) of Congregation Agudath Israel in Caldwell, New Jersey, which sought to satisfy people who lacked familiarity with the service and sought a sense of personal spirituality. Congregant Debbie Rabner epitomizes its supporters: she loves the fact that they teach "beautiful" melodies and that people clap freely during them.

Another Congregation Agudath Israel congregant, the *gabba'i*, Alan Gerberg, rather likes the idea that the congregation's main worship service has barely changed since he joined in the 1980s. He runs the traditional Friday night minyan, while the clergy lead the various other options. But the clergy come to the sanctuary service for the more important Shabbat morning service. Rabbi Silverstein is proud of the fact that even those who attend the Friday alternatives come Saturday morning for the regular davening. He has refused even to exchange the old Silverman Siddur of 1946 for its 1985 denominational replacement, *Siddur Sim Shalom*.

At Congregation Agudath Israel, the sanctuary service has seen change, but within the limits allowed by halakhah and local tradition. During its experimental period with S2K, the congregation moved the reading table to a more central position so that the people were closer to "the action." Space was easier to change than music. Paula Mack Drill, a member of the change team, recalls failing miserably at introducing a congregational melody that she had learned at an S2K convention. What did succeed was adding a healing component to the worship experience. Here was an innovation that did not compromise the integrity of the traditional service structure—it did not require leaving anything out, and no precedent had to be consulted. Having chosen to specialize in becoming a synagogue with healing at its core, the congregation even went farther. Having met Debbie Friedman at S2K conventions, the change team arranged to have her bring healing to Congregation Agudath Israel in the form of a separate service, again something that was easily achievable, because instead of an alternative to Shabbat services, it was a separate, independent, and altogether creative offering.

But Shabbat N'shamah and the healing services seem to have run their course. At first, all of these experiments received enormous clergy attention—Cantor Joel Caplan, for example, "physically used to change the space for N'shamah services," says program director Randi Brokman. "He consulted with a congregant artist about creating atmosphere." The program remains but "the candles have stopped, out of safety concerns" and "the drapery was also discontinued." Clearly, Synagogue 2000 thinking has permeated the congregation, but from our interviews, it is hard to know the ultimate fate of specific worship innovations, which seem to be dying off.

Congregation Agudath Israel's experience teaches us a great deal:

- Vital congregations make up for the inability to change tradition by adding to their offerings, both within the service and outside of it.
- If they cannot change the prayer text very much, they can and do change space.
- Alternative services spring up, but may be seen as threats to the primary Shabbat experience that the rabbi wants the entire community to share.
- To make up for limited ability to change the service, congregations change the congregants: they train lay leaders and develop a culture where familiarity with the service is sufficiently prized to motivate even those who do not lead it to at least be able to follow it.
- Music is absolutely definitive as the most experiential part of prayer. Musical change, however, tends toward congregational engagement (good davening, in the Conservative context) and may pit the cantor against the rabbi.
- Change requires people to champion it. Most especially, it needs the support of opinion molders, usually the clergy, and of specialists who import necessary expertise. Rabbis enjoy special power here: they can kill efforts at change just by ignoring them. Eventually the lay leaders get tired of fighting or move on to other issues.

BETH JACOB CONGREGATION

Beth Jacob Congregation in Mendota Heights, Minnesota, mirrored most of what we saw at Congregation Agudath Israel. It too joined the initial cohort of S2K congregations, but unlike Congregation Agudath Israel, it had no intention of even considering dramatic change—not through lack of energy, goodwill, or ability, but because of pride in the existing service. For example, S2K advocated using space to engage people. The congregation, however, had already constructed a new building that features a semicircular worship arrangement with "everyone in close" (according to founding member Harold Gillman). Additionally, ever since Rabbi Morris Allen had arrived, participation and overall competence to lead services had become primary. Here, too, the attention of the rabbi stands out as probative.

Morris had come from a smaller pulpit in Lincoln, Nebraska, where "if we got fifteen people, we were, like, thrilled. So whoever came got a part." This respect for radically democratizing service participation influenced Morris's newfound pulpit, which he had chosen over an established one, precisely because he wanted to build something with his distinctive mark upon it. Preferring to have everyone lead rather than have a perfect service dependent on professionals, he went about asking people to do whatever they could—"read Torah, if possible, or just the *chatsi kaddish* [a prayer that recurs frequently and is easy to master]."

People at Beth Jacob know that liturgical competence matters. Laura Honan, a Jew by choice, was initially intimidated by the traditional service's complexity and the fact that it was all in Hebrew. Recognizing that the full engagement she sought required further education, she studied Hebrew and worked hard to master the service's myriad details. Jeanine Lange is another Jew by choice who "didn't want to become part of something I just observe," so learned her way around and is now a regular morning attendee.

People at Beth Jacob point with pride to their singular success in training service leaders. "People became Torah readers who never dreamt [of doing it]," says Harold Gillman, who recalls that even the rabbi's wife got involved teaching people how to read Hebrew. The congregation does without a cantor on principle, Harold adds, because "without a cantor, people have to take responsibility."

The service's integrity is carefully guarded here. Shabbat morning *b'nei mitzvah* are not allowed to dominate. President Mark Savin speaks for many when he applauds the absence of "guitars and bongos." This is not a place to try lots of new things, warns educator and program director Susan Drazen. "We don't want to turn our Shabbat into something kitschy." Members are happy that Conservative congregations change very slowly, limiting their innovations to "a few things that people find meaningful, like the *mi sheberakh*" (the Debbie Friedman melody gleaned at S2K conferences). Overall, explains Laura Honan, change is decried as the "watering down" of prayer.

Still, the rabbi knows that davening alone is not for everyone; so he makes sure the quality of the food at the kiddush is good. He also launched a monthly meditation service for congregants who find traditional davening lacking. The meditation option has diminished in importance, however—one suspects because of ambivalence from the rabbi, for whom meditation is fine but hardly a goal. "People were afraid that these activities would divide the congregation," says Arielle Ehrlich, but they were permitted because it seemed more likely that without them "people would break off to form a new congregation."

Like Congregation Agudath Israel, then, Beth Jacob is a congregation that orchestrates spatial change but little else; rather than change tradition, it educates people to appreciate it. It tolerates alternative services, but prefers a single service that builds community.

What is striking here is the ubiquitous role of the rabbi, the founder of the congregation in the first place and the sole clergy member, because there is no cantor. Morris's presence is everywhere. But a strong rabbinic presence could be seen in all our congregations. Morris is just a particularly obvious example.

CONGREGATION BETH SHALOM

As the sole congregation that could not participate in a national change initiative, Congregation Beth Shalom in suburban Kansas City had to set one up locally. It is more liberal than the other Conservative synagogues mentioned here. Even though it shares the lessons drawn from its two sister congregations (Agudath Israel and Beth Jacob), it represents a bridge to the Reform synagogues that will be considered next.

The most obvious difference from the other Conservative shuls we studied was Beth Shalom's very decision to attack worship, an area most Conservative synagogues avoided. Like all the congregations mentioned here, Beth Shalom benefited from risk-ready clergy, in this case, a clergy team. Additionally, the clergy were joined first by one, and then another, determined lay ally.

Shortly after senior rabbi Alan Cohen arrived in 1989, a separate library minyan was established for people looking to exchange the cantor-led sanctuary service for good davening. While the original planners envisaged a United Synagogue Youth (USY) Camp Ramah-like format with plenty of ruach, the group that came together was older, more ritually observant, and desirous of a straightforward, traditional-style service that Josh Sosland, one of the minyan's founders, expressly describes as more "Torah centric." Emblematic of this attitude is the minyan's decision to read the entire weekly Torah portion instead of the shorter triennial selection that is followed in the main sanctuary. A large percentage of those attending began to rotate the responsibility of a Shabbat *d'var torah*. At times, they even added a preservice study session.

Like many such alternative minyanim, the niche became a clique. "The people who were there had taken ownership of that minyan," Alan recalls. "They may have had no objection to other people coming but they weren't really anxious to market it."

Meanwhile, a third minyan, part of Tefillah 2000, the change initiative that is our interest here, had begun meeting in an all-purpose room—rather than in the chapel that had fixed seats, no room for instruments, and too much formality. The impetus had come from Beth Smith, a recent widow who approached Rabbi Cohen with a proposal to memorialize her late husband: "That," recalls Alan, "is how Tefillah 2000 was born." A task force was subsequently established under the guidance of the second lay ally, Jeanette Wishna. At first, the alternative met only on Friday nights, but eventually spread to Saturday mornings and even (somewhat later still) to the High Holidays and the Festivals. Alan himself had directed the service at the beginning, but as it expanded he found himself unable to give it his full attention. Meanwhile, the congregation was going through a succession of cantors, only one of whom was inclined to attend it. He also led it some Friday nights. But simultaneously, lay members of the Tefillah 2000 task force were being groomed for service leadership. Toward that end, a study group met over a period of months; it included two musicians who attended a conference at a Reform summer camp to learn congregational melodies.

In the middle of this ferment, Rabbi Amy Wallk Katz arrived in town. She was accompanying her husband, whose employment had brought him there. At first, she began working in the shul as a volunteer. Having written her doctoral dissertation on prayer, she took a special interest in the alternative, liberal service. It had spread from Friday to Saturday by then, part of strategy 2, parallel worship performances. But it was bereft of clergy leadership, since on Saturday mornings the rabbis and cantor felt obliged to attend the main sanctuary service. When the lay leaders in training couldn't make a commitment for every other week, Amy concluded, "If the Shabbat morning Tefillah 2000 service is ever really going to grow, we need someone to devote some attention to it." So she attended regularly, provided direction, made decisions (like employing a band called *Yachad* every week), and the minyan took off.

At that point, Katz was still just a volunteer, with more leeway than the professionals. "I could do whatever I liked," she says. And she got lucky: she enjoyed exemplary lay partners and a senior rabbi with whom she consulted at every step along the way and who gave her license to move forward.

Every Shabbat morning: (1) the traditional minyan met in the library; (2) a typical Conservative service took place in the sanctuary; and (3) a liberal, creative minyan began thriving in the all-purpose room. Eventually, some Tefillah 2000 innovations made their way to the sanctuary as well; most significantly, says Rabbi Cohen, "some tunes and, eventually, the option for *b'nei mitzvah* with instruments."

In some ways, Beth Shalom was like the other Conservative congregations we visited. It too featured a traditional Conservative service, with a cantor and regular attendees committed to its continuation; and it faced the same halakhic problems, primarily whether to import musical instruments. But Rabbi Cohen stands out as a liberal within the Conservative camp. Even before Tefillah 2000, he opened a ritual-committee conversation about instrumentation, at least for Friday nights.

Here, we see the most typical response to worship discontent in Conservative synagogues: strategy 2, establishing an alternative minyan, in this case not just one but two. (In fact, a third one was added: a neighborhood minyan that met unofficially outside the shul. Its schedule was not widely circulated, and not everyone was invited to attend.) Here, too, the rabbis worried about retaining community despite multiplying parallel services.

But Beth Shalom differed from Beth Jacob and Congregation Agudath Israel. First, Rabbi Cohen did not think the sanctuary service deserved to be preserved as it was; second, being more liberal, he was more inclined toward strategy 1, large-scale liturgical innovation. Third, the synagogue boasted Rabbi Amy Katz as a member.

Amy's presence demonstrates once again the importance of professional attention and rabbinic support. When she began her volunteer work, the shul had an assistant rabbi, who, however, was a committed traditionalist and vastly preferred the sanctuary service to the Tefillah 2000 alternative. When he left, Amy was hired to replace him. But ironically, Tefillah 2000 now lost clergy support, since, as the official rabbi, she had to be with the bar and bat mitzvah families in the sanctuary. Exacerbating the situation was the weakening of lay leadership. Jeanette Wishna died, and funding began drying up.

Has Beth Shalom been noticeably changed by Tefillah 2000? Clearly, some of its creative ferment has penetrated the sanctuary service—bar and bat mitzvah families may opt to have instruments there, for example. Rabbi Cohen notes also that "on High Holidays, the change is dramatic." Whether Tefillah 2000 will have an impact on other areas of synagogue life is less certain. This was Tefillah 2000, not Synagogue 2000. Unlike S2K and ECE, an overall transformation was never the goal at Beth Shalom.

LESSONS LEARNED: THE CONSERVATIVE CAMP

Looking especially at the congregations studied here, but also taking into consideration others that worked on worship with S2K, we can say that the worship change in Conservative shuls generally unfolds in stages:

1. Some traditionalist and liturgy-competent congregants express discontent with the traditional sanctuary service, usually its cantorial centrality and the bar and bat mitzvah dominance.

2. With at least the tacit agreement of the rabbi, they form their own minyan (strategy 2).

3. The congregation adopts a change initiative for the main sanctuary service, beginning with areas that have little or no halakhic implication (strategy 3, minimal to moderate change)—like rearranging space to make the main service more engaging, or adding a healing service. Noncantorial musical alternatives may be suggested but not necessarily implemented. As it becomes clear that the main service cannot change very much, other alternatives (strategy 2, again) make their appearance.

4. The clergy begin to worry about losing a sense of overall community. Feeling tugged in competing directions, and according priority to the sanctuary service, they slowly disengage from the break-off(s), which then diminish in importance or disappear.

5. Some of the new ideas enter the sanctuary service, which, however, remains pretty much as it began.

Significantly, with the exception of our bridge congregation, Beth Shalom, sustainable ritual change in Conservative synagogues tends toward reinforcing traditionalism. Movement away from tradition runs counter to Conservative culture, so is less likely to occur; and even if it does get started, it has no davening experts to drive it—the experts are likely to be the elite clamoring for movement in the other direction. Beth Shalom succeeded only because the rabbi wanted it enough to devote attention to it. Without continued rabbinic support, liberalizing experiments are likely to fail.

Reform Patterns

Reform congregations began with much the same story as Beth Shalom. For years, laypeople alienated by a privatized Saturday morning bar and bat mitzvah service and anxious for a participatory experience instead had been establishing separate library or chapel services (strategy 2), usually combined with Torah study. They too tended to settle into niched, and even cliquish, gatherings. But here the story changes.

Conservative rabbis retained allegiance to their sanctuary services even if those services did not provide good davening. Reform rabbis felt no such loyalty. Their rabbinic mentors of the 1950s and '60s had invested their energy in childhood education and social justice, not in prayer. To the extent that they did attend to worship, they focused mostly on sermons. Having grown up experiencing what they knew was poor worship, the new generation of rabbis could not wait to attack its problems with a passion. By the 1980s and '90s, they had become senior rabbis with authority to do so.

The formative years growing up in the 1970s played an important role in what they brought to their task. The Six Day War had awakened the Reform movement's identification with Jews worldwide and brought about a revival of tradition and reclamation of Hebrew. These rabbis were also the first to spend a mandatory rabbinic-school year in Israel, visiting synagogues of all sorts and valuing the traditionalism they saw there. Instead of dismissing ritual, the new cohort of senior rabbis embraced its fascinating potential.

The 1970s had also been the era when liturgical renewal became the clarion call in churches. Influenced by this national liturgical ferment, Larry Hoffman had brought the study of worship (as opposed to liturgy as text study) to the rabbinic curriculum that these rabbis (then rabbinic students) had encountered. Some fifteen years later, a number of these alumni had come together to further their study and experiment with putting theory into practice. The Reform movement's embrace of worship renewal was, therefore, just waiting to be tapped by S2K. While Conservative rabbis approached liturgical change hesitantly, these Reform rabbis could not get enough of it.

THE CONGREGATIONS IN OUR STUDY

In chapters 4 and 5, we include two of the five Reform congregations (Congregation Beth Am, Los Altos, California, and Temple Israel, Boston) for their work in education and social justice, respectively. Here, we will focus on those synagogues (Temple Micah, Westchester Reform, and Temple Beth Elohim) where worship transformation was pivotal. But so important has worship become in the Reform movement, that Congregation Beth Am and Temple Israel could just as easily have been our subjects. Temple Israel's service grew to incorporate guitar and percussion instruments; clergy moved off the high bimah and walked up and down the aisles encouraging people to sing; the entire ambience shifted toward greater engagement, inclusivity, and joy. As for Congregation Beth Am, even before arriving there, Rabbi Janet Marder had authored an article where she argued for worship that is "joyous, dynamic, and spiritually alive."[13] When interviewed for this study, she added, "Worship life is at the heart of the congregation. If the worship is dead, the congregation is also, in a way, dead."

In what follows, however, we will focus on just the three congregations that chose specifically to work on worship, recognizing that the discussion could have encompassed the other two as well.

We saw before that worship reform can be broken down into strategy and components. We saw also that of the inanimate components, space is the easiest to address. It is no surprise, then, to see that all three Reform congregations emphasized the role of space immediately. "S2K began one year after the move to the new building," reports Rabbi Danny Zemel at Micah. "No question, the move was the defining moment of change, because for us, S2K became the vehicle to figure out how to be a congregation in our own building." Among other things, Micah had shared the old building with a church, so it had to schedule religious school on Saturdays; now it could move classes to Sunday, leaving its clergy free on Saturday to concentrate on Shabbat morning services. Friday nights changed too, since the new sanctuary boasted moveable chairs and no raised bimah. Westchester Reform in Scarsdale, New York, still had its old postwar plant with fixed pews, but it had purchased the adjacent lot where it erected a retreat space with an inviting room for worship. It too was constructed to permit worship in the round and to diminish the distance between clergy and laity. Temple Beth Elohim in Wellesley, Massachusetts, knew it needed a new sanctuary, if not an entirely new building; in fact, Rabbi Joel Sisenwine was consumed by the need for new space from the moment he arrived. In the meantime, however, the congregation relocated services to a new atrium (called the galleria) with circular seating. When he interviewed for his position, the committee chair told Joel, "I want to see standing room only Friday night." At the time, "there were about forty people there," says Joel. "We grew the number to about 130."

Since novel space permits novel choreography, people began doing worship differently. Westchester Reform initiated a family service (Sharing Shabbat) that went hand in hand with its ECE education initiative. Temple Micah moved the kiddush and candle-lighting to the atrium adjoining the sanctuary so that people could meet, mingle, and sing together even before processing inside for the service.

Neither space nor choreography, however, made the greatest difference. Nor, certainly, could it have been the prayer book (*Gates of Prayer*), which had been in use since 1975 without facilitating much notable change at all. The determining factor was music—a finding compatible with Protestant worship change as well. Rick Warren, founder of the path-breaking Saddleback Church in southern California, recalls, "If I could start Saddleback all over again, I'd put more energy and money into music. . . . The great American pastime is not baseball; it is music."[14]

Since its inception, Reform Judaism has welcomed instrumentation on Shabbat. The instrument of record back then was the organ, whose initial use in 1817 prompted a famous exchange of responses between Orthodox traditionalists and their Reform opponents. Two and one-half centuries later, the organ is again a subject of debate: this time, however, Reform traditionalists are its advocate, while proponents of new worship want it replaced by something more upbeat and inviting of congregational singing. The first instrument to emerge was the folk guitar, which debuted nationally in the 1960s and '70s—today's synagogue leaders discovered it at camp. Of late, under the influence, particularly, of Craig Taubman, entire bands have become normative. In any case, whether with guitar, band, or something else, worship renewal in Reform circles depends on music. Cello, clarinet, and flute are common and with the new generation, percussion is coming into its own.

We described above how the issue of music in Conservative congregations revolved around the fear of losing traditional nusach. The issue was joined differently in the Reform camp. There, two bodies of traditional music had evolved: not just nusach but also art music. As sophisticated musicians, cantors considered populist music simplistic, hardly, they argued, what worship of God deserves. But passivity was precisely what the new rabbis were intent on overturning. What made Rabbi Marder's article particularly controversial was the fact that she documented successful worship at four congregations, not one of which had a cantor. Many of her rabbinic colleagues were bemoaning, at least privately, cantorial recalcitrance to change, even though some cantors like Jeff Klepper had pioneered the folk music that rabbis were drawn to. The cantorial community was clearly in flux, and cantors were the key to how congregations dealt with music.

Beth Elohim's cantor Jodi Sufrin had mastered both traditional and art music, but she played the guitar as well, having been a song leader before entering cantorial school. She had been at the temple for twenty years, slowly expanding her role from a pulpit presence alone to being at the hub of congregational life. People in our study called her "the heart and soul of the congregation." She led her congregation's worship initiative, which she had been eagerly anticipating for years. What had been missing prior to S2K, she says, was "marking Shabbat with your community . . . in what is really a meaningful, warm, accepting, compelling way."

When Rabbi Sisenwine arrived, change had already begun at Beth Elohim. "I knew my strong suit was my cantor," he says, "so I spent hours on worship." Typical of the testimony we heard are the comments of congregant Nancy Belsky:

> When my new rabbi [Sisenwine] arrived, he smiled all the time; he got an assistant rabbi, who, oh my God, smiled even more than he did. . . . It became a warm, cozy place to be Friday night. They moved the service to 6 o'clock so you could go after work and have dinner afterward. . . . It kind of spoke to what Shabbat was supposed to feel like.

Westchester Reform, by contrast, enjoyed a gifted cantor for whom the new music was completely foreign. Here, the rabbi, who sought change, got lucky: being in the greater New York area, he brought Debbie Friedman to introduce healing services. He also hired Cantor Ellen Dreskin, a family educator and the national program director for S2K, who was based in New York and who played the guitar. The result was a second worship track (strategy 2) alongside the one in the sanctuary, an alternative Saturday morning minyan, really, but unlike the Conservative parallels where members could lead davening, this one required professional guidance. So the synagogue charged Ellen with running the new service and combining it with Sharing Shabbat. Like Beth Elohim, it also provided an early Friday night service after which worshipers could go home for Shabbat dinner.

TEMPLE MICAH: A CASE STUDY IN MUSIC

Finally, we come to Temple Micah in Washington, D.C., a cross between Beth Elohim and Westchester Reform. Unlike the former, it boasted no cantor at all. Instead, it had entrusted its worship to a music director and a part-time soloist.

Temple Micah's rabbi, Danny Zemel, returned from his first Synagogue 2000 conference on fire with possibility. "S2K gave a model to think about Shabbat as the result of a lifestyle rather than as an event. The lifestyle is that people are on their way home from work, and that's when people should have a taste of Shabbat."

So he too moved what had been a late Friday night service to 6:30 and engaged the congregation in Shabbat melodies that people could carry home with them. Danny recalls, "We made a change in our cantorial soloist totally because of what we learned about worship at S2K. . . . I spent a year working with her, and it just wasn't working. I wanted her to pray as a Jew instead of sing as a soloist. Meryl [the soloist's successor] prays as a Jew. And Meryl has a deeper presence. Meryl is a spiritual person."

From Danny, we see that more is at work than just engaging a congregation in song. He gives us a glimpse of the culture of experience and the new romanticism mentioned above. The nineteenth-century Romantic movement wanted art that derives from the heart and speaks to the soul. The new music of today derives its authenticity from the fact that it is the prayer of its leaders, who manage to engage congregants in it as their own personal prayer as well.

Music director Teddy Klaus now faced a dilemma. Though not a cantor himself, Teddy shared his cantorial colleagues' hesitancy "to let go of their 'performance' stature. There was always a feeling that this was 'dumbing down,' especially when it came to music." Teddy concedes that at first, he felt the same way, but eventually decided that the new music was not being "dumbed down," so much as it was serving a different purpose, "bringing prayer to people—liturgy to life."

Danny took more control over the music. He is pretty much the general and Meryl and I are the lieutenants. He makes no bones about that. He has developed a concept of the Friday evening services, and I think it is pretty exciting. It's a dynamic that goes from finishing the week, gathering together, and then focusing on the idea of creation and its "afterglow." Danny crafted this whole concept and then we've set about figuring out, "Can the music reflect this and contribute to this?"

Temple Micah's experience underscores the fact that Reform rabbis had reached the conclusion that synagogue worship was truly terrible. But cantors, overall, did not agree (Beth Elohim's Jodi Suffrin and Westchester Reform's Angela Buchdahl were exceptions). So, the most important change was not just space, or just music, or just any other *inanimate* component. It was the *human* components, usually the rabbi, and sometimes the cantor, who drove worship change by a theological and aesthetic vision of what worship should be.

Space and music followed theory. In all five Reform congregations, services became more or less "sing-through"; that is, with the exception of the Torah reading and whatever sermon or d'var torah there was, the congregation sang its way virtually from beginning to end. It was the Reform version of good davening.

Two Worship Cultures

The congregations in our study are parts of larger movements, their respective denominations; and however much or little they still achieve loyalty from lay members, denominations play an important role in socializing the clergy who lead synagogues locally and attain positions nationally from which to influence policy. They also position lay and rabbinic authority differently. At stake, therefore, are entire cultures, formed and furthered by implicit denominational understandings.

From its inception in 1873, the Reform movement in North America has taken its lead from its congregational arm, the Union of American Hebrew Congregations (now, Union for Reform Judaism). The agenda for Conservative Judaism, by contrast, has emanated from its academic address, the Jewish Theological Seminary of America. The impetus and tone of change reflect these two centers of power.

For Conservative Jews, the traditionalism of its seminary remains decisive. For Reform Jews, the voice of congregational unrest is paramount. In both cases, change trickles down through rabbis, but Conservative Judaism vests power in local rabbis who consult the tradition they learned at the seminary; while the very organization of Reform Judaism makes its local rabbis more responsive to pressures from laypeople. In both cases rabbinic influence is primary. But the locus where that influence operates is different. In Conservative Judaism, it operates at the local congregational level: the national congregational body has little say in the matter. Reform polity is equally congregational—Reform rabbis too are autonomous. But they are more closely allied with their laypeople and are responsive to models that arise in the lay organization's national and regional meetings.

Hence, the different cultures—which mirror the denominational structures. Both Conservative and Reform rabbis care deeply about the authority of traditional texts and the spiritual life of congregants. Worship negotiates that connection. Given the primacy of the seminary ambience, it seems right and natural for Conservative rabbis to give primacy to texts. Given the powerful voice of its laypeople, it seems equally right and natural for Reform rabbis to privilege congregational needs.

If a litmus test to differentiate the two movements exists, it is the issue of worship competence. Consistent with its seminary-based authority, Conservative worship is all about competence, which is treated as a goal in its own right, a full kri'ah, lay leadership of services, Hebrew ability, and the like. Consistent with strong lay organizational dominance, Reform Judaism values competence too, but only as a means toward a larger worship goal—achieving spirituality even for congregants who are barely able to follow the service.

It is no surprise then to find the Conservative and Reform movements pursuing opposite worship strategies. Both denominations establish alternative prayer groups; but Conservative minyanim showcase congregational competence while Reform equivalents depend on professional leaders to understand the appropriate worship dynamics, the means to "deliver" experientially meaningful prayer even to people without the competence to do so on their own. If these experiments include more tradition, as they usually do, it is because traditionalism is part of the experience that people in a Romantic era appreciate as a sign of authenticity. Reform's new worship *contains* tradition but does not *exist for tradition's sake*. Not surprising, Conservative rabbis prefer the strategy of minimal to moderate change; Reform rabbis prefer moderate to maximal.

These divergent cultures give rise to equally divergent worship styles. Conservative congregations remain loyal to the traditional script and choreography. Reform has radically changed both. Conservative rabbis defend tradition; Reform rabbis urge change despite it. Except in competent traditional minyanim, Conservative innovation in break-off groups tends to wane, because rabbis have greater allegiance to the sanctuary service and fear the dissolution of community. In Reform worship, changes have more staying power: rather than compete with the rabbi's official agenda, they constitute it, and thereby become the sanctuary service rather than a rival to it. Both Reform and Conservative worship strive for congregational engagement, with the battleground being music—making cantors in both movements suspicious, but for different reasons. Conservative cantors worry about the erosion of traditional nusach. Reform cantors worry about the dumbing down of sacred music. Conservative synagogues largely ignore Friday night but struggle to improve the traditional experience of Shabbat morning; Reform reinvigorates Friday night, sometimes before dinner rather than after, and has largely given up on Saturday morning.

Both denominations seek worship that is meaningful. But what does *meaningful* mean? Cultural historian Thomas R. Cole puts it well when he differentiates scientific questions from existential ones: "The scientific questions about meaning are part of the human attempt to develop logical, reliable, interpretable and systematically predictive theories. The existential questions about meaning are part of the human quest for a vision within which one's experience makes sense. [Meaningful means being able] to connect the world of public understandings with the inner struggle for wholeness."[15]

Science and religion explore alternative worlds of human experience. What experiments are to science, worship is to religion. Science tests its hypotheses by their predictive capacity. Religion does the same thing by the symbolic success of its rituals. In both cases, we, the subjects, need convincing: scientists compare prediction with result; worshipers seek to be moved while in prayer and to emerge from it with a sense of wholeness and purpose. Science reveals what we are willing to take as realities in the world, insofar as we come in contact with nature; worship unveils similar realities in human consciousness, insofar as we come in contact with God. In their own distinctive ways, Reform and Conservative synagogues seek meaningful worship that "connects the world of public understandings with the inner struggle for wholeness."

CHAPTER 4

Visionary Learning:
Schooling for Everyone

The Jewish tradition is replete with texts urging Jews to study Torah. A well-known passage in the Mishnah states:

> These are the things, the fruits of which a man enjoys in this world,
> while the stock remains for him in the world to come:
> honoring the father and mother
> the practice of charity
> timely attendance at the house of study morning and evening
> hospitality to wayfarers
> visiting the sick
> dowering the bride
> attending the dead to the grave
> devotion in prayer
> making peace between man and his fellow;
> *but the study of the Torah is equal to them all.*
>
> —PEAH 1:1 (italics added)

Though we have no way of knowing how much time *amcha*, ordinary Jews, devoted to study throughout the generations, we do know that for centuries communal leaders and members of the elite upheld the principle (if not always the practice) of *torah lishmah*, the study of Jewish texts "for their own sake." In America, however, this commitment to study took a different form. Jews valued learning as much as ever (perhaps more than ever), but the *type* of learning they sought was, by and large, secular learning, the kind of learning tied to career advancement. Perhaps the need to earn a living in a new country left little time for Jewish study, or perhaps immigrants were, as some have argued, eager to throw off the yoke of traditional obligations. Either way, the mitzvah of talmud torah (the study of Torah) devolved very quickly into the practice of sending one's sons (in the beginning it was only sons) to religious school in preparation for their bar mitzvah. While some sectors of the community maintained the practice of *torah lishmah,* and while periodic revivals of adult Jewish learning have occurred, for most American Jews, Jewish education has been seen as something children have to undergo to become *b'nei mitzvah.*

This shift from *intrinsic* to *instrumental* learning was influenced, at least in part, by the American notion that the goal of education is certification, acquiring a diploma. In the minds of parents, religious school was the equivalent of public school, and bar mitzvah the equivalent of graduation. It did not seem to matter that, according to Jewish tradition, a boy *automatically* becomes a bar mitzvah (literally an adult obligated to fulfill the commandments) at age thirteen, and that being called to the Torah is simply a means of recognizing this change in status. And it didn't seem to matter that influential Reform rabbis had even abolished the celebration of bar mitzvah entirely. The demand to have boys "bar mitzvahed" in a synagogue continued, largely unabated. If one synagogue would not oblige, parents would find another one that did.

Sociologist Stuart Schoenfeld (1988) has shown how in the 1930s and '40s local bureaus of Jewish education worked with the Conservative and the Reform movements to link the celebration of bar mitzvah (bat mitzvahs did not become popular until later) to formal Jewish study. They set standards that required a minimum of a certain number of years of study, a number of times a week. The exact calculus of how many years and hours varied, but the principle remained the same. The result: a Faustian bargain whereby religious schooling became inextricably linked (in the minds of parents, synagogue leaders, and even some synagogue professionals) with preparation for bar (and later bat) mitzvah. A 1989 study quotes a synagogue board member as saying, "Does the congregation really want quality education? Maybe we just want kids to make it through their Bar Mitzvah."[1]

Some Reform congregations fought against this trend, managing to retain the majority of their students through ninth, tenth, and even eleventh and twelfth grades with strong confirmation and postconfirmation programs. But even though this extended the students' years in religious school, it reinforced the belief that Jewish education should be directed toward a concrete goal; once "graduation day" (be it bar mitzvah or confirmation) was reached, students had no reason for further study. This contributed to the idea of the synagogue as a fee-for-service operation and tacitly invited families to discontinue membership after the bar or bat mitzvah or confirmation of their youngest child.

The Persistent Problems of the Congregational School

Because children comprised 80 to 90 percent of the synagogue learners, teachers, as well as educators to supervise them, needed to be hired (first part time, and then increasingly full time). Over time a division of labor evolved. Children's education became the domain of the educator and the relatively low-key members of the school committee; the attention of high-powered lay leaders, and in most synagogues the senior rabbi, was focused elsewhere.

Few congregational schools have been given the human or financial resources to solve their chronic problems—a shortage of qualified teachers;[2] frequent disruptions in the classroom;[3] low student achievement;[4] and dropout rates ranging from 35 percent in eighth grade and 55 percent in ninth grade, to 80 to 85 percent in eleventh and twelfth grades.[5] Many researchers and communal leaders continue to share this dismal view today. In his introduction to a study of supplementary school parents, Jeffrey Kress writes that in speaking with "colleagues and Jewish communal professionals, the very mention of religious schools would often provoke a Pavlovian smirk or rolling of the eyes. When I asked about these reactions, I was regaled with countless narratives about negative experiences in religious school or about frustrations encountered as professionals working with religious schools."[6]

Despite all of its problems, the congregational school remained relatively unchanged during the last half of the twentieth century. New programs in teacher training came and went, as did experiments with alternative settings, like retreats and day camps. The idea with the most traction, family education, was too often reduced to a series of one-shot, stand-alone programs. Sometimes, these programs related to the children's curriculum, but rarely did they relate to adults' interests, much less to worship or to synagogue life as a whole.[7] This would not surprise sociologists of public education, who have written about the persistence of what they call the "grammar of schooling," the underlying assumptions of how schools should function, despite wave upon wave of educational reform:

> The basic grammar of schooling, like the shape of the classroom, has remained remarkably stable over decades. Little has changed in the ways that schools divide time and space, classify students and allocate them to classrooms, splinter knowledge into "subjects," and award grades and "credits" as evidence of learning. . . . [This] has puzzled and frustrated generations of reformers who have sought to change these standardized organizational forms.[8]

Historians of education David Tyack and Larry Cuban offer the following explanation for the staying power of the traditional model: "The grammar was easily replicable. . . . Administrators, teachers, and students learned how to work in the system; indeed the grammar of schooling became simply the way schools worked. Over time, the public, schooled in the system, came to assume that the grammar embodied the necessary features of a 'real school.'"[9]

In her study of Jewish, Catholic, and Protestant Sunday schools, Michelle Lynn-Sachs argues that the grammar of religious schooling, remarkably similar in the Catholic, Protestant, and Jewish Sunday schools she studied, is doubly intractable. Not only do parents and administrators expect *schools* to adhere to a conventional pattern, a "grammar of congregations" exerts a strong, conservative pull on *congregations* as well. Like other organizations, congregations "tend to seek legitimacy within their field by conforming to ritualized, expected ways of operating, rather than organizing their work according to purely rational, goal-oriented demands."[10] In this, Lynn-Sachs echoes Nancy Ammerman, who notes, "As participants in a distinct organizational field, [congregations] often structure their efforts around commonly accepted kinds of programs with commonly accepted kinds of personnel."[11]

With the grammar of religious schooling taken as a given throughout the twentieth century, the education departments of the Conservative and Reform movements saw their role as developing new curricula, which they did every few years. But in the absence of qualified teachers who could bring these curricula to life in the classroom, few of them had wide distribution or long shelf lives. As a result, central agencies, federations, and foundations turned their attention to day schools, maintaining an attitude of benign neglect toward congregational schools.

This attitude has begun to shift in the past decade, due, in part, to the influence of the congregations in our study and to the change projects discussed in this book. A new generation of rabbis have embraced changes in synagogue learning as a part of a larger transformative effort.

The Revival of Adult Learning

For most of the twentieth century, relatively few Jewish adults in the United States engaged in ongoing Jewish learning. Synagogues typically had a Torah study group, an introduction to Judaism course, and little else. During the 1980s, this began to change. Jewish feminism prompted women who had not celebrated a bat mitzvah as children to "become bat mitzvahed." In response, synagogues developed the adult b'nei mitzvah class, a one- or two-year course of study that to this day is popular among women and has even attracted some men.[12]

Concurrently, the 1980s saw the development of ongoing, text-based Jewish learning in a number of newly created and widely publicized national programs that included the Wexner Heritage Program, the Florence Melton Adult Mini-School, the Union for Reform Judaism's Kallot, and in Boston during the 1990s, the *Me'ah* program, which will be discussed below. Having partaken of serious adult study, graduates of these and comparable initiatives became avid learners, turning to congregations for more. Synagogues responded with varying degrees of alacrity; in general, their response was scattershot rather than systemic. Unfortunately, this new wave of adult learning had relatively little impact on synagogue schools. Because adult education was accorded more status, it was viewed as a separate undertaking, under the aegis of the rabbi rather than the educator. Coordination between adult and children's education was rare, as was an overall vision for congregational learning as a whole.

A New, Holistic Approach to Learning

The congregations in our study were among the first to challenge these conventions. They created alternative models for the religious school that altered the grammar of schooling in significant ways. The most important of these was having parents participate in learning on an ongoing basis, along with their children. As we will see later in this chapter, these congregations also worked intensively with their teachers to rely less on textbooks and more on experiential learning; the result was that students began to behave better and actually enjoyed coming to religious school. For students in the critical post b'nei mitzvah years, these congregations adopted the principle espoused by Harvard psychologist Howard Gardner and others that one style of learning does not fit all.[13] They began to tailor instruction to the interests and needs of their students, offering a variety of ways to stay connected to the synagogue. For adults, they created rich and varied learning opportunities, with offerings for beginners as well as the most advanced students, from weekly classes to intensive *shabbatonim*.

Leaders of these synagogues realize that not all adults will participate and become avid learners, nor will all parents choose the more demanding alternative models of religious school. But leaders try to promote a culture of learning wherever they can, incorporating study into worship, even at High Holidays and bar and bat mitzvah celebrations. They continue to increase the requirements for parent education in the religious school, encountering less resistance than they had initially feared. Most important, these congregations have discovered the excitement of continual innovation, steadily producing new programs that engage more congregants in authentic learning—true to the tradition, and true to the learner's sensibilities.

In short, these congregations exemplify the principles of the visionary congregation as they apply to congregational education: They have embraced the idea of learning as a sacred obligation, not simply a prerequisite for bar and bat mitzvah. They have created a synergy between learning and the rest of synagogue life—worship, community, and social justice. They have sought to involve all members of the congregation in both learning and teaching. They have connected the subjects they teach to the issues learners care about. They constantly innovate. Above all, they continue to learn from both their successes and their failures, to think about areas in need of improvement, and to plan next steps to widen the circle and deepen the engagement of learners. Along the way, they have drawn on these principles and applied them to other sectors of the congregation: worship, community building, and social justice. It is no accident that the congregations and leaders quoted in this chapter appear in several of the others.

This chapter focuses on the efforts and accomplishments of three congregations that have set the goal of becoming congregations of learners.[14] The following, then, are the stories of how learning was transformed in these congregations—Congregation Beth Am, Los Altos Hills, California, which convened its learning task force in 1990; Westchester Reform Temple, Scarsdale, New York, which joined the first cohort of the Experiment in Congregational Education (ECE) in 1993; and Temple Beth Elohim of Wellesley, Massachusetts, where the transformation began with Me'ah, a federation-sponsored program of adult learning, in 1997.

CONGREGATION BETH AM

On a crisp November morning in 2006, Teddi Kalb celebrated her bat mitzvah at Congregation Beth Am. That week's Torah portion was *Toldot*, and Teddi focused her *d'var torah* on the scene in which Rebekah, suffering from the twins struggling in her womb, cries out to God: "If so, why do I exist?" Teddi recalled how "Rebekah's prayer encouraged me to think about how we respond to life's challenges. And what does our response teach us about ourselves and about our values? . . . Over these past couple of weeks, I've thought about where I go when I need advice on what to do. To whom do I turn and what does this teach me about myself?" Of course, Teddi noted, she often turned to her parents for help and advice. But at times she sought advice and comfort elsewhere:

In situations like that, I come to this place, this sanctuary: Beth Am. I always know that I can come here to ask my fellow congregants, not to mention the staff and clergy, about what I should do. And when all else fails, I know that I can turn directly to my tradition, to this Torah and, ultimately, to God. Sometimes just studying an ancient text or reading about how my ancestors confronted similar challenges or by simply saying something out loud in a prayer, I feel like I'm not alone.

Teddi's connection to Congregation Beth Am was forged through her family's participation in a family school called *Shabbaton*. In lieu of the usual Sunday morning classes, children in grades K–6 and their families gather on Shabbat afternoon. They begin with *Shira*, or singing, for fifteen minutes, followed by fifty minutes for *Mishpacha*, a family learning opportunity. Then the children go to grade-level classes while the adults study with one of the educators or a member of the clergy. The afternoon concludes with presentations, singing, and Havdalah. As part of this program, families are divided into small groups called *michpachot*, which typically become extended families. They join for dinner on Saturday evening after the program and attend holiday and life-cycle celebrations together.

The commitment Shabbaton demands of the parents—to attend weekly with their children rather than simply dropping them off at religious school—is steep, but the program consistently draws about a third of school-age children and their families. The presence of parents conveys the message that Jewish learning is a lifelong pursuit. Congregation Beth Am's educators find Shabbaton students more engaged than their age-mates who attended the congregation's Sunday school program. Reflecting on her experience as a parent in Shabbaton, Susan Wolfe wrote:

Shabbaton has demonstrated to our children that Jewish learning is not only for children; we are involved in their learning, and in our own. When they go to religious school, we go to religious school. When we come back together, we each have an experience to share on a common Jewish topic. Additionally, we are practicing what we preach: We tell our children that Shabbat is a time for relaxation and study; each Shabbat, we relax and study with other Jewish families at our synagogue. . . .

Our vocabulary of *brakhot* (blessings) has increased dramatically. The prayer before study, the prayer before snack, and all of the Havdalah blessings are now ours. Similarly, our Hebrew word-stock is far more extensive than it would be without attending an education program with our children. . . .

But perhaps the most meaningful outcomes have been personal. As much as anything I have learned at Shabbaton, I have learned how very much I have yet to learn. I discovered the depth of my hunger to further my understanding and appreciation of our Jewish heritage.[15]

Wolfe went on to describe how she and her husband found opportunities for continued adult learning.

Thinking back on fifteen years of Shabbaton, its first director, Lisa Langer, comments, "A huge number of adults who had never ever done Jewish learning before became engaged in Jewish learning. It built friendships and community because people saw each other week after week. These family groups became *chavurot* [small communities] for many families. For a lot of people it became their connection to the synagogue. . . . Shabbaton transformed the leadership; at one point, at least 90 percent of the board had participated in Shabbaton."

One indication of how important Shabbaton has become to the synagogue, and not incidentally of how it has *changed* the synagogue, is what took place during the 1990s dot-com bust in Silicon Valley. With 10 percent of the congregation out of work, the synagogue needed to cut its budget. Coincidentally, the educator who had directed Shabbaton had resigned, and no money was available to replace her. Rather than eliminate Shabbaton or cut back other synagogue offerings, the senior educator approached two lay leaders, both of whom had taught in Shabbaton, hoping they would step into the breach by volunteering to coordinate the program. One of these, Ann DeHovitz, recalls her reaction: "I would never have thought of myself as a person to take the job. But once I was asked, not only was I highly flattered, I couldn't say no—the thought of the program going away was out of the question; it was such an integral part of our lives, and a very important part of the congregation. It's an alternative that meets such a huge need."

Ann and her co-coordinator, Daryl Messinger, threw themselves into this work, saving the program and, despite the fact that they were unpaid volunteers, becoming part of the synagogue team. The economy eventually improved and the paid position was restored, but the tradition of volunteer coordinators remained. Daryl, who is also a former president of the congregation, notes that when parents see how hard the volunteer coordinators are working, they are more likely to volunteer themselves. They think, "I need to be involved and help make this happen." The level of involvement increases across the board, as people volunteer for other synagogue programs and initiate activities. This "virtuous circle" enables a visionary congregation to become even more responsive.

Congregation Beth Am's leaders knew that Shabbaton, however powerful, was just the first of many changes they needed to make. For parents whose children attend religious school on Sunday morning, they created Toldot, in which parents learn what their children are learning, albeit at a higher level. Each year about two hundred learners participate in this program, studying in ten to twelve different courses over four to six sessions.

Because middle schools had begun to assign more homework, and because increased traffic congestion lengthened the drive to the synagogue, it became increasingly difficult for children to attend religious school two days during the week (in addition to Sunday or Shabbat). In response, Congregation Beth Am created *Tzavta* (an Aramaic word meaning "together"), a program in which students attend religious school two days during the week (rather than three, as before) but maintain the same number of contact hours through a series of twelve Friday night and Shabbat morning family events. Each of these includes *t'fillot* (worship services), a meal, and separate classes for children and adults. Within a few years, all families opted for Tzavta, which was expanded through seventh grade. Over the years Congregation Beth Am has become not only a congregation of learners but also a "self-renewing congregation,"[16] a congregation that is both proactive and reflective and embraces experimentation, with leadership that works collaboratively. When faced with a perplexing or difficult situation, the leadership convenes a task force to deliberate over an extended period, bringing recommendations to the board or one of its committees. Since its original task force in 1990, Congregation Beth Am has convened task forces devoted to adult and teen education, the Sunday religious school program, worship, and the bar and bat mitzvah.

Not all of Congregation Beth Am's experiments have been equally successful, and some, while initially successful, have proven difficult to sustain. In an effort to create a greater sense of community in the school and hire teachers who could serve as role models for both students and their parents, Congregation Beth Am established the Congregant Teacher Institute. Two cohorts of teachers went through the program, including a number who had been or would soon become board members. Though the synagogue was pleased with the quality of the program's graduates, funding for the program ran out after two cohorts and the educators' energies were pulled in other directions. Several years later, a staff development program aimed at creating a learning community among the teachers met with great enthusiasm but ultimately met a similar fate.

One other failed experiment is worthy of our attention, because it raises an interesting issue—the degree to which adult learning can and should be "curricularized." Around 1995, as Shabbaton was becoming a permanent fixture, the synagogue's leaders began thinking about next steps in adult learning. The professional staff created a map of lifelong learning, a list of the subjects with which a well-educated Reform Jew should be conversant. Many meetings spanning several years produced a sheet of paper, about 30 x 45 inches in size, divided into many cells each filled with subjects ranging from Hebrew decoding to theology. The size and density of the map made it unwieldy, both physically and intellectually. More problematic was the fact that it intimidated the few lay leaders who saw it. Linda Kurz, a member of the adult learning task force, says, "Delineating all the things an 'educated' Jew *should* know by a certain age was fraught with problems, and I was very concerned about how people would respond. There was a strong suggestion that we hand it out at a community-wide meeting, and I said that [would] be a disaster."

Since then the map has been used only rarely and indirectly. Rabbi Josh Zweiback, senior educator at the time of our interviews, believes that "it continues to have an impact, but its influence is marginal, not central. We use the map to help us think more clearly about content areas that we need to do a better job of and about our educational theme each year."

Ongoing adult learning now includes Shabbat Torah study (which draws between 120 and 150 people); Shabbat afternoon salons (discussion groups); adult classes that parallel childhood learning in religious school; Hebrew at six to eight different levels; and family offerings like Shabbaton and Tzavta. In addition, during the week the rabbis and educators offer courses on topics of interest. But the goal of a totally comprehensive education program has proven elusive. As we will see, Westchester Reform Temple is beginning to struggle with the same issue.

Still, Congregation Beth Am's leaders continue to think up new ways to involve more adults in learning, just as they continue to think of ways to innovate children's education. In the past two years, they have experimented with a Shabbat morning minyan that includes a *parashat hashavu'a* (Torah portion of the week) program for children, a theater-based alternative to the weekday afternoon religious school, and a program specifically targeted to young adults called Roots, which features its own salon.

To date about a quarter of the synagogue's congregants (a total of 1,475 member units) participate in some form of adult learning on a weekly basis, while many others are exposed to ongoing learning through worship as well as various family education programs. Is the glass three quarters empty or one quarter full? How many of their members will they entice into greater learning? The culture of the 1990s has definitely changed, but more changes lie ahead as the synagogue attempts to bring more adults in from the periphery to the core.

WESTCHESTER REFORM TEMPLE

On Rosh Hashanah, 5755 (1994) shortly after Westchester Reform Temple joined the first cohort of ECE, Rabbi Rick Jacobs delivered a now-famous sermon entitled, "The End of Religious School as We Know It" (a riff on then-President Clinton's promise to "end welfare as we know it"). "Once upon a time," Rick said, "we Jews were known as the people of the Book, but in truth we have become the children of the Book. Too many of us have a thirteen-year-old's understanding of Judaism." To change this he pledged, "Together with the best and brightest Jewish educators of our time, we are going to think creatively about how we can do even better as a congregation in creating and sustaining a living Jewish community with learners of all ages. In this bold undertaking we must be ready to end Religious School as we know it; we can no longer afford to do the same old things and hope it will be good enough."

At a 1995 ECE retreat, the core planning group at Westchester Reform heard representatives of Congregation Beth Am speak about Shabbaton. They loved the idea of a family school but wanted to make prayer a more integral part of the program, "to create a sacred community through shared prayer and learning." Why not hold the program on Shabbat morning? The result was Sharing Shabbat.

Every Shabbat morning, nearly two hundred people stream into Westchester Reform's Center for Jewish Life, a Victorian house adjacent to the congregation's main building. Set aside as a retreat house, its ground floor was designed as a quiet and spiritually inviting prayer space. Sharing Shabbat features a service with lots of congregational singing, short explanations of particular prayers by the rabbi, and a d'var torah by one of the families. Some children sit on their parents' laps; others snuggle. The singing is rousing, the mood alternately tranquil and exuberant. After the morning kiddush at the conclusion of the service, parents go to one of two ongoing classes for adults while children proceed to grade-level classes. An hour later, the group reconvenes for sharing and group singing.

Westchester Reform parents at Sharing Shabbat echo their counterparts at Congregation Beth Am's Shabbaton—surprise and delight that the Jewish tradition has so much to offer. In the words of Bob Miller, "This was a perfect idea in order for us to share Shabbat and be together as human beings. It was one of the first opportunities I had to study with my wife. The worship was certainly very accessible, filled with music. Being a musician it was a very easy entree. I have to say it was the first time that I felt spiritual in a congregational setting."

Weeks of praying and studying together over seven years has had a profound impact on the children as well, as Rabbi and Cantor Angela Warnick Buchdahl, who led the service for a number of years, explains, "You just listen to a kid who went all the way though Sharing Shabbat for ten years, she's now in college. She said, 'Everyone's surprised that I'm a Reform Jew because I'm leading the services at Hillel.'"

With Sharing Shabbat well established, drawing roughly 20 percent of the synagogue's children, Westchester Reform's leaders asked themselves what they could do to revitalize learning for everyone else. They wanted to involve parents in the Sunday morning religious school, but knew they couldn't ask for the same level of commitment, so they began to require four sessions of adult learning a year for religious school parents. Then they created *Likrat Shabbat* in which students prepare Shabbat dinner for themselves and their parents a number of times each year. In its first year leaders assumed that if they required children to come on a Friday afternoon, parents would expect class to be cancelled on the following Sunday morning. But it turned out that parents did not expect any such quid pro quo. They then began inviting parents to the Sunday morning service at the beginning of religious school. Rick recalls:

> Did we think that people were going to park their cars and not go straight to tennis? Walk their kid in and sit with their kid at t'fillah at 9:00? The answer is no, but we started by doing Havdalah in the atrium, because [according to the halakha] you could do Havdalah until Tuesday noontime. It's not the most inspiring thing to do it Sunday morning, because you miss the magic of the evening, but it was the great hook, because people had to walk their little kids into the atrium, and we were in a big circle. And we had the spices and the candle, and you walked in with your gym clothes and someone pulled you into the circle. So we did that for a whole year and the model was: school begins with a ritual. Then we beefed it up to be a morning service, and now more parents stay than before—between half and two-thirds. And a lot of them stay because they participate in their own class.

In 1997 Westchester Reform received a grant from the New York UJA, the federation's Commission on Jewish Identity and Renewal to redesign their high school program and offer an array of options, from drama to social action to Jewish philosophy. Reflecting on this program, Rick says:

> I had an assumption that serious Jewish kids went to confirmation, and the rest was all kind of candy that wasn't worthwhile. So we had this

really serious confirmation program, but kids who didn't go into it, they just were dropped out of the airplane. And we were sitting in some staff meeting and we said, "How is that responsible? How is that a good thing? Some of the most devoted kids might have, for other reasons, no desire or no social comfort in confirmation."

Now the congregation offers multiple paths of both informal and formal learning that is better suited to who the youth are, asking "Which path is going to be the good path for you?"

But reconfiguring high school was not enough, because too many children were dropping out already during middle school. To keep these kids engaged, Westchester Reform offered them much more time to socialize—over pizza dinners, for example. Says Sorel Loeb:

> As an educator, I hate to present minimal expectations, but I think with kids in eighth and ninth grade the most important thing is to get them breathing Jewish air. That's what eighth and ninth graders do when they come in the building. They're here with other Jewish kids and lots of great Jewish role models and they're breathing Jewish air. How much content are they learning in eighth and ninth grade? It's an open question.
>
> Some kids come because their parents make them, of course, but most kids come because they just want to be here. . . . I don't really care why they come in the building. Basically, what we know is that if we can get them here and keep them coming back, by the time they get into tenth grade and eleventh grade they're going to be ready for more serious Jewish content.

A fortuitous byproduct of all this experimentation is that the teachers have been drawn into discussions of new content and new teaching methods. In an effort to forge a stronger connection between children and teachers, Westchester Reform now has teachers staying with the same class for at least two years, challenging them to think more broadly about content. In addition, teachers now have an opportunity to observe one another, a practice that has led them to adopt new teaching techniques.

In keeping with its vision of lifelong congregation-wide learning, Westchester Reform offers a spectrum of classes, from one-shot lectures to daytime and evening classes that run for four to eight sessions. One of these, Rabbi Jonathan Blake's Torah class, has seventy-five participants at midday and another seventy-five in the evening. Jonathan, who came to Westchester Reform in 2003, found that "everywhere I looked, people were interested in learning." A highlight is the annual *Yom Limud*, a day of learning for the entire congregation, which includes a guest speaker, three different breakout sessions, family education, a book and Judaica fair, and a series of learning stations in which fourth and fifth graders teach everyone else. Attended by more than four hundred adults as well as all the children in the religious school, Yom Limud serves as the kickoff for the year's theme (such as "Israel at 60," or "70 Faces of Torah").

As at Congregation Beth Am, not all of Westchester Reform's experiments have taken root. For example, *Ivrit Lamishpacha*, in which parents studied Hebrew with their third graders, attracted a small but enthusiastic group the first year; however, it failed to attract a sufficient number thereafter.

Of greater concern is that alumni of Sharing Shabbat neither feel comfortable attending services with newer families nor do they feel welcome at the formal bar or bat mitzvah service in the main sanctuary. Thus the habit of Shabbat attendance, built up over many years, quickly erodes. Westchester Reform's leaders are trying to respond to these families.

In 2008 Rabbi Jonathan Blake, with Sorel's assistance, formed a task force to rethink and reshape adult learning. At the initial meeting, the task force's charge was phrased in terms of five Cs:

Cohesiveness: How do the pieces of the program fit together?

Constituencies: How do we maximize the number and type of participants?

Comprehensiveness: How well are we covering the waterfront of learning? (Note the similarity to the issue of curricularization that arose at Congregation Beth Am.)

Credits: How can adult learners sculpt an individualized program that allows them to attain certain identified benchmarks?

Community: How do we create a community of learners?

Westchester Reform Temple, like Congregation Beth Am, has entered an era of continuous innovation. While appreciating how far they have come, they are always looking for the next challenge.

TEMPLE BETH ELOHIM

Temple Beth Elohim's transformation into a congregation of learners began in 1995 when Barry Shrage, executive vice president of the Boston's Combined Jewish Philanthropies (CJP), met with a group of lay leaders and gave a memorable speech. Terry Rosenberg remembers:

> Basically he embarrassed us into thinking seriously about what Jewish identity meant. He said, "How is it that Jews in America, who are among the most highly educated in the history of Jewish life, who know Rembrandt from Monet, can name five Shakespearean plays don't know Maimonides?" I didn't know who Maimonides was, so I'm sitting there thinking, "Who the ** is Maimonides? What he is saying is true.". . . This was the kicker—I was embarrassed at my own Jewish ignorance. Having taken so seriously every other aspect of my life, how is it that I didn't apply the same diligence to my children's Jewish education, or, for that matter, mine?

Having faced their "Jewish ignorance," the synagogue's lay leaders began looking for adult study that was both intellectually challenging and spiritually nourishing. Terry formed a women's Torah study group in her own living room. Recalling the work of Rabbi Alan Ullman, who was hired to lead a number of synagogue classes, she says, "He really understood how to make Torah meaningful and relevant to people's lives. Alan tapped into that trend. He took us by the hand, and together we took baby steps—discussing each piece of text with voices that we could understand and to which we could relate. He was right there with the Torah saying, 'This is meaningful. Here's how it's meaningful.'"

Soon after that, Temple Beth Elohim became the first congregation to host Me'ah, CJP's adult education program, which offers one hundred hours of Jewish learning taught by scholars at nearby universities over a period of three years. During its first year, so many Beth Elohim members wanted to join Me'ah that they had to offer two classes of twenty-five each; since then, a new cohort enrolls every three years. As of this writing, the synagogue boasts over 350 Me'ah graduates, in addition to about three hundred adults taking twenty or so ongoing classes each year.

Joel Sisenwine, who came on as senior rabbi in 2000, knew that the next step would be tackling children's education, which, by all accounts, was dismal. Because the retention rate after bar and bat mitzvah was less than 25 percent, and attendance for those enrolled was "maybe 50 percent on any given week," he decided to start there, hiring Rachel Happel, a newly minted graduate of Brandeis University's Hornstein-Heller dual degree program in Jewish Communal Service and Business Administration.

Realizing that an entirely new approach was needed, Happel set about researching alternatives but was disappointed to find that "there wasn't a whole lot going on that was different." She says, "I started thinking about how would you create a program that was experiential in nature, that would interest kids, that would get them involved, that would have a flexible enough schedule for them to be able to come with good attendance."

The *Havayah* (experience) program, as it came to be called, has both a confirmation track and a la carte options, allowing teens to be involved in some of the programs without having to commit to the entire package. In the confirmation track, students in grades eight through ten are required to attend two out of three weekend retreats and enroll in one of several chavurot (fellowship groups) designed "to combine a great experience that excites the kids with something that has deep substance Jewishly," explains Happel. Each *chavurah* meeting includes an activity, like rock climbing, with the study of a related text, such as a reading from Abraham Joshua Heschel on radical amazement. Other chavurot include the Jewish Actors' Workshop, Youth Choir, Tastes of Judaism (cooking), *Madrichim* (teaching assistants in the religious school), and *Telem* (which focuses on social action and social justice). Within a few years of instituting Havayah, Temple Beth Elohim's post-b'nei mitzvah retention rate rose from 23 percent to 70 percent.

In 2002 the synagogue hired Alison Kur as its congregational educator. Alison, a career changer, could be a poster child for the new Jewish educational initiatives of the past two decades. As a lawyer, she oversaw a large staff working in state government on child support enforcement. But when a new governor instituted policies in which she didn't believe, she began looking for other work options. To her surprise, she found that what intrigued her most was not law, but Jewish education. As a participant in the Wexner Heritage Foundation's Boston cohort, she had had powerful experiences of adult Jewish learning. As chair of the board of the Rashi Day School, she had participated in a change effort of the Rhea Hirsch School of Education entitled "Jewish Day Schools for the 21st Century," and thus knew firsthand the challenges and possibilities of educational change. Given the severe shortage of congregational educators, she might have found a job immediately but chose instead to study for a master's degree at Brandeis's Hornstein program. She recalls how she had her eyes set on the position at Temple Beth Elohim (TBE) two years before the job became available: "I was looking for a particular kind of culture, one that was excited about experimentation and that was willing to engage in a process that would bring all of the constituencies together in partnership. . . . And TBE was that kind of place. . . . It's an entrepreneurial congregation. They enjoy experimentation. They were ready."

Given a strong mandate for change, Alison convened a task force, leading them through a yearlong process. They read widely, engaged in a range of visioning activities, and set their priorities for change. They chose to start with sixth and seventh graders, re-placing Sunday classes with *Ma'asim Tovim* (good deeds), in which students work in small groups on local *tz'dakah* (charity) projects. Alison explains, "The mitzvah part of bar [and] bat mitzvah is re-ally important. We wanted the kids to feel that they have the power and the opportunity to make change in the world; that they *should* do it, that in the Jewish tradition it is an imperative to do so."

Their next task was to revamp *Limud* (study), the K–5 reli-gious school, whose curriculum according to one parent "con-sisted of coloring, more coloring, and more coloring." It was not entirely clear at the outset that the Limud program would remain in existence; Rabbi Joel Sisenwine fully expected that it would be dismantled and replaced by an alternative model. But Alison felt strongly that many parents would prefer the traditional religious school and would not participate in an alternative, arguing, as Joel recalls, "You can't let [Limud] die. We have too many people in the program. It's unfair to them to have their children learning in a program that's not excellent."

Though Alison's reconstruction of Limud began soon after her arrival, the process was greatly accelerated in the fall of 2005, when Judy Avnery came on as Limud director. In just a few years, the change was dramatic. Two high school students reminisce, "When we were in elementary school and middle school it was kind of boring. We all hated it. But the religious education program got a major overhaul, and . . . the temple was starting to do all sorts of great new things and I was jealous. I wanted to be a part of that because all of a sudden I saw kids that were liking Sunday school. I'm TA-ing [serving as teaching assistant] for a grade; they're learning the stuff that I never got to learn about then."

To achieve these changes, Judy increased the number of staff development hours from sixteen to twenty, devoting this time to modeling and practicing teaching methods that address multiple intelligences.[17] She worked intensely with the teachers, rehiring only those who were not resistant to the new teaching modalities. She required that teachers send her lesson plans three or four days ahead of time, and she still spends considerable time refining the plans that need work. She also instituted greater communication with the parents, such as regular e-mails giving detailed information on their children's progress and material covered. A father recounts his pleasure at being informed of his children's progress on a regular basis: "You felt like you were a participant in the classroom."

Even as Limud was being transformed, Beth Elohim began piloting an alternative to the Sunday program, *Beit Midrash* (house of study), which centers around students reading Jewish books and completing a related set of assignments with their parents at home. Age-graded cohorts are brought together every six weeks, and regular *tikkun olam* (social justice) opportunities are provided for families. This kind of flexibility is particularly appealing to three types of parents: those who want to be more involved in their children's learning; those whose children attend day school but who want them to be connected to the synagogue community; and those whose children's learning disabilities prevent them from being in the regular Limud program.

Temple Beth Elohim has made great strides in a very short period of time; its leaders are painfully aware of what still needs to be done. Every time we interviewed her, Alison stressed that the education program at Beth Elohim is a work-in-progress. As she explained in the fall of 2007, "It's iterative—it's going to continue to move.... One of our best practices is that we we're not satisfied ever with exactly how it is. We haven't landed, and I don't think we ever will."

Common Themes

Cutting across the stories of the three congregations highlighted in this chapter, as well as the other congregations in our sample, are common principles of a new approach to learning and a common set of factors that make it possible to translate theory into practice.

PRINCIPLES OF THE NEW
APPROACH TO CONGREGATIONAL EDUCATION

The new approach to congregational education, exemplified by the congregations profiled in this chapter, is based on six principles: (1) Jewish learning for its own sake (torah lishmah), (2) connecting the Torah of our people to the torah of our lives, (3) experiential learning, (4) offering a range of choices, (5) weaving learning into all synagogue activities, and (6) increasing the numbers of learners and the levels of learning.

Torah Lishmah (Jewish Learning for Its Own Sake),

Though congregants might join primarily for the bar or bat mitzvah of their children, leaders of these three synagogues are committed to the principle of torah lishmah, the intrinsic value of Jewish study. They entice adults into learning by highlighting the benefits to be gained—spending quality time with their kids, being able to talk with their kids about what they are learning, deepening their understanding of Jewish life, exposing them to highly regarded academics and new ideas, connecting them to the clergy (all three congregations find that this is a big draw), celebrating an adult bar or bat mitzvah, and being part of a community of learners. Different motivators work for different learners; taken together, they have shifted congregants' expectations.

Connecting the Torah of Our People to the Torah of Our Lives

The synagogues in our study have embraced the notion that the study of Torah (writ large) will enrich and illuminate the lives of their congregants. The goal is not simply to have them ingest content but to connect the text and their deepest concerns and aspirations. Alan Ullman, the legendary teacher of adults at Temple Beth Elohim, explains:

> So, the dance is: I'm trying to get people to hear the voice in the text. But then, the next step is for them to hear their own voices and then to get them into a conversation with the text. And not to make the text say what they want it to say, and not to make themselves say what people think that they may want to ask. But to actually get them to ask what's in their hearts and to listen to what the text would say in response.

Experiential Learning

John Dewey's dictum that experience is the basis of all true education has been the watchword of progressive education for more than a century.[18] In keeping with this principle, the synagogues profiled in this chapter strive to make learning—especially learning for children, but also learning for adults—an activity that has not only a cognitive dimension but also an affective, spiritual, social, and practical one. One might call this approach one of enculturation rather than one of instruction.[19] Congregation Beth Am's Josh Zweiback puts it this way: "Now we're thinking a lot more about enculturation, which doesn't mean that content is unimportant but that the feelings and the experience and type of community we're creating, and having students and families feel they are a part of what we're doing here, and feel connected to Judaism and to the Jewish people. All these affective things are really important, and we think a lot about them."

This emphasis on experiential learning is most evident in Temple Beth Elohim's Havayah and Ma'asim Tovim programs, which engage teens and preteens in activities such as social justice, hiking, and acting. But it is also found in a myriad of other activities, such as students in the temple's Hebrew classes forming letters with clay and with their bodies or building a scale model of the Second Temple with Legos, as the entire school did one year.[20] Westchester Reform's Likrat Shabbat, in which students prepare for Shabbat together, and the *Hagigah* (celebration) program at Congregation Beth Am, which centers around a theatrical production, similarly seek to connect Jewish learning to engaging and memorable experiences.

Offering a Range of Choices

In their conclusion to *The Jew Within*, Steven M. Cohen and Arnold Eisen compare Jewish professionals to "operators of a transit system":

> Jewish institutions face a formidable task in this period of voluntarism and mobility. They must have a range of options available to every individual at every moment, so that when he or she is ready to seize hold of Jewishness or Judaism, the right option is there to be had. . . . A bus must be ready and waiting at the bus-stop at the exact moment that the prospective Jewish rider appears. The fleet must be sufficiently large to be there whenever wanted, and it must be sufficiently diverse to take account of the diverse tastes and needs of its potential clientele.[21]

This is one of the inspirations for our three congregations, who try to address the diverse interests of their learners. At Westchester Reform, children have a choice between classes on Sunday and family school on Shabbat; at Congregation Beth Am, these options plus a third, a theater-based program, are offered; at Temple

Beth Elohim, an alternative program centers on reading books at home. The range of possibilities for adults is even broader. In all three congregations, Hebrew is offered for beginning, intermediate, and advanced students. Text study is available on Shabbat, on Sunday mornings, at lunchtime, and in the evening; each time slot attracts a different crowd. For those who can't attend an ongoing class, there are more intensive learning opportunities. And those who can't, or don't, make time for a separate class will still encounter learning as a part of worship, mitzvah day, or the work of a committee.

Adhering to this principle leads to some surprising, and even uncomfortable, decisions for the educator. Alison Kur observes:

> When I first came here, I thought, "We're never going to do any one-shot deals." I really don't like them, philosophically. But I've learned that we have to have some one-shot deals, because there are some people who learn that way. That's what they're looking for. What I've really learned is that in a community of this size, for the adults, people are all over the place. . . . What works here is a very broad range of opportunities for people to engage in. That is a challenge, but it's also exciting.

While three other congregations in this study offer fewer options for children, they do attempt to reach adults in a variety of ways. Congregation Agudath Israel, Caldwell, New Jersey, is building a new center of lifelong learning; its adult learning brochure for 2007–8 is fourteen pages long, and includes both Me'ah and Florence Melton Adult Mini-School courses. Learning is integral to Temple Israel's Riverway Project for young adults in the Boston area; in the past few years the synagogue has applied Riverway's organizing principles to empty nesters. And it too offers a seemingly endless list of courses and programs. All this requires money, and the cost of many of these courses (though by no means all) is partially offset by modest fees. Temple Beth Elohim is, we believe, unique in charging fees of one- to five-hundred dollars for courses taught by outside guests (courses taught by the clergy or educators are free) and in setting a threshold for enrollment below which the course is not offered.

Smaller and less wealthy congregations are typically more limited in what they can offer. At Beth Jacob Congregation in Mendota Heights, Minnesota, the rabbi offers courses primarily for beginning and intermediate learners. Arielle Ehrlich, one of the more advanced learners, is somewhat frustrated by this situation, though she understands it:

> I don't go to the rabbi's classes too frequently. . . . [They are] often too basic. And they're terrific, but I've done many years of formal and informal study. . . . There are many others who also have too much background to be in the class. . . . That's one failing that I see at the shul: that there isn't an "above intermediate" level class. There's only so much you can offer, and the people who could teach advanced classes are already taxed teaching classes that benefit a greater number of people.

In contrast, Temple Micah in Washington, D.C., compensates for its size and small staff by empowering their congregants to coordinate and lead a number of study groups.

Weaving Learning into All Synagogue Activities

As noted in chapter 2, one of the hallmarks of a visionary congregation is a holistic approach. Torah, *avodah,* and *g'milut chasadim* are linked not only in the brochures and on the website but also in the congregants' experiences. The conventional division of labor with the rabbi responsible for worship, the educator for learning, the social action committee for social justice, and so on is certainly more efficient and cost-effective. But the congregations featured in this chapter, like the other five congregations in our study, link these functions more organically. Worship services are an integral part of children's learning at all three congregations in this chapter, as they are at Temple Micah. On Shabbat mornings at

Congregation Agudath Israel, learning opportunities for every age run parallel to the service. As we shall see in chapter 5, fifth- and sixth-grade students at Temple Israel are a key part of *Ohel Tzedek*, the synagogue's social justice effort; leaders of Ohel Tzedek's other initiatives regularly emerge from the ranks of its parents.

Conversely, learning has also entered the sanctuary. Some congregations, like Westchester Reform and Beth Shalom in suburban Kansas City, have incorporated participatory text study and explanatory comments by the rabbi into worship to the point where participants describe their service as "Torah centric."

Learning has increasingly become part of the agenda at committee meetings. Alison Kur was asked to bring a regular text teaching to meetings of the finance committee at Temple Beth Elohim. Marjorie Miller, a former president at Westchester Reform, notes that learning has become integral to all synagogue meetings, to the dismay of some participants: "A committee member does a d'var torah before every meeting, even Finance. Some people think it is a waste of time. But it is all part of the learning community. Now Torah is really alive, our religion is alive, our temple is energized."

As this quote suggests, infusing learning throughout all synagogue activities is not always so easily accomplished. When Temple Beth Elohim educators tried to insert learning into mitzvah day, they encountered a great deal of resistance from the lay committee responsible for it. Overall, though, learning is slowly expanding beyond the education wing and into the heart of all the synagogues' activities.

Increasing the Numbers of Learners and the Levels of Learning

Whether by nudging, requiring, or enticing, the three synagogues we have focused on in this chapter aim to increase the universe of learners and to have these learners engage more deeply with core Jewish content on an ongoing basis. Congregations go about this in different ways: Westchester Reform has instituted new requirements for parent attendance at certain religious school programs; Temple Beth Elohim has increased the number of days that religious school is in session and broadened its adult learning opportunities; Congregation Beth Am has cut the number of days of instruction but substituted Shabbat dinners, Shabbat family learning, and an expectation that students learn Hebrew decoding primarily at home.

When a congregation succeeds in motivating more adults to learn, its culture begins to change; adult learning comes closer to being the norm rather than the exception. For this reason, both Temple Micah and Westchester Reform offer classes for new members. Rick Jacobs at Westchester Reform explains:

> When people join, if they already sit in the back and don't get right *in* there, the reality is that in five years, they'll probably be in the same dis-connected place; and when their kids go through the program, they'll be ready to step out. They're already comfortable on the margins. How do we yank somebody right away? They're in the door five seconds, we pull them into a learning experience, make community out of it.

These six principles combine to form a new vision of Jewish learning. Individually, none of these is new—some, like the concept of torah lishmah, go back to Talmudic times; others, like experiential learning and the notion of connecting the torah of our lives to the Torah of our people, are nearly a century old. Taken together, the six principles form a set of benchmarks against which all programs of congregational education have begun to be judged.

ENABLING FACTORS

What factors contributed to this cultural shift? Here, too, are several commonalities: a task-force process that culminated in a shared vision of congregational learning, abundant resources, and high-caliber lay leaders.

Task Forces to Rethink Learning

Congregation Beth Am, located in Silicon Valley, is rich in entre-
preneurs and management consultants. They adapted the notion
of a learning task force from organizational theorist Edgar Schein,
who advocates that businesses create "temporary parallel learning
systems"[22] to investigate new approaches and find new solutions.
The advantage of a task force, Schein explains, is that it can create
synergy between stakeholders who don't ordinarily have sustained
contact with one another. The most reflective and cooperative
representatives of each constituency are invited. Because the work
of the task force does not include quotidian tasks like oversight or
budgeting, its members are freed to think in new ways. A limitation of the task force, discussed in the literature on institutional
change and experienced in both ECE and S2K (Synagogue 2000),
is that it can easily become an insular, elite group that loses touch
with the constituencies its members represent. For example,
members of the S2K task force at Congregation Agudath Israel,
inspired by their experiences at an S2K retreat, attempted to lead
their fellow congregants during services in a *nigun* (wordless melody). Not only were they unable to inspire the congregation to
sing but they also managed to alienate some of the congregation's
members, as was recounted in chapter 3.

Modeling its change processes after those that worked at Congregation Beth Am, the ECE directs its congregations to form task
forces at the outset. Westchester Reform found that its ECE and
S2K task forces were such effective vehicles for change, it convenes
them whenever a new direction is needed, rather than simply relying on the professional staff.

By the time Alison Kur arrived at Beth Elohim, task forces had
become the norm among those interested in synagogue change, so
she convened one as her first order of business. To this day, Alison
relies heavily on some of the task force's original members to help
generate and evaluate new proposals.

Community Resources

The maxim "It takes a village to raise a child" might be paraphrased, in this context, as follows: it takes the resources of the larger community to transform synagogue education. Temple Beth Elohim is the most obvious example of this principle; its success is due in large part to Boston's Combined Jewish Philanthropies' active interest in synagogue life. Recall that CJP executive Barry Shrage challenged the synagogue's leaders to educate themselves, and that CJP's Me'ah program has inspired and continues to inspire those in leadership positions. CJP grants have paid the salaries of several new educators for the first few years of their tenure. In addition, the local Hebrew College provided partial funding for a pilot program in teachers' professional development. Last but not least, four of the current educators are graduates of Brandeis's Hornstein program in Jewish educational leadership; their shared language and understanding of Jewish education has surely facilitated their collaboration. While few synagogues in the area have maximized these kinds of resources as effectively as Beth Elohim, without these resources, change would have come much more slowly, if at all.

Westchester Reform has benefited greatly from its proximity to New York City, which allowed it to bring in Hebrew Union College (HUC) interns and a plethora of rabbis, cantors, and academics on a regular basis. In particular, it formed an ongoing relationship with CLAL (the National Center for Jewish Learning and Leadership) to offer high level classes for its adults. In addition, a grant from the UJA-Federation of New York enabled Westchester Reform to launch its high school program.

Congregation Beth Am's resources were internal as well as external. Eddie Reynolds, a congregant who is a management consultant, planned and facilitated the first task force.[23] Subsequent task forces and planning processes have been led by a number of organizational development experts who are members. Congregants based at Stanford University helped design the teacher training efforts; an evaluation expert from Stanford led a workshop in "empowerment evaluation," a technique the synagogue now uses regularly.[24] In addition, the synagogue's educational offerings have been enriched by its association with the Berkeley-based Lehrhaus Judaica, an American heir to Rosenzweig's institution; seed money for several key staff members was provided by grants from the San Francisco-based Koret Foundation; and the synagogue's long-standing connection with HUC's Rhea Hirsch School of Education has enabled it to hire a seemingly endless number of alumni.

Can other congregations learn from the experiences of these three? To some extent they can. Many congregations have comparable resources that are as yet untapped, including wealthy donors and congregants with specific areas of expertise; and there is reason to believe that congregational education is poised to receive a larger share of the philanthropic dollar. Few federations, however, have invested as heavily in congregational education as those of Boston and New York. (Kansas City, home of Beth Shalom, is another.) Temple Beth Elohim has six full-time educators and an assistant rabbi who devotes a third of her time to working with teenagers. Westchester Reform has two full-time educators and an associate rabbi who spends considerable time on adult learning. Congregation Beth Am has three full-time educators; in addition, two of its three rabbis hold masters' degrees in Jewish education and devote a significant portion of their time to teaching and educational planning. When vacancies occur, these congregations have no trouble filling them; by dint of their innovative programs and stellar staff, they have their pick of rabbis as well as educators. In recent years, a number of local efforts, like NESS (Nurturing Excellence in Synagogue Schools, a project of Philadelphia's Central Agency for Jewish Education), and LICSP (Leadership Institute for Congregational School Principals, a joint project of Hebrew Union College and the Jewish Theological Seminary), have begun to work on professional development for congregational teachers and educators, with some notable successes. But much remains to be done in this area.

Strong Lay Support

The *type* of lay leaders invested in congregational learning makes a big difference. Religious school committees typically run bake sales and coordinate room parents but do not provide any genuine leadership, much less serve as catalysts for change. The synagogues profiled in this chapter have their worker bees too, but the key to their success lies in lay leaders who are visionary and analytical and have clout within the congregation. When Judy Avnery, director of Temple Beth Elohim's Limud program, required matching funds for teacher education, her committee provided assistance by lobbying the board and by soliciting contributions. The synagogue's alternative model of the religious school, Beit Midrash, is paid for by a donor who is a congregant. Congregation Beth Am and Westchester Reform can offer similar stories.

Lay leaders share more than their financial and political acumen. At Temple Beth Elohim, key members of the original task force serve, even today, as Alison Kur's closest allies and advisers. At Congregation Beth Am, the education steering committee is cochaired by the senior educator and a board member whose portfolio is education. It includes the lay coordinators of Shabbaton and others who invest considerable time and energy in policy decisions. Responsibility for leading text study rotates among all the members. And when a particular book or article is discussed, everyone reads it.

The lay leaders in these congregations exhibit another critical trait—they welcome experimentation and understand that experiments sometimes fail. Their job, as they see it, is to support the educators in their role as change agents. Sometimes this means advocacy with the board; at other times it means making the educator aware of problems that need to be addressed. When we interviewed him at his workplace, Jim Heeger, then president of Congregation Beth Am, had just gotten off the phone with Josh Zweiback. Though the purpose of the call was to schedule a meeting, Jim also inquired into plans for the performance review of a staff member. "I try to add value every time we talk," he commented.

CHALLENGES THAT REMAIN

For all their successes, the congregations described in this chapter face a number of perennial educational challenges: hiring high quality teachers, providing learning opportunities for adults at a range of levels, and dealing with congregants who resist change.

The Shortage of High Quality Teachers

Alternative models, new curricular approaches, and parent involvement are key ingredients of good congregational education, but the quality of an educational program rests, in the end, on the quality of its teachers. Finding excellent teachers for adults has not posed a serious problem for our congregations. Finding and retaining excellent religious school teachers, however, has. Even when a school runs double sessions and teachers are given additional responsibilities as tutors or youth group leaders, the number of hours they spend in a synagogue rarely exceeds twelve hours a week. By its very nature, religious school instruction is a part-time job.[25] Synagogues must therefore recruit their teachers from a population with limited training whose primary commitments lie elsewhere: college students, underemployed adults, day school teachers, public school teachers, Israelis living in the area, retirees, and congregants. Some of these teachers have good Judaica backgrounds; others have good teaching skills. Rarely do they come with both.[26]

Whatever their background, all of these teachers require training, mentoring, and support. Our three congregations take this responsibility seriously, but they often face an uphill battle. Temple Beth Elohim, for example, hires many students from local colleges. They are eager and enthusiastic learners, but they graduate in a few years, only to be replaced by a fresh pool of inexperienced students. Congregation Beth Am recruited congregants but was unable to maintain its training program due to a lack of funds.

Taking Adult Learning to the Next Level

Despite impressive gains, much work remains in the area of adult learning. Roughly three-quarters of the adults at all three congregations are *not* engaged in ongoing Jewish learning. Is this recalcitrance just a reality of congregational life, or can the equation be changed?

At the other end of the spectrum are adult learners who are ready for learning at a higher level. The advanced learners at Temple Beth Elohim are fortunate to have Hebrew College nearby. Advance learners at Congregation Beth Am do not enjoy that advantage and are frustrated. This is one of the reasons Susan Wolfe, an active participant in the Shabbaton family school for seven years, left the program when her youngest son was enrolled. "The level of learning doesn't seem to stretch. We aim for the lowest common denominator because we want to be inclusive." She understands that it would be expensive and somewhat divisive to hire a second teacher for the more advanced adults, but believes that this is a challenge the congregation must face. Amy Asin, a former president who was also a Shabbaton parent, shared this concern at our interview with her in 2004: "We need to make a strategic decision about adult learners who have gone beyond basic—how do we manage our resources, and deal with both beginners and advanced learners? . . . Of course this is a wonderful challenge to have, and I celebrate it." As we went to press, Amy reported that her small chavurah within Shabbaton had begun to study together once a month and that, in five of the families, one parent participates in Torah study with the rabbi every Shabbat.

The demand for advanced learning is compounded by the fact, noted by educators in all three congregations, that congregants prefer learning with the professional staff rather than with one another. The two smaller congregations in our study are the exception: at Temple Micah several groups meet on their own, such as one that reads Israeli poetry; Beth Jacob also has study groups that meet without the rabbi, though these tend to be small and informal. Rabbis and educators at the other congregations are struggling with this issue. Susan Werk, educator at Congregation Agudath Israel, notes, "If we [the professionals] are not there doing it, then they don't want to do it. They very much need us there, which is something I'm working on right now, because I don't think it's healthy, but that's what's going on." Josh Zweiback at Congregation Beth Am calls it a "culture of expertise" that goes well beyond the synagogue: "We want experts for everything. And when you don't perceive your fellow congregant as an expert. . . how do you open someone up to the idea that that person has some wonderful torah to teach you. How do you do that?"

Congregants Who Resist Change

There will always be pockets of resistance to change, and in each of these congregations one can hear complaints about the cultural shift. Some who have minimal Jewish knowledge feel insulted by the implied message that they are not good Jews. Some who joined the synagogue just so their children could be "bar mitzvahed" ignore the new requirements; others simply leave. Ina Bauman, a lay leader at Congregation Beth Am who interviews each family that leaves the synagogue, reports, "Many who are leaving won't put the reason they are leaving on the form, but will tell me. Some of their reasons are: 'I want my children to be educated, but I want them do other things. I don't want the synagogue to be the center of their lives.'"

Though Temple Beth Elohim has many adult learners, they tend not to be the parents of teens. The synagogue's leaders worry that they are having more of an effect on the children than on their families. Ronnie Haas, vice president of congregational learning, is concerned that "there [is] a whole group of kids who are more engaged than their parents and the challenge is getting the parents to agree to sign them up for a program and/or bring them to temple. Not all parents understand what's happening here."

REACHING HIGHER AND HIGHER

Organizational development specialists advocate beginning with "low-hanging fruit"—introducing changes that are easy at the outset. The innovations at Congregation Beth Am, Westchester Reform, and Temple Beth Elohim might seem daunting to other congregations but were relatively easy for them. Most impressive is that these synagogues continue to set their sights higher and higher, rolling out new programs every year or two.

Relatively easy changes for some synagogues might be much more challenging for others. For some congregations, a reimagined religious school or a fourfold increase in the number of adult learners is much higher fruit, maybe even out of reach. But to the extent that they are truly visionary, congregations keep trying. To paraphrase another famous verse from the Mishnah (Pirkei Avot 2:16), these congregations believe that, though they may never finish the work, neither are they free to stop trying.

CHAPTER 5

Visionary Community: *Tikkun Olam* and *G'milut Chasadim* from the Inside Out

This chapter will focus on three distinct though intertwined dimensions of community life: *tikkun olam*, *g'milut chasadim*, and community. The first two are vital areas of congregational life and each one represents a different dimension of communal belonging and responsibility. The third, *community,* is often used synonymously with *congregation*, as if a dues-based membership covers both services and relationships. This chapter takes a closer look at these three areas of congregational life and will illustrate the ways in which they are neither simply opportunities for good deeds nor a byproduct of membership. Instead, all three are interrelated, mutually constitutive qualities of visionary congregations.

Building Community

In functional congregations, caring and social action are often the purviews of different voluntary committees staffed by people passionate about one of these areas, while community building rarely even attracts that level of attention. Often the work of these three areas is delegated to relatively independent committees, each of which operates in its own corner of the functional congregation. Tikkun olam is often thought to deal with people on the *outside* of the congregation, nonmembers, including non-Jews, while g'milut chasadim focuses on those *within* the congregation. This differentiation illustrates precisely the segmentation that characterizes functional congregations. By contrast, visionary congregations understand that tikkun olam and g'milut chasadim are ethical imperatives that shape the way in which members of the community relate both to one another and to the community at large. In short, visionary congregations succeed by approaching each in terms of the other two.

Although the glue of any community is relationships, synagogues have historically spent little intentional energy on strengthening relationships between their members. To approach congregational life with relationships at the center is to reconsider the dynamics of tikkun olam, g'milut chasadim, and community not as incidental but as central. Visionary congregations are able to build community on a large scale by attending to relationships on a smaller scale. Likewise, they understand that a commitment to social justice can be energized by relationships and concerns that are personal rather than abstract. Finally, they are committed to integrating an ethos of caring throughout the congregational community rather than sequestering it in a committee.

The value of community in congregational life is so strong that both the Experiment in Congregational Education (ECE) and Synagogue 2000 (S2K) used the language of community in their methodologies. ECE advocated the use of a *community conversation*, hosted small groups, usually in people's homes with selected members of the temple, to discuss the synagogue and members' vision of Jewish education. According to Peter Wang, the community conversation at Westchester Reform Temple, Scarsdale, became such an effective model for people to speak about their hopes and concerns for the temple that they adopted the term for their congregational culture and have since held community conversations on issues not connected to either ECE or education.

Likewise, S2K understood the importance of small groups, advocating that each meeting begin with a check-in. Check-in set a tone of intimacy and honesty among members that allowed them to transcend the formalities of functional congregational meetings. Amy Lipsey of Congregation Agudath Israel explained, "During check-in, everyone understood that what was said was confidential. People shared personal information, such as marital and health concerns. More so than the study portion of S2K, the check-in strengthened personal connections and created close ties." The check-in helped strengthen individual relationships as well as the sense of connection to the congregation as a whole. The relationships formed in these meetings became one of most influential and lasting effects of S2K on the congregation.

Both check-ins and community conversations had aspirations beyond supporting connections between individual congregants, yet some of the most powerful effects of these frameworks appear in the individual relationships they helped create. Likewise, tikkun olam, g'milut chasadim, and community present opportunities for mitzvot, but they also provide powerful frameworks for enabling deeper connections between individuals. This is not incidental. Whether emphasizing an ethic of caring among members, structuring individual conversations with the purpose of effecting change, or simply creating opportunities for informal socializing, efforts that treat tikkun olam and g'milut chasadim as central to the life of the community enrich the entire life of the congregation and distinguish functional congregations from visionary ones.

Tikkun Olam and Social Justice

In the past decade, much attention has been focused on community service and social justice as two potentially powerful modes for American Jews both to connect to their own religious and ethnic tradition and to effect change on a larger scale. Shifra Bronznick and Didi Goldenhar's 2008 publication *Visioning Justice* chronicles many of the ways in which these fields have expanded in scope and scale since the year 2000. Some of the issues that have become most prominent on the collective Jewish social justice agenda are poverty, human trafficking, human rights, Israel, sustainable development, health care, affordable housing, environmental change, and homelessness. Long-standing organizations as well as those of more recent vintage have begun to address these issues, among others, and they hope to create momentum for social justice in many areas of Jewish life.

Historically, synagogues have been the locus of Jewish social justice activity. From the earliest Jewish settlements in America, the synagogue served as a place for worship, for gathering, and for collecting and disbursing charity. Charity was primarily meant for their own as, in 1655, the Dutch West India Company granted Jews permission to settle in New Amsterdam (soon to be New York) "so long as they do not become a burden to the company or the community." In effect, Jews were permitted to reside in New Amsterdam as long as they tended to the needs of their own community. This ethic persisted throughout subsequent centuries as American Jews developed a robust infrastructure of charitable organizations dedicated primarily for attending to the needs of other Jews, both in the United States and abroad.

Jewish charities proliferated around the turn of the twentieth century and federations formed to coordinate charitable efforts. In the wake of World War II, that mission began to change as congregations started looking outward instead of inward. In addition, as the struggle for civil rights rose to the top of the American social and political agenda, rabbis and their congregations remained important players. The Jewish community adopted the language of the prophetic tradition, especially in the Reform movement. The establishment of the Union of American Hebrew Congregations' Religious Action Center in 1961 is evidence of the commitment to social justice by congregational bodies.

In the wake of the civil rights movement, Jewish social justice efforts turned to Israel and to the plight of Soviet Jews. Synagogues again became important loci for organizing, meeting, and supporting these causes throughout the 1970s and 1980s.

But with the collapse of the Soviet Union in 1989, Jewish social justice activists often found themselves without any large-scale issue around which to rally. Concurrently, the desire to effect local change through congregations settled into social action committees that typically organized congregational food or clothing drives or one-time direct service opportunities. This approach to social action is typified by "mitzvah day," an annual event in a congregation's calendar dedicated to performing mitzvot, understood as "good deeds" generally of the charitable kind.

In the past five years, in reaction to these circumstances, a more nuanced vocabulary has developed to describe the variety of issues and causes in which Jews participate. Generally, *social action* has come to refer to one-time, direct-action opportunities: food and clothing drives, making sandwiches for the homeless and hungry, working at a homeless shelter, and so forth. *Social justice* refers to interventions that address the root causes of injustice and typically involve more labor-intensive and slower-moving efforts. Rabbi Ronne Friedman of Temple Israel in Boston explained the difference between social action and social justice in practice. "It's not a 'mitzvah day.' There's a place for that. That's not anything bad. But it's not a solution to what we need to do; it's a feel-good, better-to-do-that-than-not-to-do kind of thing, but not a transformation." This distinction is helpful for discerning between different synagogue-based efforts to effect change.

To be sure, none of the leaders or laypeople we encountered during our fieldwork advocated getting rid of social action or abandoning direct service commitments. Congregations are full of people who advocate both direct service opportunities and longer-term social justice projects, and each has its benefits. All of our visionary congregations have active social action agendas that only sometimes reflect an orientation toward social justice work. Rabbi and Cantor Angela Warnick Buchdahl offered some examples of how her congregation, Westchester Reform Temple, engaged in direct service: "Social action ... [is] a really big piece of our identity as a congregation. ... This year [Rabbi Jacobs] preached during the holidays about Darfur, and it's become a driving mission. . . . We raised $100,000 within the two months after that to build a hospital through AJWS [American Jewish World Service]. There's going to be a march on Washington April 30, [2006,] and we've already bought Amtrak tickets."

Margie Miller, also of Westchester Reform, framed the congregation's activities similarly: "Our social action committee has extended its mitzvah day to the entire year. Members of the congregation volunteer by cooking for the homeless, the elderly, the handicapped. . . . Teens and adults tutor in day-care centers and perform in nursing homes. Before our board of trustees meetings, we pack nutritional bags to be sent to kids in shelters."

Betsy Broder explained how at Temple Micah in Washington, D.C., the social action campaigns relate to holiday celebrations:

> Following on "my father was a wandering Aramean," [from the Passover Haggadah] we now do a drive at Passover time to purchase duffle bags—proper suitcases for kids [in foster care] so that they felt better going from place to place. At Chanukah we adopt families through local social services programs and shop for their selected gifts. . . . And at the High Holidays we purchase thousands of pairs of underwear for clients at a local homeless shelter. The upcoming b'nei mitzvah class organizes this annual effort.

Members of Beth Jacob Congregation in Minnesota also spoke proudly about their involvement in issues of social justice. They joined with American Indians to oppose state highway department plans to build on sacred Indian ground; they marched at the state capitol for immigrant rights and Darfur; and they held "Social Justice Shabbat," featuring an afternoon of conversations about illegal immigration, which included lawyers and advocates from the broader community, who explained the issue to the congregation as it pertained to their lives and their city.

As successful as these direct service opportunities are, the leadership of visionary congregations often recognizes that the efforts

are short-term fixes that ultimately fall short of their broader vision of social change. But also important, they fall short in their
ability to cultivate relationships and build community. Rabbi
Elaine Zecher framed the difference between social action and social justice work explicitly in terms of an ethical and communal
difference between an event where "it feels good, it's great, you
take a lot of pictures and give everyone credit, and then everyone
forgets about it," and an opportunity to "create a sustainable relationship that is based on the human power to imitate the divine."

Zecher's congregation, Boston's Temple Israel, has been deeply
engaged in one of the most robust community organizing and
social justice efforts of any congregation in the United States. The
congregation prided itself on its long history as a social justice
congregation. Long led by rabbis with strong social justice commitments, Temple Israel absorbed some of that ethic and assumed
the identity of a justice congregation. Rabbi Pesner explained,
"Rabbi Gittelsohn preached the famous sermon on Iwo Jima and
against the Vietnam War, and Rabbi Mehlman used to fly to the
former Soviet Union and smuggle things in and people out, and
Rabbi Friedman had done this historic inclusion of gay and lesbian people and did the first gay marriage ten years before anyone was talking about that." This legacy had become an important
part of the temple's identity, but it became clear to the clergy that
the temple's social justice commitment had ossified as social action, and when Jonah joined the clergy, he inherited the social action portfolio.

By his own admission, Jonah was not a "social justice guy" in
rabbinical school and had inherited the portfolio largely on the
basis of his junior status among the temple's rabbinical leadership. But he felt encouraged by the temple's senior rabbis, and
with support from key players outside the temple, Jonah began to
ask pressing questions about the place of social justice in the life
of the congregation, beginning his investigation with the social
action committee. He learned that "people who care about an issue . . . want to do their issue" and that the members of the com-

mittee were not interested in going to meetings to discuss vision and direction. The social action committee disbanded, though Jonah's questioning continued. He framed his investigation with three "agitational" questions, paraphrased as follows:

- Is Temple Israel's social justice legacy real? Is it real for us?
- Do we believe that social justice should address more than just superficial projects that don't get at root causes?
- Shouldn't it be integrated with worship and learning?

Jonah's three questions—though posed within the specific frame of social justice work—echo three of the six characteristics of visionary congregations. In the first question, he is asking his congregation to be *reflective* in their assessment, not simply to rest on the history that they have inherited. The second question articulates an intention to providing *meaningful* opportunities for engagement. The third question takes a *holistic* approach to social justice and posits how to integrate it with other areas of congregational life.

At the urging and suggestions of community organizers Orit Kent and Meir Lakein, Jonah became more involved with Greater Boston Interfaith Organization (GBIO) through which he had opportunities to meet members of Boston's non-Jewish clergy, who shared a wealth of experience about congregation-based community organizing. Temple Israel had long been a member of GBIO, but often approached its involvement as just one of the many projects that Temple Israel does, rather than a fundamental quality of the congregation itself. In an effort to follow up on his agitational questions, Jonah managed to raise ten thousand dollars to hire a part-time organizer, Jenny Oser.

Like a professional educator or a professional cantor, a professional organizer comes with a highly specialized set of skills, and hiring Oser indicated a commitment to innovative social justice work at the temple. Oser quickly developed a relational organizing campaign. She explained:

It would look like any other campaign. It would have a start and a finish. It would have a leadership team. We would do leadership development. Those folks would be trained at how to run a campaign. And the campaign itself would be relationship building. We would set a goal—we want to have five hundred conversations over three months . . . [and] to see what common themes people were talking about in these conversations. We would then bring people together in a big way at the end to ratify whatever the common themes were that we heard, and roll out an action platform and say, "These are the things that are deeply and widely felt at Temple Israel, so we're going to act on them."

Perhaps more important than just creating a base for action, Jenny understood that this relational organizing campaign would not succeed if it were divorced from other areas in the life of the temple; so she, along with Jonah, devised a strategy that would include prayer and learning as integral parts of the campaign itself. "Every single time this leadership team would gather or bring people together either in one-on-one conversation or in big group check-backs or these roll-outs, there would be worship and there would be study. So, there would always be some blessing or some ritual. And there would always be some text of Torah to reflect on to study or to ground our conversations."

They kicked off the relational organizing campaign on Martin Luther King's birthday, January 15, and agreed that it would run through Passover. At the conclusion of the campaign, Temple Israel had exceeded its goal, hosting 807 one-to-one conversations and four community check-backs to report on the conversations that had taken place. Additionally, house meetings, or gatherings held by congregants at their homes, were dedicated to a similar purpose. They played a crucial role in the organizing campaign and provided another space for sharing concerns and cultivating relationships.

If nothing else, a few hundred temple members sat down with one another and had a chance to speak about their lives and share their concerns. Had that been all, that effort alone would have strengthened the congregation. But these conversations took place within a larger organizing campaign, which meant that these 807 newly invigorated relationships became Temple Israel's greatest strength in advocating social justice. The conversations had generated a wide array of topics that concerned members of the temple: Israel, affordable housing, health care, public education, gay and lesbian equality, the isolation of seniors in the community, and a handful of other concerns. Capitalizing on the concerns of temple members meant mobilizing the network of relationships created during the campaign and activating the network of GBIO partners to "do one major action that would show people that this stuff is real, . . . [and it] addressed root causes," Jonah recalled.

> Throughout the temple, people were talking about homelessness at one end of the spectrum, and then members of the temple whose kids couldn't live in the area because they couldn't afford it and were moving far away. Out of that came a three hundred person action at the temple with seven state representatives, where we got our state reps to sit on the bimah. We studied texts on housing and [the] homeless in the Jewish tradition. We prayed together, we brought in our interfaith partners, and we got our seven state reps to support the one hundred million dollar affordable housing trust fund, which was passed. We did it together with GBIO that got a lot of the other reps and senators from outside of our area.

This action resulted from a commitment to an issue that was strengthened in two ways by the relational organizing campaign initiated a year earlier. First, the relationships developed through the one-to-one conversations made for a sense of solidarity that the congregation had rarely experienced before. Second, because the decision to act on affordable housing emerged from congregants' personal concerns, not just their general sense of justice, much more passion was devoted to the effort.

The combination of a more tightly knit community and the expression of their collective concerns resulted in two significant revelations for the temple. First, they discovered the effectiveness of collective organizing for leveraging political power. Both the temple and the city realized the political potential of such community action. Second, they realized that it reversed the traditional clergy-led structure. Ronne observed that in the past the clergy's interests more often drove the social action committee's agenda. "It was . . . more top down than bottom up."

In the affordable housing campaign, the idea to organize an action emerged "bottom up," from the membership instead of the clergy. And the bulk of the organizing effort did not lie with the clergy but with a group of lay leaders. Jenny attributed much of the success of Temple Israel's campaign to the contributions of one such leader, Fran Godine, who "was a main mover in inciting the congregation." Fran and her friends recruited "a group of fifteen people who knew everything about what this was meant to be—the vision, the picture—before coming to an initial meeting."

Meir Lakein at GBIO further explained the significance of relational organizing to developing leaders:

> Good organizing requires a commitment to the idea that if you are a leader and you bring in other leaders, that doesn't mean you have less power because now you have to share responsibility and authority. Instead, now you have more power because you're a leader of other leaders, and in that way power is expansive because everyone can have more power, more ability to act on behalf of themselves and their institution.

The affordable housing campaign pushed the congregation to reflect on its own identification as a social justice congregation and to reconsider how they approach social justice work. Meir recalled Ronne's comments during the brief evaluation that immediately followed the affordable housing action, where he challenged the congregation to see themselves and not only their rabbi as part of Temple Israel's social justice story:

I just remember [him] saying something like this: "Ever since I came here I always heard these stories, you know 'Rabbi Gittelsohn marched, and Rabbi Gittelsohn went to this rally, and Rabbi Gittelsohn did [something else].' And until today it never occurred to me to ask, 'Did anyone else in this shul do any of this stuff with him or go anywhere with him or was it just him?' I don't want to be the one out there by myself doing it. I want to have people in the temple doing it together." And that was a key moment. It was the highest level of endorsement for this model.

Other successful actions followed this major action on housing, and at some point during these campaigns, the social justice efforts of Temple Israel were organized under one umbrella called *Ohel Tzedek*, which houses eight individual organizing efforts among the temple's members.[1]

Ohel Tzedek continues to use relational organizing to create new initiatives according to the desire and will of temple members, although not every issue receives the same attention or prominence because of the bottom-up approach. Some of the groups gathering under the banner of Ohel Tzedek have been meeting for a while without a culminating action, while others—like the affordable housing group—have disbanded shortly after successful actions. Still others have met for a long time before identifying an opportunity for action. One such effort resulted from a house meeting conversation focused on the housing issue. Four to five people met initially and over time began to focus on children's issues. One person in the group, Martha Chason-Sokol, had what she described as "a real passion about children and educational funding." The group grew to include sixty people and became a very powerful chapter of the state organization Stand for Children.

Since the interview, Temple Israel's chapter of Stand for Children has largely disbanded, but the emergence of such a large group remains a strong example of the community organization effort at Temple Israel. Perhaps as important, Martha's personal transformation (which is discussed in chapter 6), resulting from her participation in Stand for Children, remains a powerful example of how community organizing can change not only the dynamics of the congregation but also the lives of individuals.

The individual relationships, born out of one-to-one conversations, continue to be central to the congregation and its social justice organizing efforts. Steven Goldman explained the nature of these relationships as he recalled a recent one-to-one conversation (which Temple Israel calls a *mifgash*) with Rabbi Jeremy Morrison who was "wary" about the relational meetings having a hidden agenda and predetermined outcome:

> [Jeremy asked,] "Is this really a relational meeting, or is there an ask at the end of it?" I felt really comfortable to say, "No, actually this is a mifgash campaign, this is about building relationships." But it's not about building relationships purely to build community. There are other avenues to do that. Our eventual goal is social action. So it's a public relationship as opposed to a really personal relationship.

Steven's characterization of the mifgash reflects the intentional approach to community organizing at Temple Israel. Sometimes, a mifgash is part of a directed campaign geared toward a specific goal, and sometimes, it is part of a sustained, if low-level, campaign to create or strengthen the relationships within the congregational community.

Temple Israel leaders have continued to employ the tenets and methods they learned from GBIO and have integrated them into other areas of temple life. In recent years, Temple Israel has used relational organizing to reimagine how social justice is taught in their religious school and their high school. When the temple board underwent a significant restructuring, board members employed methodologies of relational organizing to strengthen relationships that could withstand serious disagreements and significant change. When Jonah left the temple to help start Just

Congregations, the Union for Reform Judaism's national social justice effort, the temple sought and hired a new rabbi who had experience in community organizing to replace him.

One of the lessons here is that simply taking an intentional approach to the organization of one's congregational community will change a congregation's culture, as it enables extant structures to grow in new directions. Beginning with relationships fuels the community by infusing it with energy on an interpersonal level. However, combining a commitment to the congregational community with sustained attention to social justice enables efforts normally considered valuable for their effects beyond the walls of the congregation to have internal effects as well.

Marshall Ganz, a professor at Harvard's Kennedy School and an important advisor to Temple Israel, explained the symbiotic relationship between social justice and community building in terms of the holism of sacred purpose.

> If it's social action without a connection back to worship, . . . it's disconnected then from the source of motivation and energy. Or [if] people are acting out of values that they acquired experientially, but they have lost the capacity to articulate that experience and therefore recreate it and draw energy from it, it's like being alienated. The worship experiences ought to give us courage to engage the challenges of the world around us.

Visionary congregations have adopted three essential concepts that characterize their commitment to social justice and community organizing. First, they believe that their community derives from something beyond mere membership and includes the relationship between the congregation, its members, and their city or larger environment. Second, they understand that community building is a process that requires intentionality And third, they tie the work of community building to a sense of sacred purpose that is, necessarily, larger than simply creating a community for its own sake.

Caring Community

Evidence of a strong congregational community is hard to identify and difficult to trace because it often happens on the margins
of a congregation's formal programmatic structures. It is simply
easier to count people than it is to measure the strength of their
relationships. Despite this challenge of measurement, the congregants themselves are often quite clear that they feel either a part of
or apart from any given community and the aspects of that community that provide meaning and connection.

At Temple Micah, Washington, D.C., the sense of a congregational community is tied closely to its commitment to social
justice and its sense of sacred purpose. This tripartite relationship—community, social justice, sacred purpose—illustrates how
an ethos of g'milut chasadim can strengthen the community internally, even when the force of the action is not dedicated toward the congregational community directly. The story of Josh
Seidman is illustrative in this manner. Josh and his wife joined
Temple Micah in 1993 and almost immediately both began serving on the board of Micah House, a transitional, supportive home
for homeless women in recovery from substance abuse, that is an
independent nonprofit organization supported by Temple Micah
and its members. Soon, Josh became the president of the board
and expressed his understanding of the relationship between social justice work and sacred purpose: "I was president of the Micah House board and I very much believe [that] is God's work . . .
[and] I [brought] that spiritual mindset to my board meeting. . . .
We started off beginning every session with some sort of prayer
or poem or song or whatever. I made it a point to only do it myself the first time and then ask different board members to read
it." Soon, Josh became more directly involved in the congregation.
Micah House was not the work of an isolated group but an integral part of the congregation's identity and—almost as important—an avenue of entry into the congregational community.

Yet, Temple Micah's social justice work is not only valuable because it helps draw people into the life of the temple. On its own, Micah House continues to be valuable to the women it serves, regardless of its impact on the temple and its community. However, the way in which Josh articulated Temple Micah's sacred purpose through social justice and community building indicated that when congregations approach each of these endeavors holistically, everyone benefits.

Congregation Agudath Israel in Caldwell, New Jersey, offers a different account of the relationship between g'milut chasadim and community building. When S2K organizers approached Rabbi Alan Silverstein to ask his congregation to participate in the first conference, in 1996, Alan jumped at the chance. Alan handpicked a team of doctors, nurses, and social workers who would represent Congregation Agudath Israel at the conference and steered them to S2K's curricular healing track because he understood that the congregation would face new needs in the area of health and healing in the years to come. Following the conference, Congregation Agudath Israel launched a number of journey groups,[2] brought in the well-known songwriter and singer Debbie Friedman to lead a healing service, created a position for a congregational nurse, and invested in establishing a health and healing center at the MetroWest JCC. Each of these initiatives offered new avenues for the congregation to engage in meaningful interaction through concerns for health and healing.

Although the healing services were initially quite popular, they eventually dwindled in size. By contrast, other efforts thrived. The congregation signed on to the idea of having a congregational nurse and raised money to pay for her services one day per week. Other congregations also saw the advantage of having a nurse on staff and joined with Congregation Agudath Israel to create one full-time position. Karen Frank, a member of Congregation Agudath Israel's S2K team, was hired to fill it.

Congregation Agudath Israel approached the issues of health and healing with a broad sense of what healing could mean. Instead of thinking about healing from within the structure of existing committees or health-care occupations, Congregation Agudath Israel created a position that wed a concern for individual health to the strength of the congregational community. With this innovation, Congregation Agudath Israel reached outside its own community to engage other congregations and enable them to benefit from Karen's position as congregational nurse. In addition, she had a platform not only for helping individual members but also for channeling that help through individuals' congregational memberships.

Although at the time, she was the only congregational nurse in the country, Karen did not work alone. Creating the congregational nurse position coincided with and complemented the efforts of Congregation Agudath Israel's caring committee, a group charged with responsibility for g'milut chasadim within the congregation. Abby Landau, a long-time organizer of the caring committee at Congregation Agudath Israel explained how they work in collaboration with Karen, hearing from her when she encounters a situation where they need to be involved, as well as alerting her to needs they hear about. "She's sometimes the first person to find out about a need and then she will call us in. Or many times we will have heard about somebody in need and we'll call her. . . . So it works both ways, but very closely, hand in hand."

Joyce Musnikow Harris, the long-time chairperson of Congregation Agudath Israel's caring committee, emphasized that the caring committee's sense of responsibility extended not only to working with the nurse and the rabbi or educator but also to the membership:

It was a lot of *bikkur cholim* [visiting the sick] work, predominantly with members of the congregation. Many congregants wished to be assisted by the caring committee without the knowledge of the synagogue staff. The confidentiality and the privacy that would be afforded people has always been a common thread from the very beginning to today. But the importance of that is crucial. There are people in the congregation that we have assisted and the rabbi and the cantor do not know.

The integrated efforts of the caring committee and the congregational nurse illustrate the ways in which they worked cooperatively while remaining independent. Yet the ethos of relationship building remained central to both. Irene Edelstein explained:

> We had a nascent caring committee, but with Synagogue 2000, we really launched a very active—and it remains to this day—active, wide, involved caring committee that has done everything from arrange meals to drive people to chemotherapy treatments, and they've done it and they continue to do it. And a lot of people were trained—and they continue to have training—and the caring committee really became an important aspect of our synagogue. It brought out some new people. It connected us to people.

Congregation Agudath Israel's success lay in its ability to work on three levels simultaneously: creating innovative positions, having talented people available, and building relationships one at a time. None of the elements stood alone. Congregation Agudath Israel strove to shift the work of the caring committee into a broader ethos of a caring community in which *caring* could become a central pillar of communal life. Fostering an ethos of a caring community meant adopting an approach to community building that integrated sacred purpose and an ethic of caring.

This shift to a broader ethos of caring could begin to happen because of Congregation Agudath Israel's innovative approach to healing, which drew on congregational resources, a visionary rabbi, and an emerging emphasis on interpersonal relationships. Rather than seeing the caring committee as a kind of "subcontractor" for g'milut chasadim within the congregation, journey groups and the emphasis on healing contributed to the congregation's ability to see health, healing, and caring as central to congregational life. Supported by a network of tighter relationships between members, Congregation Agudath Israel could begin to see itself holistically and in terms of its sacred purpose as a caring community.

Building Community I: Relational Organizing

At the core of these two examples is a logic of *relational organizing*. The term derives in part from the world of community organizing and in particular the work of the Industrial Areas Foundation (IAF). Rather than imposing an organizing agenda from above, the IAF "does indeed use a radical tactic: the face-to-face, one-to-one individual meeting whose purpose is to initiate a public relationship and to re-knit the frayed social fabric."[3] Attending first to relationships changes the perspective of the congregation and congregants and alters the frameworks within which tikkun olam, g'milut chasadim, and community building all take place. These three dimensions of congregational life reflect and refract one another, drawing strength and creativity from each effort. The central issue here is that each requires intention and attention to the relationships that comprise any congregation.

Of the congregations we studied, the one that has the most developed approach, is Temple Israel of Boston, owing in large measure to its relationship with the Greater Boston Interfaith Organization, an affiliate of the IAF. The strategy of relational organizing has informed their approach to almost everything, from social justice to restructuring the temple's board. Rabbi Jeremy Morrison, who runs the Riverway Project (the temple's young adult programming), explained how he approaches relational organizing "as a way of getting at ritual and learning, in particular, to build internal community," as opposed to "external social justice work."

Rabbi Ronne Friedman of Temple Israel succinctly captured the ways in which the ethos of relational organizing has changed the congregation: It has empowered people "to organize internally for things they want." The congregation and especially the staff have a new consciousness of "the responsibility to . . . connect with greater numbers;" and the "network of *chavurot* have committed themselves in a sense as a confederacy of groups that support one another's projects. There's this sense that there is an instant network of support that goes beyond the *chevre* or smaller group, which in turn serves as the spearhead or the vanguard of a particular activity." Ronne emphasized that the impetus for much of this change came from social justice work with GBIO, but he situated that effort holistically among other changes that have taken root in both the staff and the membership.

By contrast, Congregation Agudath Israel employed a similar approach but under quite different circumstances. In the wake of the Synagogue 2000 conference, Congregation Agudath Israel instituted a number of journey groups. Participant Debbie Rabner recalled, "The focus was on healing, and a lot of it was on how you visit people who are sick, and what you can do to help. And people bringing stories from their own lives and things like that. But it was personal. You got to know the people in the group very well. I knew many of them, but not all of them [before the group]. I still feel very close to everyone."

Rabbi Paula Mack Drill, a member of Congregation Agudath Israel's S2K team, explained the impact that journey groups made on her and her team: "Part of the transformation. . . is that we had this group of thirty people having this extraordinarily wonderful learning experience and sharing of personal lives that wasn't a self-help group but was really based on this vision of our shul being a caring community. The meetings were all in my house. They were very sacred. People didn't miss [them]." People's commitment to their journey groups evidenced a commitment to one another and to the congregation as a whole. Paula explained: "It was a subtle change in language and the way we saw each other."

Karen Frank recalled how she applied some of the lessons from her journey group to her professional life as a visiting nurse:

> When I would visit Jewish patients, I suddenly felt that I could ask if they would like me to sing *mi sheberakh*, or I would ask them about God, or I would ask them how is it going to be, not being able to get to the synagogue this Rosh Hashanah. Because I was Jewish and because I was very actively Jewish, I was able to ask them questions they felt so happy to be able to discuss with somebody, which really all had to do with their illness in the context of their spiritual life.

In the wake of the success of journey groups, Congregation Agudath Israel strengthened its commitment to building relationships by hiring Randi Brokman as its program director. To some degree, Randi served as the congregation's social coordinator and saw to it that the congregation welcomed "each and every person." She put this ethic into action even at the level of membership applications. When members join the congregation, they complete a form that asks for their basic contact information as well as their interest in specific ways to become involved in the synagogue. Debbie Rabner, a member of the *chesed* (caring) committee, created a spreadsheet to capture this information, and she distributes the new member names to the relevant committee chairs, who follow up with the person. She says, "I did that with every aspect of the synagogue. Sisterhood would call each new member and invite them to come with someone who was already involved. It helps people connect and not feel uncertain when they are new." Randi, who had been a member of the congregation for ten years before becoming its program director, focused on individual people and their interests rather than trying to fill the congregation's calendar with more and more programs.

Though responding to different needs and working from different methodologies, Congregation Agudath Israel and Temple Israel both adopted the intentional approach of community organizing in order to create opportunities for members to talk face-to-face and strengthen individual relationships at their respective congregations. Focusing on the face-to-face dimension of congregational life as a vehicle for tikkun olam or g'milut chasadim has proven to be a radical departure from standard committee-based efforts. Turning their attention to individual relationships has provided a framework and a strategy for changing not only individual areas of congregational life but also the culture of the congregations discussed above. Other congregations have witnessed similarly powerful effects from less obvious efforts to build community.

Building Community 2: Kiddush Matters

Following the logic of relational organizing means attending to individual relationships. For the IAF and Temple Israel, this means highly structured, if personal, conversations that often takes place within a larger campaign or other such framework. However, relational organizing can also happen in less structured environments—*less* structured, as opposed to *un*structured. Insofar as we are talking about building communities, the congregation provides a framework for social interaction, but often that is not sufficient for building the relationships that fuel thriving communities.

For smaller congregations and minyanim, meaningful interaction is relatively simple because there are simply fewer people who tend to be more homogeneous. Long-time members of Temple Micah and Beth Jacob speak fondly and a little wistfully about the days when everyone knew everyone else. Now that these congregations have grown to about four- to five-hundred member units, the question arises as to how to manage demands in a less intimate setting. For Temple Micah, this question has arisen around the number of b'nei mitzvah. Rabbi Danny Zemel recalled how one couple whose attendance at services had been minimal floated the idea of starting a davening group in their home and wondered if it would have Danny's blessing. He told them, "I can't stop you from doing anything, . . . [but] I don't think it would have my blessing. We're a community here."

Other congregations have faced similar issues, whether around b'nei mitzvah or in response to a desire for greater diversity in worship styles—as with Sharing Shabbat at Westchester Reform in New York or Tefillah 2000 at Congregation Beth Shalom in Kansas City. In some cases, such as that of Westchester Reform, the situation has not been resolved, and a split remains between the Sharing Shabbat crowd and the main sanctuary service. There are no easy solutions to these problems, but providing an opportunity for congregants to build relationships with one another is a popular strategy among visionary congregations.

Beth Shalom, Beth Jacob, and Temple Micah have addressed this problem by emphasizing the importance of kiddush as a time and place for the membership to gather, interact, eat together, and schmooze. Kiddush is where community happens. Andrea Kessler explained the importance of kiddush at Congregation Agudath Israel:

> I know this is going to sound silly, but part of what many people really enjoy about Shabbat, especially if they didn't grow up with much of a background, like my husband, is kiddush. People stay for lunch. People eat. People connect with one another and catch up with friends. It's something that we do. If it's a *simchah*, everybody participates and everybody shares in the joy together. It makes you feel 100 percent part of a community.

Congregation Agudath Israel invests in kiddush to ensure that there is a fairly substantial spread even on *Shabbatot* without specific celebrations. In addition, it has a policy that every kiddush— even those in honor of specific events (like b'nei mitzvah)—be open to the entire membership. Alan Silverstein is clear about his intention. "We have people who come from various towns, so I want to create a virtual community on Shabbat." Rabbi Morris Allen at Beth Jacob shares this philosophy: "I had big fights about the importance of kiddush. From the start, we don't allow families to leave shul after a bar or bat mitzvah. The kiddush is in shul, everyone is invited to the same kiddush. Whether you're an invited guest or not, you get the same food."

Jeanine Lange, of Beth Jacob, who describes herself as a bit of a loner, explained how the congregation reached out to her at kiddush, but continuing to participate was difficult. "For a long time I would just slide out after the service and not go because that was tough." When she decided to convert to Judaism and began meeting with the rabbi weekly, she knew she needed to be part of kiddush, part of the community. "One day . . . I was . . . standing there and Grandma Zelda came up and said, 'Come with me,' and dragged me off. . . . That made it a lot easier after that. Sometimes it's just the simple things."

Simple, to be sure, but not accidental. Both Morris and Grandma Zelda took advantage of kiddush to encourage congregants to connect to one another. Although certainly not relational organizing in the strict sense of the term, kiddush institutionalizes interaction as an important tool for community building.

Creating Community 3: Tending to the Margins

Informally, kiddush does important community work, insofar as it provides a venue for people to speak with one another casually. However, other aspects of congregational life, like lay leadership or ritual participation require a bit more structure. Yet these areas, too, benefit from the logic of relational organizing by turning away from large-scale issues and toward the relationships that constitute the community.

At Beth Jacob, Rabbi Morris Allen works hard to create a sense of openness, welcoming, and warmth to which most congregations aspire. Darlene (a pseudonym), a long-time member of the congregation, explained how that sense of openness and warmth fostered a stronger and more diverse sense of community: "A variety of people are involved in the leadership. And I think that's wonderful. Again, that's a strength of the shul. It's not just the people that have been there for the last ten years, eleven years, fifteen years. It's new people. It's people who have only been there a couple of years, who are willing to come in and to lead. In all sorts of ways."

This ethos is, in part, a response to the congregation's location in Saint Paul, a place known for having families with deep roots. Laura Honan, a Jew by choice and member of Beth Jacob, explained how Beth Jacob fits into the city's social landscape: "The Twin Cities is the kind of place where everyone has their gazillion relatives and the friends they've known all their lives, so it's not the easiest place to break into as an outsider. Beth Jacob, though, has a high percentage of people who came from other parts of the country and want to build community here, so we are open to newcomers." Arielle Ehrlich, who grew up in New Jersey, described her experience at Beth Jacob in similar terms. "It's just a really warm community. People were very quick to take me in."

An environment like this is not accidental; the rabbis at every one of our visionary congregations play a crucial role in the culture of their congregations. This is not to say that the rabbis dictate what happens, but rather that the rabbis lead by example. Each one takes it upon him- or herself to engage in relationship building to strengthen the congregational community. Morris is exceptionally good at reaching out toward the margins and inviting people into the community's center. Louis Newman, a long-time member of Beth Jacob, offered this example of Morris's commitment to community building:

> At the end of services every Shabbat morning, Morris invites anyone who is a newcomer to stand up and introduce themselves, and invites people to introduce guests that they have with them. . . . This is not a

great big place where nobody is going to notice you if you're a first-time person. You're going to be noticed, you're going to be welcomed. There's going to be somebody at the door to greet you when you come in. It's that kind of place, and I think it's been that kind of place pretty consistently for many years.

Rabbi Danny Zemel of Temple Micah embodies a similar thoughtful approachability. Jodi Enda explained her first meeting with Danny, while she was "shul shopping" following the birth of her daughter:

I talked about how my husband wasn't Jewish, and I had just had a baby. And [Danny] was great. I went to services a couple more times, and my husband went to services, and I decided it felt like a warm, friendly community. It was a place where my daughter could have a similar experience to the one I had growing up, where she could know the rabbi and he would know her. And she would feel that she had a place there.

As in the case with Temple Israel above, intentionality about community is crucial at Beth Jacob. And their leadership embodied that commitment. Educator Susie Drazen explained Beth Jacob's "biggest cultural issue":

Everybody doesn't know everybody. We need to be more planful on greeting people. We're a great congregation for saying, "Hello. How are you?" But we need to remember them when they come back to us. Making sure new people have someone to sit with at services and at kiddush. Making sure people get phone calls about programs, and someone to greet them when they get there. We need to make sure they have a seder and a place for the high holidays.

Everyone had ideas for how best to address maintaining a sense of community within the congregation. Jeanine Lange explained the need to "make sure that we keep moving people around a little bit," suggesting that they turn people over like a farmer tills soil, "to keep people involved but to keep moving [them] around" so that programs and activities don't stagnate. This was something of a leitmotif in our interviews with members of Beth Jacob. Morris worked hard to ensure that people who seemed marginalized found their way into congregational life. During our fieldwork, we saw this occur in a number of ways, from inviting someone for an aliyah at the daily morning minyan to asking a teenager who had recently returned from Israel to lead a part of the Saturday morning service. Morris's attention to his members has become a model for continual congregational community renewal by looking beyond the "usual suspects" at its core, and instead always looking outward toward its margins.

Morris explained this practice in terms of the congregation's commitment to lay-led worship:

> Is it perfect davening? No, but it's pretty good and he's gotten better. I knew [that a certain congregant] couldn't do "*ve tegaleh, ve tera-eh* [a particular prayer] . . ." But I knew that if I empowered him to say that, he could start calling people up to the Torah, because the person who is our normal *gabba'i* wasn't there. So then he can start doing that, and he said the *chatsi kaddish* [a prayer that is often said], and pretty soon, it'll be pretty natural for him. I'm pretty intentional about this stuff. I do that with all sorts of people.

Morris's approach to building and sustaining community has succeeded at Beth Jacob and continues to infuse the ways in which the congregation sees itself in both ritual matters and lay leadership. He continued, "We have engaged and involved people, and brought people into the core of synagogue life and to leadership who otherwise, economically, would be considered marginal."

This attitude was echoed in a story told several times about a donor who wanted to make a significant contribution, provided he would be honored with a plaque bearing his name, but the congregation turned him down because putting names on things would intimidate some members. Sensitivity to the congregation's economic diversity not only exemplified Beth Jacob's commitment to the diversity of its members and a generally modest disposition but it also represented the ongoing commitment to the relationships at its core.

Beth Jacob is not the only one of the visionary congregations in our study to adopt a "no plaques" policy. Westchester Reform, Scarsdale, New York, and Congregation Beth Am, Los Altos Hills, California, follow a similarly modest approach to acknowledging the generosity of its membership. A handful of members at Temple Micah even semiseriously offered "No Plaques" as the congregation's motto. This ethos of equality helps to foster a sense that everyone is valuable and that everyone can contribute in his or her own way. Rabbi Danny Zemel explained how this sensibility translates into opportunities to engage congregants. "Everybody's a *macher*, nobody's a macher. That's the sense of the place. . . . I ask anybody to do anything. I think people have a sense of that."

That sensibility is a crucial part of cultivating a congregational community. Respecting and facilitating relationship building, whether through engagement in formal campaigns and social justice work like Temple Israel or through more informal strategies like those at Beth Jacob, benefit the congregations in dramatic ways. The constant tending to margins, of attending to the individual needs of people to take on responsibilities within the community, both illustrates and models the kind of work necessary to create community consciously and to maintain the relationships that constitute it.

Creating Community

To launch any of these efforts, the leadership has to know its own community. Danny Zemel explained:

A rabbi's got to be an expert in his community. A rabbi has to have a certain level of Jewish expertise, but if you're not an expert on your community, you can't be a successful rabbi. So I know this congregation better than anybody else. I understand what the zeitgeist is better than anybody else. I think about it. I talk to everyone in the congregation more than anyone else. If someone asked me "What's your area of expertise?" I'd say, "Temple Micah."

At our visionary congregations, the leadership—both professional and lay—understands their congregations and their needs. The fact that Danny "talk[s] to everyone in the congregation more than anyone else" allows him to know his congregation and his community, and it is crucial to his ability to initiate changes that will strengthen the community.

Knowing how the congregation understands itself allowed Alan Silverstein to push for healing and enabled Jonah Pesner to challenge his congregation to rethink its historical relationship to social justice. Morris Allen is keenly aware of his congregation's place in the Twin Cities, and Danny, too, understands his congregation's identity and values its commitment to Micah House. The significance of this knowledge cannot be underestimated, because the ability to build community rests on the best possible understanding of the community's identity and its vision of its future.

But the story of the relationship between tikkun olam, g'milut chasadim, and community building cannot end with talented leaders. Visionary congregations are committed to reflecting on their situation and to reconsidering their direction. This means thinking about the community within the congregation in relation to the larger community of which the congregation is a part. In essence, this means not relying on membership numbers as an indicator of communal strength, but looking to the strength of personal relationships that are the glue of the community.

Visionary congregations, led by reflective leaders, are ripe with opportunities for congregants to build relationships with one another. Whether they look to intervene in issues of social justice or hope to create a caring community, their efforts to effect change begin with building relationships. Whether as structured as the IAF methodology of relational organizing or as unstructured as a kiddush that makes people want to stay and eat, tilling the social soil of congregants increases opportunities for individual engagement and builds strength within the community itself. Tikkun olam and g'milut chasadim are intimately tied to the strength of the community, and the community draws its strength from those larger values. But the values of justice, kindness, and even community cannot begin to take cultural root without attention to building community, one relationship at a time.

PART 2

Achieving
Congregational Change

◆ ◆ ◆

CHAPTER 6

Transformation in Practice: Moving toward Change

At some point during our research, a group of rabbinic students visited Boston's Temple Israel, one of the model synagogues studied here, but an example of what Hebrew Union College professor Sam Joseph, who consults with many congregational boards, calls "Nimitz-size synagogues." Joseph has in mind the U.S. Navy's largest category of aircraft carriers, named after Admiral Chester W. Nimitz, which, he explains, take twenty miles to turn around at sea. "It takes Nimitz congregations twenty years to do the same," he says.

Temple Israel, then, is a Nimitz congregation: it occupies an entire square block in the heart of the Harvard Medical School Longwood area, is a home run away from Fenway Park, and employs four full-time rabbis to serve a membership of 1,600 family units.

But Temple Israel has turned around. For one thing, it leads the way nationally in social justice organizing; for another, on their way home from work Friday nights, parents stop off for services, plunk their kids down to crayon over sheets of paper spread out on the sanctuary carpets, and then sing their way through joyous and participatory prayer. And if that were not enough, its Riverway Project has set the standard for engaging young adults in Jewish life. Temple Israel thinks differently: its standard for success goes beyond a list of programs. It was a natural stop for the students.

Amazing Grace: What Counts as Transformation?

While in Boston, the students also visited Grace Chapel, one of the many megachurches that have revolutionized American religion since the 1980s. Talk about Nimitz-size! Every weekend, some eight thousand worshipers arrive, bringing with them double that number of Sunday school children. During the week, people by the hundreds come and go, for social action projects, concerts, youth group events, and a host of other activities—all of them intended to strengthen evangelical Christian identity. What makes Grace unique is that the high profile megachurches normally cited as exemplary—Southern California's Saddleback, for example, or suburban Chicago's Willow Creek—were built from scratch, as unfolding visions of pastors who had constructed new churches because they had given up on changing old ones. Grace, however, is like Temple Israel in that it has undergone transformation from within—a perfect parallel for the rabbinic students to consider.

What especially struck the students was Grace's Sunday school, an entire storey that had been painted in carnival colors, and then outfitted with the latest technology to permit not just classroom activities but stage performances as well, mounted against the backdrop of impressive props and professional acoustics. Equally impressive is the church entrance, which opens onto a living-room-like area for guests to gather and leads into a state-of-the-art coffee bar that serves only fair trade coffee harvested by unionized labor.

The students appreciated both visits, but on the way back to the hotel, one of them wondered aloud, "Temple Israel probably has the same budget as Grace. How come Temple Israel still looks like Temple Israel while Grace looks like Grace?"

The student was observing that even the transformed synagogues in our study do not look or feel revolutionary, whereas megachurches do. The comparison does not imply that synagogues should be either churches or mega,[1] but it does force the question of what we mean by transformation. Our samples look more like the mainstream churches described in a 2006 study tellingly labeled *Christianity for the Rest of Us*—that is, not like the megachurches.[2] It defines transformed churches as becoming "mindful" of their theological raison d'être, rather than pursuing activity for activity's sake.

It is helpful to contrast *transformative* with *additive*, an approach whereby new programs simply get added on to old ones, with no underlying shift in synagogue values or culture. Transformative change, by contrast, alters the nature of everything the synagogue does. It pervades every aspect of synagogue life—its committees, worship, policies, and personnel. And it does so over time. As committees turn over, new members take the change for granted, rather than revert to the way of thinking that preceded the change. As current clergy retire or leave, successors are chosen with the transformative model in mind—the clergy adapt to the culture, the culture does not adapt to the clergy.

When speaking of change, however, differentiating substance from form is important, a distinction that becomes clear if we realize that asking what constitutes a transformed congregation is like inquiring after the definition of a good novel. One kind of answer is *substantive*, identification in terms of content: I like *War and Peace*; you like *Moby Dick*. Substantive definitions are arbitrary. So, too, with synagogue transformation. We, the authors, want transformation to accord with the substantive criteria we call *visionary*; others may think transformation should accomplish something else. *Substantive* identifications of transformation are a matter of taste.

Another kind of answer is *formal*. Both *War and Peace* and *Moby Dick* are great novels because they share certain agreed-upon formal criteria—they must prove lasting, let us say, or have memorable characters and a consuming plot. Chapters 3–5 of this book discuss the substantive definition of change that we were after—the particular ways that we thought transformed congregations ought to think. We called such congregations *visionary*. By contrast, this chapter handles the *formal* characteristics of transformed congregations, the process whereby synagogues engage in transformation regardless of what transformative end they choose. People may legitimately take issue with our *substantive* preference for visionary, without, however, questioning the *formal* qualities that define transformation. The transformative *process* that is the subject of this chapter is independent of the transformative *goal*: it is a route toward a new way of institutional thinking.

- A transformed congregation *thinks differently* about absolutely everything: it has different criteria, different processes of analysis, different approaches to problems that arise.
- This change in thinking is *pervasive*; that is, it may have begun in one area of synagogue life, but eventually it shows up throughout the system, even in the infrastructure of how the synagogue does business—its board, its offices, its website, everything.
- It demonstrates this change *over time*, not just in the first flush of success.

Transformed synagogues are recognizable by a new mode of thinking that pervades the entire institution and lasts through time.

Another way of describing it is to say that transformation affects entire cultures, the taken-for-granted way of just "the way things are." A culture is like a backdrop for a play—foggy old London for Sherlock Holmes or the wide open spaces for a cowboy story. It frames the way actors go about their business on stage: Sherlock Holmes cannot show up in a Wild West shoot-out. Additive change is like tinkering with the script—Holmes boards a railroad train instead of a horse-drawn carriage. Transformative change alters the actual backdrop. It moves Sherlock Holmes to modern-day New York and makes him into a contemporary detective, a woman perhaps, whose PhD in forensics outfits her to use computer technology to solve her cases. Synagogues that do not attend to their cultures get frozen in time. They limit their imagination to the arbitrary limits of the past. The transformation process allows them to question the unquestionable by opening up dramatic possibilities that the old backdrop would never allow.

We researchers have long wanted to know how synagogues accomplish such transformative change. How do you go about questioning what you do not even know is there? Thanks to our interviews with people in the eight synagogues described in this book, we think we can now say a good deal about it.

This notion of *different thinking that pervades time and culture* was implicit in both the Experiment in Congregational Education (ECE) and Synagogue 2000 (S2K). ECE helped synagogues become not only congregations of learners but also self-renewing congregations: institutional systems that learn from their experiments, constantly bettering what they do. S2K challenged synagogues to become *sacred communities*, where relationships mean more than programs and Jewish values drive every aspect of synagogue life. Guided by these criteria, we found eight congregations that demonstrated cultural transformation.

How do synagogues get there? We are not discussing *dysfunctional* synagogues, remember—places that cannot hold a rabbi, that are saturated with internal squabbles, or that in other ways display signs of institutional pathology. We would hardly expect transformative greatness from these. Our topic is *functional* congregations, by which we mean congregations that function well and have the luxury of thinking about doing more. Not all functional congregations are open to transformation, in large part because their very success means that they have nothing to propel them into going beyond what they know and do already. Synagogues are not profit-making enterprises that can never rest content with last year's quarterly earnings; nor are they not-for-profit charities like March of Dimes or Jewish Federations, which exist to expend contributed capital and can compare a current campaign with what was raised formerly. Synagogues have no such evident measure of success. They are *not-for-profit institutions with no readily apparent bottom line.* If almost everyone is happy—and almost everyone is, in highly functioning congregations where members join expecting exactly what the congregation is so good at providing—what would possibly drive synagogue leaders to dream of change?

But some good synagogues do dream anyway, and find themselves going from *functional* to *visionary*. This chapter traces their journey—from the emergence of leaders to the day the synagogues look back to discover a genuine culture shift. Our story begins with the emergence of visionary leadership, without which change never gets off the ground.

How Change Started

Even transformed synagogues begin with ordinary people drawn to synagogue life to educate children, meet friends, "get a bar or bat mitzvah," or just do what they think Jews ought to do when they move into town. Some members then encounter a turning point where they find themselves looking for something more. We call these *nodal moments*, junctures in life where people look for new directions. They are open to finding something in synagogues that they never knew was there. Paula Mack Drill of Congregation Agudath Israel in Caldwell, New Jersey, likens these moments to blowing glass where at a critical point the glass is "hot and you can mold it. That happens," she adds, "when people are at really critical junctures."

Those critical moments take different forms. Nancy Belsky at Temple Beth Elohim in Wellesley, Massachusetts, had earned a degree in counseling psychology and "was in my own psychoanalysis professionally," she says. "It was a wonderful complement to Jewish study, because psychoanalysis doesn't tend to be spiritual. . . . So I was open to searching in general." Thinking of the other women who joined her synagogue's change project, Nancy opines, "There's more meaning to life than the responsibilities that we accomplish every day. . . . [The women in the synagogue's change project] had beautiful homes, their husbands were successful, they might have been successful in their own name, and yet they were feeling like that wasn't enough." Martha Chason-Sokol was drawn to Temple Israel's initiative on organizing for health care. "I remembered, 'Wait, I was without health insurance when I was an artist in New York City.'" But even more, "It helped in my personal life because my son has special needs. . . . So learning how to advocate publicly enhanced my ability to advocate personally for my family." For Beth Elohim's Terry Rosenberg, the critical moment was when "my daughter became a bat mitzvah. My father, who had died several years earlier, was a very big influence on my life and I found myself thinking of him and what it would mean to him to witness his granddaughter's bat mitzvah. I became very melancholy about it all." Everyone encounters nodal moments at some time or other. Great synagogues appreciate this human encounter with life's inevitable voids. What they offer is not just more programming but also an opportunity to matter.

Mattering has two sides. *Internally*, it denotes a personal sense of wholeness, satisfaction that all's right with the world. One can label that feeling *spiritual*, a word that comes up with some frequency in the testimonials of people we met. It was also couched in terms of *community*, a word with almost mystical overtones for those we interviewed, indicating that they had found a place to belong. *Externally*, people sense that they matter to others—they make a difference to the synagogue community and to the larger world beyond it. Our chapters on worship, learning, and social justice relate directly to this human need to matter. *Mattering internally* is associated with learning that runs deep, and the consequent conviction that one is connected to tradition, to a past, and even to something that might be called transcendent. *Mattering externally* derives from being part of a healing community and a force for social justice. Regular Shabbat services take on an additional dimension of reflecting and celebrating how people matter in both ways.

In the congregations we studied, congregants at nodal moments then met unusual leaders—generally, though not always, rabbis. These leaders fell into one of two categories: leaders in their own nodal moments and leaders expanding their original visions.

LEADERS IN THEIR OWN NODAL MOMENTS

Leaders in their own nodal moments are rabbis or laypeople who had reached their own transitional stages of life, felt something lacking, and cast about for an opportunity to reinvest their energy in an important cause. Anthropologists call these life opportunities *liminal*, a term derived from the Latin *limen*, meaning "doorway" or "threshold," because these are threshold moments when the potential for creativity is highest.[3] At Beth Elohim Harold Kotler, who was recently retired and gifted with vision, energy, and know-how, threw himself into initiating synagogue change. At Congregation Beth Shalom in suburban Kansas City, Beth Smith found herself memorializing her late husband at services that "were awful; I mean the old men raced through it." So she approached Rabbi Alan Cohen about "designing a service that would be interesting to both young people and others who weren't totally immersed in the traditional service." The rabbi had reached the point where he feared that "in ten years I won't have any congregation in the main sanctuary." So he joined forces with Beth.

A particularly common nodal moment corresponded to what has traditionally been called a midlife crisis.[4] Our study regularly turned up rabbis for whom going through the motions as busy synagogue clergy was easy, but who missed the sense of challenge, to the point where the prospect of more business as usual threatened to squelch their reason for becoming rabbis in the first place. Because upward mobility in the rabbinate generally correlates with age and experience, and because only senior rabbis have the power to determine overall synagogue policy, this midlife crisis was actually experienced by rabbis who had recently accepted, or grown into, a senior rabbi position.

Indeed, the most likely, though not the only, profile of transformative rabbinic success is senior rabbis in midcareer who become unwilling to settle for just *functional* and feel comfortable enough in their position to risk large-scale change. Rabbi Janet Marder came to Congregation Beth Am in California as such a person. She had directed the largest region in the Reform movement, seen a plethora of synagogues struggle with worship, written her own manifesto on the subject, and then moved to Congregation Beth Am to put her dreams into motion. Rabbi Rick Jacobs too had recently moved to a senior rabbi post at Westchester Reform Temple in New York. In Washington, D.C., Temple Micah's long-time Rabbi Danny Zemel was reaching the point where he felt he had to make dramatic changes where he was. Unlike Rick and Janet, who had recently arrived at their positions, Danny had long ago settled *into* it without settling *for* it.

LEADERS EXPANDING THEIR ORIGINAL VISIONS

Some of the rabbis we met had founded the congregations they were in and needed no nodal moment to push their original visions forward. Rabbis Alan Silverstein at Congregation Agudath Israel in New Jersey and Morris Allen at Beth Jacob in Minnesota fall into this category. Alan had designed—and was now directing—a "traditional egalitarian Conservative shul" with *t'fillah* at the center. He knew, however, that the pastoral aspect of synagogue life needed work, so he opted for S2K's track on healing. Morris had decided against a comfortable suburban position precisely because he wanted to develop a traditional Conservative synagogue—not unlike Alan's, but smaller. He too was always looking for a new way to do things better.

Synagogues have always recognized the power of nodal moments, since it is precisely those moments that get marked through life-cycle ceremonies like weddings, bar and bat mitzvahs, and funerals. But they do not adequately appreciate the power those moments have to catapult a person into long-range commitment to a cause. The ceremonies, and preparation for them, exist in a vacuum. Except for bar and bat mitzvahs, no active synagogue involvement is required in advance, and parents of bar and bat mitzvah children are more likely to drop than to enhance their membership when the bar or bat mitzvah ceremony is over.

More important still is the fact that most adult nodal moments—moving into town, children off to college, changing jobs or careers, and midlife crises in general—have no Jewish ceremony associated with them. These are the occasions when competent and experienced men and women are most likely to dedicate themselves to a new and exciting way to make their lives matter. Yet synagogues allow them to pass without suggesting that the place to matter most can be the synagogue.

Most synagogues operate on inertia—at best, adding a program here or there, or a new best practice they have heard about. This inertia becomes institutionalized as normative so that even when challenges mount or things go wrong, synagogue leaders are apt to think that the answer lies in more additive change. They initiate a program, tinker with schedules, or add a staff member to do what is being done anyway, but better. And they return to business as usual. Members will come and go, dropping in on each other's nodal moments, but never imagining that the synagogue is a place to satisfy their own adult yearning to matter.

Visionary synagogues know that business as usual can put you out of business. The business that ends up failing is not the synagogue, which usually manages to survive and may even be quite functional, but the larger enterprise we might call the Jewish *project*, making Judaism itself matter, personally and globally. Great congregational leaders make sure they stay in *that* business by taking pride in, but never resting content with, what they already have in place. Always in search of other creative and critical voices, they offer adults in nodal moments opportunities to matter.

Of Rabbi Alan Silverstein, a congregant says, "He picked people to join the Synagogue 2000 change initiative because he felt they were on the cusp of something or were looking for something." He offered a chance to matter more than momentarily by rethinking the synagogue obligation to the Jewish project.

How Change Spread

Additive changes are local—specific to the religious school, the sanctuary, the sisterhood, or men's club. They are initiated by individuals who hold positions of authority in whatever realm they affect. Religious school directors, for example, add weekly assemblies or prayer services; cantors change melodies; boards adopt new budgetary processes. Transformative change, by contrast, infiltrates the entire synagogue culture and requires a growing network of people committed to spreading its influence. That network begins when the committed leaders we have been describing become what we called gadflies with "D'n'A."

GADFLIES WITH D'N'A

The change agents we met were not failing leaders who had no choice but to do something different. On the contrary: they were senior rabbis or lay leaders at the top of the synagogue heap. Membership was booming; there was no obvious reason to change course. But our leaders felt differently: they were possessed with D'n'A—*discontent and ambition*. Their discontent focused on what are usually taken for signs of success: the three Bs—busy, big, and boisterous. Without a vision, however, their ambition to go beyond activity for activity's sake had nowhere to go, no specific direction to take.

Founding rabbis expanding their own original visions have usually already built reputations for trying out novel things. Transformation initiatives are just the latest example. They encounter little resistance from congregants who became used to experimentation a long time ago. Less fortunate are the nodal- or midlife-moment rabbis who move into established congregations that are not their own from the outset. They have to convince the laity to undertake what may seem a radical departure from what has settled in as normative institutionalized inertia.

The rabbis we studied sometimes reverted to radical measures to get congregants' attention. Rabbi Rick Jacobs at Westchester Reform Temple gave a sermon entitled "Ending Religious School as We Know It." He accounced, "Guys, the thing is broken and we're going to fix it, and it's not about changing Hebrew school by fifteen minutes or getting a new Hebrew textbook. That's little thinking." Things needed more than tinkering; they were broken beyond repair. Rabbi Elaine Zecher at Temple Israel jokes that people sometimes need to perceive an institutional "trauma to make things happen."

Either noisily or quietly, the nodal- and midlife-moment rabbis thus became gadflies intent on shaking things up. ECE and S2K became important because they arrived from the outside with a ready-made motivational language to denote goals on one hand (sacred community) and processes on the other (community conversations). "It's not about programs," people began saying. It's about "transformation," "culture change," "thinking differently," "the Jewish project," and the like. We will see later that individual synagogues eventually added their own localized language. Also, some of the adopted vocabulary stuck, while some did not. "Congregation of learners" proved lasting; "self-renewing congregation" lacked traction.

Congregations took advantage of whatever outside initiative they could find. Westchester Reform, for example, began with ECE, but at the same time, says Peter Wang, "there were a couple of congregations around the country doing Synagogue 2000; we were kind of shadowing it, and doing some of the same stuff." When their initial experience ended, the synagogue redid S2K. Unable to formally participate in S2K, but inspired and assisted by Rabbi Rachel Cowan who knew all about it, Kansas City's Congregation Beth Shalom created its own initiative, Tefillah 2000. Wellesley's Beth Elohim began with *Me'ah*, an educational experiment developed through its federation. It did not seem to matter which initiative congregations chose, as long as there was one to choose—and as long as it was seriously transformative.

Change began, then, with at least one gadfly, someone, moreover, who was well enough positioned in the system to engage others. We do not mean to imply that these individuals *alone* perceived the need for change. They were frequently nudged along by others. But it took a well-placed gadfly to convert the nudge *about* change into a movement *toward* it. At Congregation Beth Am, for instance, a board member on retreat asked why the synagogue was satisfied by mediocrity in its children's education. The rabbi capitalized on this dissatisfaction.

ASSEMBLING TEAMS

Gadflies who fly alone are likely to crash. Knowing this, the change initiatives guided them as they went about the necessary task of assembling a change team. Rabbinic school, it turned out, had taught its rabbis little about the process of team building. Indeed, past generations of rabbis were more likely to lead change from the pulpit by dint of a charismatic rabbinic persona. Not so the leaders in our study, who worked quietly behind the scenes and made common cause with others.

Alliance building did not erode rabbinic authority: these rabbis were every bit as appreciated as their more solitary forebears. But over time, the nature of rabbinic authority has changed. Where once it was *ascribed*, part and parcel of the title Rabbi, it is now *achieved*; and rabbis achieve it by their authenticity in representing Jewish tradition and by building honest, trusting, and transparent relations with lay leaders.

As described above, support often came from people who were themselves at nodal opportunities in life. These moments are intensely personal and were met in equally personal ways: handwritten letters or even phone calls from their rabbis requesting participation. In most synagogues people bubble up to the top of the institutional hierarchy by virtue of long years of service, commitment, and stamina but not necessarily competence. By soliciting people personally, the wrong people could be excluded; and for the right people, only a personal appeal would work, since the best candidates were usually already invested in other projects that had gotten to them first. Terry Rosenberg at Beth Elohim recalls Harold Kotler telling her, "'I want to change this place. I want interesting creative people with great ideas. . . .' On that basis I went, and the rest is history."

At this point in most of our congregations, a subtle sense of elitism galvanized those selected. Joining initiatives spearheaded by nationally known personalities with reputations for being on the cutting edge had a certain cachet. Just being chosen brought a rush of excitement. According to Rabbi Rick Jacobs, his team felt like a "little heated core of really great bold thinking. . . . People would say, 'ECE is going to be the wave of the future. . . . We're the chosen few.'" Temple Micah's Josh Seidman encountered the same sense of being chosen. "There was a little bit of an 'inside the group, outside the group' thing. There was the group that was studying and there was the rest of the congregation."

At times this elitism proved a stumbling block as a gap opened up between the team and everyone else. Josh returned from his initial S2K conference to find other congregants looking at us "like we were from Mars. How do we bring back that sort of excitement and spiritual connection without scaring people? We had already scared our families." In Caldwell, the change team "inflicted" upon the congregation a song they had learned while at the conference, only to fail miserably. Teams went through a process of visioning ahead of the congregation and then realizing the need to slow down and bring the rest of the congregation along with them.

TEAM FIELDWORK

The Talmud boasts a famous story of how Hillel solved a halakhic question by recommending, "Go out and see what the people are doing." That is precisely what the newly assembled synagogue teams did, sometimes in the most remarkable places. Rick Jacobs told everyone, "We're going to go anywhere in the country or even to Israel. . . . Go to church. Go to a synagogue. Figure out what's happening." Harold Gillman at Beth Jacob Congregation remembered "a church down the street over here. We went in and said, 'Wow! We like that. A semicircle. Everybody is close in.'" Pointing to his own congregation, he observed, "As you see, that's kind of how we are too." Congregations that failed to change also examined alternatives, but they found reasons why what they saw would not work, whereas congregations intent on change found something that would. "Don't adopt; adapt" went an S2K motto. Visionary congregations adapted; functional congregations didn't.

NEW CONVERSATIONS . . . WITH NEW PEOPLE

Change entails a lot of work, over a long, long time. Why did people do it?

There were important exceptions to the rule, but most of the people who joined the teams and stayed around to do the work were the regulars, the loyalists who do everything else at the synagogue. This was just the latest challenge for which they stepped up to the plate. We do not know much about those who worked for a while and left. We can, however, say why people stayed, beyond the usual selfless motive that inspires good people to stick with any task worth doing.

A huge attraction for team members was the challenge of a new set of conversations, in part made possible because of the exceptions mentioned above—the presence of people who joined teams without ever having become part of the loyalist circle before. In part also, the two change initiatives introduced these conversations by injecting a new language of discourse. ECE favored a five-part process of *readiness, visioning, experimentation* with low-hanging fruit, *outreach* throughout the congregation, and *exploration* of new initiatives.[5] What especially caught on was *community conversations*, small groups akin to focus groups and designed to communicate the congregation's vision or to test out new program ideas.

The means of fostering such conversations varied. S2K used a curriculum of study to introduce new concepts; ECE sent consultants to have discussions at each synagogue site. S2K framed the synagogue as sacred community; ECE projected the possibility of a "self-renewing congregation." S2K brought teams to large-scale conferences where they talked about synagogues differently. Ritual opened new avenues of conversation in S2K; small-group conversations were focal to ECE.

The conversation changed not just in kind but also in level—think of it as raising the conversation ante. Conversations, that is, managed to get beyond such usual board issues as an unhappy bar-mitzvah family or a leaky roof. "As a clergy staff, we sat around and shared our theology with one another," says Rabbi Zecher. "By understanding what each of us believed, we were then able to translate it into our work within the congregation. We had graduated from the ordinary to the sacred."

The lure of new topics went hand in hand with the excitement of new voices. In most synagogues, the work is done by a close-knit network of regulars. ECE and S2K made it possible for synagogues to add new people without threatening those already there. Since the topics were new, no one was privileged with having already developed expertise in them—they entered the conversation as equals. The result was a double gain for the inner circle: new things to discuss and new voices in the discussion. S2K's curricular conversations took place among teams where many people had never met one another before. To every meeting, it added a personal check-in on how everyone was doing, thereby deepening commitment to one another and not just to the issues under discussion.

But S2K suffered from having no formalized system of broadening the conversation beyond the teams themselves. Without consciously attending to the issue of expansion, teams run the risk of becoming their own insular conversation circles. ECE, by contrast, set up conversations over coffee with a salon ambience (the community conversations) to broaden the constituency. "Community conversations," says Peter Wang, "had become part of our vocabulary. Whenever something arises, we say, 'Maybe we should have a community conversation about it.'"

Conversation continued beyond the synagogue walls. "We felt an instant connection to other families in the synagogue," says Bob Miller at Westchester Reform. If I saw somebody on a train or in the community, we would have something in common. It was a nice connection." S2K occasioned the same exhilaration, and not just within individual teams. Since S2K worked with several area-wide synagogues at once, members of different teams would run into one another while shopping or picking up kids from school, and stop to compare notes. Making friends is one of the prime reasons people join synagogues in the first place; working in a change process met that need.

MUTUAL DISCOVERY

Discussing new ideas on a level playing field is often referred to as *collaborative learning*. We have to be careful how we use that term, however. In some circles, collaboration denotes a flat leadership style whereby everything bubbles up organically from group process. We did not find that here. In most cases, change was driven by a single and singular visionary, and except for Beth Elohim's Harold Kotler, that person was the rabbi. Even in Congregation Beth Am, which, as we will see, was the most process oriented of our congregations and the one that most approached this populist collaborative pattern, Rabbi Rick Block generally determined what direction the change would take.

Some rabbis found the collaborative challenge different from the way they had been trained by mentors of a different generation. One rabbi recalled a senior rabbi once advising him not to register opposition at board meetings, since he could let board directives fail just through lack of follow-through. By contrast, the rabbis in our sample were strikingly transparent. They were collaborative, by which we mean they treated lay leaders as genuine dialogue partners, honing the vision together and supporting and encouraging one another. The most striking contribution of the team, says Terry Rosenberg, "was that we provided a safety net for experimentation. . . . We basically said to the rabbi, 'You can do something really radical in the synagogue and if anybody gives you a hard time, you have the whole Synagogue 2000 initiative behind you.'"

Sometimes, a team attracted a deviant member, someone whose personal needs interfered with team process. Rabbis had to walk the fine line between sustaining an effective team and maintaining sensitivity to the needs of individual members. They spoke to the difficulty this issue raised, sometimes agonizing over the solution at which they had arrived. One S2K congregation chastened the program's initiators for failing to anticipate the dilemma that such a problem would present to rabbis. "Someone on our team uses the process for her own ends, frustrating everyone else while doing so. The team wants me to get rid of her, but I am her rabbi too, and I am not going to tell her to just get lost." Generally, as we shall see in greater detail below, they learned to dismiss truculent members of their professional staff, but they lived with a certain amount of ambivalence toward volunteers, where both professional and pastoral concerns came into play.

Having assembled the teams, rabbis were then faced with entrusting laypeople with duties they were used to doing themselves. One rabbi quoted a colleague as saying, "Let them do it; if it doesn't work, it doesn't work." But most were not so laissez-faire. They delegated leadership and responsibility to others but remained intimately involved with everything the team did, especially when it came to representing Jewish tradition. Team members acknowledged the absolute necessity of hearing the rabbi's authentic Jewish voice. They were not charting a new course alone; they were helping the rabbi do it. On the one hand, people regularly deferred to the rabbi as the religious expert; on the other, they were taken with the rush of mutual discovery, excited to have been approached as experts in their own right—often, in fields that the rabbi knew little about. Beth Jacob's Susie Drazen remembers board meetings: "We're ping-ponging stuff off each other and sharing information." It was "like we were in a lab," says Rabbi Zecher at Temple Israel, "in constant motion, a living laboratory."

A remarkable finding in our interviews was the extent to which individuals gave credit to each other rather than taking it for themselves. Everyone helped everyone else feel proud. Harold Kotler, for example, hardly mentions himself in referring to "the juggernaut," as he calls it, that he set in motion. Instead, he refers to Amy Gorin, who was "wonderful," and Terry Rosenberg who "took the ball and ran with it." Cantor Jodi Sufrin, also at Beth Elohim, says of her rabbi, "It starts with Joel Sisenwine." For his part, however, Joel knows Jodi had been there a long time before he arrived; he calls her his strong suit, whom he was fortunate enough to inherit. Congregants regularly credit rabbis; rabbis never credit themselves.

What Change Teams Did

As the teams began the actual work of transformation, old models of institutional organization threatened to get in their way. Most synagogues work with an outmoded system of authority based on early twentieth century models of corporate efficiency[6]—the ubiquitous model of a triangle. As a model of management, the triangle represents a broad-ranging staff at the bottom; then fewer and fewer members of middle management (cantor, executive director, assistant rabbi, and school principal, for instance) higher up; and at the top, a single CEO rabbi with ultimate and lonely responsibility for everything that happens. A parallel triangle represents lay authority, which oversees management. At the bottom is the congregational membership as a whole. As it rises, the triangle thins out with committee members and chairs. At the top is an executive board led by the synagogue president. Communication takes place vertically in both triangles: problems filter up; solutions filter down. Horizontal communication occurs primarily at the top, where executive board members (representing chairs of committees) communicate with the rabbi CEO or, possibly, with the relevant middle management responsible for whatever is at stake.

Even in the corporate world, this triangular structure has been under attack as being relevant only to an industrial economy where interchangeable goods are manufactured in an assembly-line process.[7] It is hardly efficient for synagogues that value learning, prayer, spirituality, and social justice as their visible signs of success. The transformational change sought by ECE and S2K focused on reevaluating the structural components that constitute this old-fashioned triangular system. It began with a new look at authority that was implicit in the kind of teamwork the two initiatives encouraged.

DECENTRALIZING AUTHORITY

As one would expect from the teamwork described so far, roles became less firmly defined while boundaries of assigned activity became more fluid. It was no longer clear, for instance, where the rabbi's work ended and the cantor's began. Jodi Sufrin says, quite happily, "For quite a few years, I functioned like a silo. I now find that I am busier than ever, but not in the realm of synagogue music. I'm a full member of our clergy team and am involved in all aspects of temple life from teaching to pastoral work. For example, the caring community team falls under my portfolio." Once a congregation opens its mind to the many ways it can carve up what it does, new perspectives open and boundary fluidity becomes normative. We call this phenomenon *the decentralization of authority*.

At Temple Israel, each of the four rabbis was given a personal portfolio of responsibilities. Says Rabbi Zecher, "You need to be able to say, 'I have this portfolio, Jonah has another, Jeremy has another one still. Yet they're all fluid." At Temple Micah, responsibilities that had once been assumed to lie with the professional staff were transferred to congregants. Celia Shapiro explains that if a group of people decides to initiate a new activity, "all they have to do is tell the board, and the board says okay and they set up a group. For instance, last year a bunch of people wanted to read [the Israeli poet] Yehuda Amichai. They simply went ahead and did it. Similarly, some congregants who like to ski organized Temple Micah Ski Club ski trips."

It bears repeating that rabbinic authority did not suffer—even in Temple Micah, where congregants were set free to determine their own religious destiny and innovation did not have to be processed up the triangular ladder. What Rabbi and Cantor Angela Warnick Buchdahl says about Westchester Reform Temple was true wherever we looked, "The clergy here are pretty much revered."

DEZONING THE SYNAGOGUE

Triangular authority systems assign synagogue activities to specific management personnel who are overseen by lay committees. The two of them work in tandem but without necessarily considering what is happening elsewhere in the synagogue. The result is *institutionalized zoning*: each sector of synagogue life operates independently, revolving around its own director of programming (for music, the cantor; for schooling, the educator; and so on). This system impedes novel thinking, since those with power to effect change are located inside hermetically sealed bubbles of activity. The big picture is known—if it is known at all — only to the central planners: the rabbi and president (who do not necessarily talk regularly with each other and who may also have conflicting visions of success). Ordinary congregants rarely think to initiate good ideas, since the bureaucratic journey to the locus of authority does not seem worth the effort. People participate in the synagogue's offerings or not, but take no responsibility for what these offerings are—any more than they try to determine the movies playing at the local theater.

Functional congregations hew closely to zoning, because zoning is precisely what allows them to function efficiently. Spatially, the school wing runs smoothly but separately from the sanctuary; organizationally, the ritual committee need not consult with the education committee; and the cantor and education director have little to do with one another. But life is holistic. The purpose of religious school is for students to be initiated into a life of prayer; minyan members (the worshipers) enjoy studying. Stretch these examples and you get skiers who pray in the morning and study in the evening. In the functional synagogue, no single zone encompasses study and prayer, so they do not get planned together; and the ski slopes, which are outside the synagogue, do not show up as the synagogue's concern. When portfolios overlap and their holders communicate, zoning limitations disappear, permitting combinations of activity never before imagined.

EXTENDING SPACE

A ready sign of decentralization is the breakdown of spatial inhibitors. Temple Israel's Riverway Project moved outside the synagogue and into people's homes; Westchester Reform converted a neighboring building into a retreat center and is still in a decade-long process for making the synagogue into a campus. Congregation Agudath Israel posted signs to orient congregants to a space made more fluid and welcoming. Josh Seidman says of Temple Micah, "In that first year we probably had twenty different configurations of chairs in the sanctuary"; then they moved the *oneg Shabbat* (refreshments) to the beginning of services and into the gathering area outside the main-floor sanctuary, rather than the social hall downstairs.

RESCUING THE RABBI

An enormous benefit of decentralizing authority is that it relieves the rabbi from the burden of being the sole and final determiner of everything. Celia Shapiro says of her rabbi, Danny Zemel:

> He can experiment more freely, consult more broadly, and decide more easily what to spend his working time on. The people he works with are far less lonely, take much more responsibility, and achieve far more satisfaction. Committees work together or actually dissolve in favor of task forces initiated by anyone at all who chooses to activate the website in favor of a Jewish idea that just might work.

One need not spend much time in rabbinic circles, and even seminaries, before encountering conversations on burnout and self-care. These are not signs of clergy "unions" trying to cut back on hours, work, and responsibility. They are reflections of congregational life that has made rabbis into unwilling CEOs at the expense of their calling: to study and teach Torah, provide counsel to those in need, oversee worship and spiritual growth, ensure a congregational conscience, and the like. Transformational thinking addresses this shortcoming by allocating responsibility throughout the synagogue system and applying spiritual and moral values to the way things get done. The result is a synagogue reenvisioned from being a fee-for-service institution into a community that shares responsibility for remaking lives in the image and service of God. Only an infrastructural overhaul will accomplish that end.

HIRING AND FIRING

Even the most spiritually directed synagogue will find that change strains old staff arrangements and leads to two options. The easier of the two is expanding professional capacity by making new hires; much more difficult is the challenge of firing, retiring, replacing, or otherwise going around people who, in some cases, have worked in the synagogue for years but are unable to accommodate to the new ideas and demands.

Obviously, expansion requires financial means; but it equally relies on an appreciation of local resources. "All politics is local," one-time Speaker of the House Tip O'Neill is said to have remarked. All transformation is local too, even if the national change initiative is not. Our synagogue leaders had a feel for their surrounding milieu, the local ecology, as we call it, and drew on its resources to meet personnel needs.

Wellesley's Beth Elohim, for example, benefited from Boston's successful Me'ah program, a curriculum of adult study offered first at the city's Hebrew College, then at individual synagogues. Without help from its Jewish federation, Combined Jewish Philanthropies (CJP), Me'ah would have been beyond their financial reach. But the CJP helped, in part because of its remarkably forward-thinking director Barry Shrage, for whom learning is the centerpiece of Jewish excellence. Even Barry, however, would have been stymied without Boston's local specialty: its many Jewish university professors who were easily tapped to provide a spectacular faculty for Me'ah's adult classes.

In the same vein, Westchester Reform's successful ECE initiative took off because, says Bill Blumstein, "People moving into the Scarsdale area have the perception of Scarsdale being a great place to educate their kids. Educational change would be something that they would welcome." Rick Jacobs says, more bluntly, "Scarsdale's only industry is schools." Westchester Reform had yet another local advantage: access to New York Jewish professionals with expertise in whatever the synagogue needed. For more than twenty years, Rick had been studying ritual and worship as part of an alumni group that included many of the leaders in the field. Informally, he was in touch with most of them. "Larry [Hoffman] is a neighbor," Rick confesses, "so we'd drag Larry over a couple of times and it began to reshape worship."

But music was the key to reshaping Westchester Reform, and in that regard Rick was frustrated. Before his arrival, the temple had hired Stephen Merkel, an extraordinary cantor (tragically, he died before this study was completed). But his gifts did not extend to facilitating the participatory music that the new Reform worship style demanded. Fortunately, the temple had hired Angela Warnick Buchdahl, both a rabbi and a cantor, whose proficiency did include congregational singing. Midway through the transformation process, it added Rabbi Jonathan Blake, who was also adept at leading the new music. Additionally, Cantor Benjie Ellen Schiller, a professor of Reform cantorial music at Hebrew Union College and a leading advocate of the new worship style, lived just a town or two away. So too did Cantor Ellen Dreskin, who, as we saw, directed the S2K programming nationally, specialized in participatory worship, and became a family educator in addition. Finally, Debbie Friedman, the composer behind much of the new music and a spectacular worship leader herself, lived in nearby New York. Ellen Dreskin summed it up by saying, "Rick places his vision above all else and never hesitates to seek the assistance of skilled leaders in all areas."

Harder than hiring was firing. At times people who did not like the way things were going left of their own free will. But usually people stayed, and when that occurred rabbis had to make hard decisions about the professional team they inherited, letting people go if necessary. Sometimes, as with Westchester Reform, one of the team members (the cantor, in this case) was unable to retool but played a valuable role elsewhere. So rather than taking apart the old worship team, the rabbi established a parallel one—in this case, people expert in experimental worship, who among other things provided a healing service and ran the alternative Shabbat morning learning plus worship experience called Sharing Shabbat.

Synagogues are often loath to replace professionals or staff because romanticized notions of congregational family cloud sober analysis of synagogue excellence. David Wentworth at Temple Micah analyzes the problem well:

> Small not-for-profit institutions, including religious organizations, often ignore the fact that they also have to function as businesses. If they don't successfully manage practical and financial matters, they often cannot function well at their intended purpose. . . . Too often decisions are not made on a rational basis, they're made for emotional reasons. . . . At the core, these institutions are small villages where everyone knows everyone; it is synagogue as family.

Concerns like these became issues for teams who felt responsible for the ideas they generated but had no authority to hire or fire. Unable to plan without considering staffing limitations, they had to contend with the fact that many synagogues are indeed like families, or at least like mom-and-pop stores, where efforts to alter staff priorities or change job definitions are apt to be resisted and decisions to change staff or clergy can be divisive to the point of being nearly impossible.

Even large and corporate-style synagogues are generally not as impersonal as outsiders might suspect. The professionals and the regulars who make up the committees and the board have probably known each other a long time. Lay leaders are likely to come from a relatively small number of families who, over the years, rotate key congregational positions. The staff, the teachers, and even the professionals and clergy may well have been there "forever," building personal relationships with each other. The decision to challenge job descriptions, alter priorities, and ask people to risk moving outside their comfort zone is apt to be resisted.

RECOGNIZING LOCAL ECOLOGY

Another issue that the teams faced as they went about their business of suggesting wide-ranging innovation was how to factor in their own local ecologies—an issue already mentioned above. We can now expand on what we mean by noting that ecology has three interrelated aspects: opportunity, need, and availability.

- *Opportunity* answers the question, "What, given our uniqueness, will probably succeed?" An inner-city synagogue with a history of demanding social justice will more readily launch an initiative to fight neighborhood poverty than a synagogue in the suburbs, where rampant poverty is harder to see and less likely to be admitted.
- *Need* determines the answer to the question, "What are the specific components required to satisfy the opportunity?" The inner-city synagogue in question may require funding for a professional community organizer.
- *Availability* is an analysis of the resources that might be found to meet the need. Lacking a budget for such a professional, the synagogue may know of a foundation that funds such efforts or an area school of social work that might adopt the new position as an internship.

Take the example of Me'ah, mentioned above. Wellesley's Beth Elohim is composed of highly educated professionals—hence the *opportunity* to institute an advanced program of continuing education. To succeed, it would *need* teachers and money to pay them. Boston's many universities with Jewish Studies programs offered the *availability* of teachers; and the openness of Boston's CJP to Jewish education within synagogues suggested CJP as a likely candidate to make the necessary funding *available*.

Successful teams found that the first step in addressing problems was a thorough inventory of the local *opportunity*. Temple Israel's *opportunity* derived from the large number of as-yet unconnected young Jewish adults in its neighboring Riverway area; it also inhabited the most liberal state of the union, a natural environment for social justice initiatives. Westchester Reform's opportunity arose from its town's reputation for good schooling. Congregation Beth Am benefited from its Silicon Valley start-up mentality.

Central also to considerations of *opportunity* were the natural proclivities of their clergy: Congregation Beth Am's Rick Block was passionate about education. Temple Israel's cantor, Roy Einhorn, played the guitar and was willing to expand his usual cantorial repertoire to include congregational singing. Beth Elohim had its own accomplished cantor, Jodi Sufrin, anxious to engage congregants in worshipful song.

Having identified *opportunity*, each congregation then addressed *need*, followed by a survey of *availability*. Beth Elohim urgently needed a new rabbi who would be on board with the change process that Harold Kotler had begun; they knew of one nearby who might be available. Later, its foray into education turned up the need for new educators, which it found in Rachel Happel and Allison Kur, two recent graduates of Brandeis University's Hornstein program. Temple Israel needed personnel for Riverway outreach and social justice. Partially because it is in Boston, a desirable location for young Jewish professionals, it benefited from ready availability of Rabbis Jeremy Morrison and Jonah Pesner for Riverway Project, its outreach to young adults, and *Ohel Tzedek*, its social justice organizing.

Synagogues prefer tapping local people who are already known entities rather than advertising broadly, the way businesses do. In many major cities, such as New York, Los Angeles, and Boston, local expertise abounds and the Jewish community is small enough for everyone to know everyone else. Besides, for synagogues on small budgets, a national search is financially unfeasible, and the low salary they offer—often part time and without benefits—will not entice full-time professionals to uproot families and relocate.

Relying on *purely* local availability may have a downside. Small communities lack the abundance of local expertise that larger metropolitan areas enjoy. Also, synagogues may hire locally for the wrong reason: still mired in a mom-and-pop store mentality, they feel more comfortable remaining within the extended local family than going outside the neighborhood. Local recruitment worked for the congregations we studied. But we suspect that without a national search, some synagogues settle for who they can find rather than who is really available.

FINDING FUNDING

Tapping ecological opportunity sometimes required nothing more than encouraging volunteers to expand their involvement, like Congregation Agudath Israel's Paula Mack Drill, who later went on to become a rabbi in her own right, or shifting the responsibilities of the professional team already in place, like Congregation Beth Am's Rabbi Josh Zweiback, who was made senior educator. But it usually cost money, and even our congregations with means struggled raising it. Rabbis frequently found it hard to get lay support for anything that had financial implications, because even though synagogues are the primary portal into Jewish life, they are also grossly underfunded, with budgets strained or even overdrawn. Boards worry about keeping existing programs going, let alone adding large-scale initiatives on top of them. So rabbis became fundraisers.

When Temple Israel's Riverway project began, the temple had no budget for it, but with three rabbis and a cantor already in place, the board was unlikely to entertain the idea of bringing on yet another rabbi. Rather than give up, however, Senior Rabbi Ronne Friedman found a donor and funded the project off budget. Now it is budgeted and the pride of the temple community. Congregation Agudath Israel's Alan Silverstein found federation funding and used his rabbinic discretionary fund. Paula Mack Drill says, "Every huge pilot grant that's out there in the universe, our synagogue is into it." Another example is Westchester Reform, which had to raise money for a director of education, a position that was expanded to include three full-time professionals plus a secretary.

For the most part, however, rabbis approached their own congregants for funds while avoiding the perception of a "4M" bias: Making *macher* money matter. "You could not cause a bigger fight at Congregation Beth Am than to even suggest that you name something," says Eddie Reynolds. "We do have a few named funds, but that took several years to agree upon." Beth Micah, too, prided itself on not being like its neighbors, where, as the congregants saw it, "the machers get the best seats." Micah's Celia Shapiro boasts, "We are plaque free. . . . The big machers here are the four-year-olds."

Small congregations with less wealth had to look inward for volunteers. At Temple Micah, religious school is partially staffed by parents and other volunteers; and in order to add instruments to Shabbat services, music director Teddy Klaus appealed to congregants, successfully, to form a pick-up band. At Beth Jacob, which has no cantor, Rabbi Morris Allen prides himself on recruiting lay prayer leaders. The shul runs, he says, "by a lot of smoke and mirrors."

STRIVING FOR EXCELLENCE

Teams were taught to recognize that they could ill afford mediocrity. Almost everyone enters a synagogue at one time or another, if only for life-cycle events; and when they arrive, synagogues are on trial. To thirty-year-olds, either the synagogue looks like the one their parents joined (and they will not), or it demonstrates that it has gone beyond that. Both ECE and S2K were careful to model excellence themselves. "The ECE program itself was very professional, very thoughtful," recalls Bill Blumstein of Westchester Reform Temple. Westchester Reform participated in ECE and then in S2K, about which he adds, "I think people whose very first experience was with Synagogue 2000 were blown away; they thought it was so great."

The lesson is clear not just for synagogues but also for national organizations and initiatives that seek to command synagogue loyalty: they must be well funded and run with excellence. This appreciation of excellence is especially germane to a computer generation whose plethora of choices permits it to harbor expectations that prior generations couldn't.[8] Transformative change is more than shifting direction; it is becoming more demanding about everyone's job, even the volunteers, all the while maintaining the family sense of mutual love and concern. That is hardly an easy balance to maintain.

Synagogues that change have to bite the bullet—gently, if possible; firmly, if necessary. Beth Elohim replaced a rabbi who was slated to retire in a few years. In Beth Shalom, the assistant rabbi left and teachers were let go. Temple Micah's professional choir was retired and the former soloist replaced. In Westchester Reform, Bill Blumstein recalls, "Teachers who would not buy in to the changes had to be replaced. We got rid of the choir. With new thinking about education, we replaced the director of education."

How Change Teams Spoke

We have seen what change teams did, but equally important is understanding how change teams spoke. We saw above how they were carried along by the excitement of new conversations prompted by categories of discussion that the change initiatives introduced. We turn now to the language that change teams themselves developed as they thought deeper about what they were doing. On the one hand, teams were entirely autonomous, able to say whatever they wanted. On the other hand, they were all influenced by the same cultural currents at work everywhere. It is no surprise, therefore, to find our teams across the country drawing on common ways of speaking about spiritual change.

The important point to keep in mind is that the language we are discussing here was not mandated by S2K and ECE. It arose spontaneously in all of the groups that were part of our study. By attending to it, we get a good understanding of the spiritual search that undergirds the general movement toward transformation in the decades spanning the twentieth to the twenty-first century.

Without saying new things, congregations cannot think new thoughts. That seems counterintuitive, but philosophers of language have demonstrated that in order to think, people need a language to frame the thinking. We make progress not by arguing better but by speaking differently. That is why, for example, we fumble for the right word when we have an idea—not to express the idea as it already exists, but to capture a word that provides the shape of its existence. Old words just recycle old thoughts. Without shaping old issues in new language, thinking about them in a new way is very difficult. And without a new way to think them through, we are doomed to the dismal experience of deja vu, over and over again.

This framing language arose as the teams attended to two complicated but related tasks: *encoding the present* and *enstorying the past and future*.

ENCODING THE PRESENT

We human beings are gifted with language—medieval Jewish philosophers even characterized us as *m'daber*, "the species that talks." It is human nature, then, not just to have experiences but also to *encode* those experiences in sentences. How we encode them matters greatly. An obvious example is whether we think we are *facing a crisis* or *meeting an opportunity*. A less obvious example is the metaphor we use when framing any particular topic for conversation. Take the suggestion that a congregation institute a Shabbat morning service separate from the one in the main sanctuary. Functional congregations that think in terms of programming will address this as a question of *what they do*: decisions will follow from such questions as space availability, staffing potential, political cost of alienating a particular side in the debate, and economics of providing two separate spreads of food following.

Visionary congregations are not immune from such concerns, but they focus the conversation not just on *what they do* but also on *who they are*. Are they a congregation that honors diversity? Will separate services divide them into competing communities? Teams were therefore taught to think not only about *activity* (what the synagogue does) but also *identity* (who the synagogue is).

Put another way, we can say that functional synagogues define success as getting more and more people to do more and more things. Visionary synagogues question the value of the "more and more things" that the "more and more people" do. Going shopping and seeing a movie respond to the question, "What do you want to do?" Jewish worship, learning, and social justice address the question, "Who do you want to become?" They inform that deeper and more pervasive layer of what we call identity.

Once, our identity was a given, part of what we were born with—things like religion, race, class, and sex. Less and less, now, are these considered fixed. At the very least, their salience is now negotiated.

When identity was inherited, it had no moral implication; now that it is what we make of ourselves, it is equivalent to what philosopher Charles Taylor calls claiming "moral space."[9] Once characters in a play that someone else set down before we were born, we have now become authors of our own stories. People *belong* to functional congregations the way they belong to health clubs and frequent flyer programs. People *identify* with visionary synagogues by throwing in their lot with what the synagogue *is* rather than just by showing up briefly for what the synagogue *does*. What language, then, did the visionary congregations in our study use to express what they thought it worthwhile to *be*? We call that language encoding the present.

To begin with, they overwhelmingly used words of *joy*. People have memories of synagogues where their childhood education

was useless and exhausting; where their rabbis were distant, pon-
tificating, and foreboding; where community was never discussed,
let alone expected; where they were made to feel guilty for all their
nots (not attending services, not knowing enough, not keeping
Jewish law); and where being Jewish was beset with memories of
anti-Semitic persecution. Visionary synagogues promise joy instead of sadness, worth instead of guilt.

We also found people using words like *deliberate, intentional,*
and *passionate.* They wanted to *experience,* to *share,* and to *search.*
They were on a *journey,* entering new *portals* and *gateways* that
would prove *meaningful* and *fun.* Clergy did not differ from laypeople in that regard. Cantor Jodi Sufrin, for example, who is
"busier than ever," is also "having fun."

As we have seen, our era, like the nineteenth century, can be
labeled Romantic in that it promotes feeling over logic and subjective meaning over objective truth. Unless prompted, our respondents, clergy and lay, rarely spoke conceptually, therefore.
With few exceptions, such as Rabbi Elaine Zecher's description
of Temple Israel "following a Martin Buberesque [view], which is
God happening through human interaction," we heard little theology. S2K introduced the goal of *sacred community*, a term that
resonated deeply with our teams. But teams were hard put to say
exactly what it was. It usually meant a fuzzy sense of welcome and
belonging, patterned somehow after a God who was only faintly
understood but was certainly loving, caring, accepting, and non-
judgmental. Here was a trend already foreseen in 1959 by social
critic Will Herberg, who perceived that for most Americans, faith
in God was becoming "not faith in anything, just faith itself, faith
in faith . . . a miracle drug trusted to bring mental health and
peace of mind."[10] It did not exclude universal concern for others, but overall its goal was self-realization—the search for "meaningful experiences" in text study or "good davening" in worship.
Nancy Belsky recalls, "It became a very warm, cozy place to be
Friday night. I feel good. I like to spend my time in a place that
feels good."

As we saw in chapter 2, finding meaning is paramount. But meaning assumes *authenticity*, another word that team members discussed a good deal. Authenticity, however, has developed two contrary but complementary senses. Once, we thought a thing authentic if it corresponded accurately with an objective standard outside itself—a Rembrandt is authentic if it displays the telltale signs of Rembrandt's actual paintings; otherwise, it is a fake. We take suspected art objects to experts to have them authenticated—declared authentic, according to the appropriate standards for artistic authenticity.

Now, however, people identify *authenticity* with getting in touch with their inner feelings, their real selves, their appropriate aspirations, whatever it is that makes them who they *really* are. This has been labeled the search for "expressive individualism,"[11] the sense that we are entitled, and even mandated, to express our own uniqueness. "No wonder people *shop* for shuls"[12]—not just to find the best rabbi or school but also to express the person they really are (modern Orthodox, egalitarian, socially concerned, and so forth). Differently put, we can say that people resort to *style*, the almost limitless ways to dress, outfit our homes, and pursue experiences that are "the real us."[13] When we think we have captured that essence, we call it *authentic*.[14] We expect the institutions we frequent to support our self-expression as the authentic people we imagine ourselves to be.

In this second and more common way we think about authenticity today, things are authentic if they are personally meaningful. Teams in our study wanted their synagogue to be authentic in that sense—it would stand for some authentic personal identity of the people who belong; it would reflect whatever they thought they wanted their innermost selves to express.

The two meanings coalesce, however, because authentic selves require roots in an authentic past—otherwise, they falter on the quicksand of convenience. Our teams therefore balanced the personalist vocabulary of meaning with bedrock values drawn from Jewish texts. The Hebrew word *pe'ah* denotes the four corners of the field where the rabbis instructed farmers to leave unharvested sheaves for the poor, so Rabbi and Cantor Angela Warnick Buchdahl says of Westchester Reform's *tz'dakah* (charity), "We thought we'd actually have built-in collection areas in the four corners of the room—like pe'ah in the four corners." Everywhere in our study, we found traditional Jewish vocabulary mined for terms that connect what people now do to what our ancestors once did or thought. Congregation Agudath Israel's new service is Shabbat *N'shamah*—"Shabbat for the soul." So too, Beth Elohim's high school program is *Havayah*, "experience," and Temple Israel's social justice organizing is Ohel Tzedek, "tent of righteousness." Elsewhere, we found programs entitled *Morashah, Tzavta,* and *Mercaz.*

Language need not be text based. Sometimes just a memorable one-liner will do. Our congregations invented catchy summaries of what they were about. "If it's not broken, break it," was Temple Micah's watchword. Cantor Jodi Sufrin strives to give people "Shechinah moments." Jenny Oser at Temple Israel uses the language of speed dating to define her organizing for social justice as "speed one-on-ones."

Sometimes these one-line mantras expressed the synagogue's mission. "We do *Shabbes*," says Paula Mack Drill; Jonah Pesner comments, "We are the justice congregation." Rabbi Elaine Zecher draws from "destination weddings" to get "destination synagogue," suggesting that people are willing to drive past other synagogues to be part of a community that meets and exceeds their expectations. These slogans are cheers, says Rabbi Rick Jacobs, "ways for the team to be cheerleaders for the next incarnation of Judaism."

No wonder synagogue change appeals to people in nodal moments, the times when their identities are in transition. Their search for personal authenticity becomes rooted in something permanent and deep: the synagogue and its changing mission. Sometimes, they find this certainty in texts. Other times, they locate catchy one-liners that justify their search—either from Jewish tradition ("We do Shabbes," "the justice congregation") or from the general culture that feels so comfortable ("destination syna-gogues," "speed one-on-ones").

ENSTORYING PAST AND FUTURE

Encoding is the way all of us discuss what we do and who we are in the present. But synagogues also exist in time, and because people *belong* to them, they come to identify with the synagogue as an en-tity with a past and a future—an institutional life story stretching backward to the founders who created it and forward to genera-tions yet to come.

Identities are like autobiographies. Change is the equivalent of composing new chapters, which must be consistent with what came before: characters cannot magically metamorphose into al-together different people and the plotline must be recognizable; that's why we call it a plot*line*—it must follow a believable trajec-tory. As communal selves, synagogues in change develop such a story, plotting a next chapter that is sufficiently new to be trans-formative, but never so revolutionary as to constitute a completely novel self. So the change teams in visionary congregations did not just encode their present; they also *enstoried* their past.

Synagogues took care to remain true to their story even to the extent of not crediting the outside interventions too much, for fear of sounding as if they were simply copying someone else—a betrayal of their institutional integrity. At Westchester Reform, for instance, Peter Wang knows "the real engine driving this [Cen-ter for Jewish Life, the on-campus retreat center the congregation built] . . . reverts back to the ECE roots as ultimately nourished by Synagogue 2000." His rabbi knows similarly that the congregation did "Larry Hoffman's prayer curriculum," but he says also, "We didn't want to hear people complain, 'Oh, it's another ECE, or S2K thing'; so we called it WRT 2000."

The search to remain true to the synagogue's authentic in-stitutional self sometimes prompted recollections about a syna-gogue's history; on other occasions people synopsized their story in terms of congregational culture. Congregation Agudath Israel began as the vision of its senior rabbi—what Paula Mack Drill calls "an observant Conservative community" where "everything spun around" its life of prayer. "We didn't want to change that." At Micah, David Wentworth uses both: as to *history*, he remembers the use of voluntary teachers, saying, "We're small, and we had no money"; as to *culture*, he notes that Micah's antiestablishment ethos is "very much the ethic of the whole structure. It's fundamental to who we are." The word *ethic* matters. These are identity stories, and identity is, as we saw, "moral space." But Micah has always drawn sustenance from its rabbi—that too is part of the way it sees itself. Celia Shapiro links Rabbi Danny Zemel's centrality at Micah to the days of his predecessor, Rabbi Bernard Mehlman. "I think, then as now, it was a *very* rabbi-driven congregation. And although there was a board, I think it fairly much rubber-stamped whatever Rabbi Mehlman wanted us to do." So, too, Louis Newman connects Beth Jacob's past with its rabbinic founder: "One of the things that makes this synagogue distinct, frankly, is that it's got a long history already, even though it's not an old shul. Rabbi Allen has been enormously successful at creating programs that are substantive, that draw in people, and making the synagogue accessible and appealing."

Mel Kronick at Congregation Beth Am tells a story about its past that is the very opposite of a rabbi-driven culture: "When I went on the board (around 1983), I was told that there was a tradition that it was a lay-led congregation, a partnership with mutual respect." He is concerned that "in the last few years, we've gone over to a situation that is moving over to a professionally led congregation." Long-term member Ina Bauman feels similarly: "We are just sort of rubber stamping things. . . . A [fellow] committee member said, 'It's ridiculous. I didn't join the committee to figure out who would bring the cookies.'" Bauman is left behind ritually as well. "So many long-term members feel alienated by the new direction in worship," she says, so she "had a hand in creating the alternative 5 p.m. service" with the old prayer book—a service designed, in Ina's view, "to keep one hundred to two hundred of the disaffected from leaving."

To be culturally disaffected is to disagree with the people writing your synagogue's next chapter. The disaffected may feel their marginality in worship especially, a ritualized activity that by its very nature displays symbolic issues of identity. Of all the changes introduced by reformers in the nineteenth century, for instance, the introduction of an organ generated the most debate. Several S2K congregations specifically avoided changing services because they knew the heat generated even by seemingly moderate experiments like changing the seating configuration and trying out new music. But they can equally object to the visionary congregation's activities elsewhere, its emphasis on being a congregation of learners, for example. As we saw in chapter 4, Ina's exit interviews with congregants who leave include someone who says, "I want my children to be educated, but I want them to do other things. I don't want Congregation Beth Am to be the center of their lives."

How do visionary congregations handle the terrible loss experienced by people who feel "disenstoried"—longstanding members, perhaps, who suspect that the next chapter in the synagogue's history has no place for them? The issue does not arise with newcomers who can join elsewhere if they disagree with the synagogue's direction. But old-timers are apt to resent being sidelined while their beloved congregation changes course. At Congregation Agudath Israel, traditionalist Alan Gerberg admits that Shabbat N'shamah, the alternative service, "is not my thing; I don't need to dance around and jump up and down and do those kinds of things." But he rests easy, knowing that the main Shabbat morning sanctuary service will remain virtually untouched. At Beth Shalom also, even though Rabbi Cohen was "firm from the beginning that alternative forms of service were positive," he carefully guaranteed stalwarts that they would always have "their place" to daven the way they always had.

Rabbis make difficult decisions as to how much to accommodate the disenstoried. Elaine Zecher balances the responsibility "to care for everybody, and be extra conscious of all those being left behind," with the recognition that at some point people have to decide "if they want to be left behind or if they want to actually make the adaptation to the changes."

The decision to become a visionary synagogue is tantamount to projecting the synagogue's next chapter but it may take some of the characters by surprise. Even members who do not actually fight it may not readily understand it. Teams were advised to expend enormous effort explaining the new twist in the synagogue's plot, to "Repeat, repeat, repeat."[15] Pastor Rick Warren says of his now-legendary success, Saddleback Church, that every ten days or so he has to reiterate the message of what the church stands for.[16] The rabbis in our study too had to keep the message fresh in people's minds. As Rabbi Rick Jacobs says, "Every three to four years we do an ECE primer for lay leaders, but it is also for my colleagues." The characters in the story, lay and clergy, all too easily fall back into the default mode of being functional, not visionary. That is, after all, what they have been doing for years.

What Synagogues Accomplished

If we want synagogues to be merely utilitarian—the religious equivalent of stores that provide merchandise or factories that manufacture goods—we should be perfectly happy with functional. But the authors of this book hold synagogues to a higher goal. Think of synagogues as institutions dedicated to making the world a better place (*tikkun olam*), acting as God wants us to (performing mitzvot), informing life's search for meaning (torah), and the like. The Talmud asks *ma'i m'akev*—"What gets in the way" of achieving such worthwhile goals? That question should be put to synagogues. Most synagogues pay lip service to these overarching values, but because they are merely functional, they have only limited success in achieving them. Why is that?

The answer lies in the fact that institutions, like individuals, develop defense mechanisms that resist therapeutic attention to organizational personality defects. They manufacture ways to deny self-destructive behavior rather than face up to it.[17] Meanwhile, damage metastasizes. Personal gains squeeze out public well-being; honest assessment of human resources declines; insecure personalities protect themselves by scapegoating others. Misunderstandings are papered over until they fester and explode, transparency disappears, efficiency declines, healthy public debate deteriorates into insidious off-line conversation. Transformative synagogues come to terms with these deep systemic fault lines. How do they do it? They are led to do so by "sofly charismatic" visionaries, and by healthy, open minded cultures that are embedded in their corporate structure.

CORPORATE OR CHARISMA?

One way to chart systemic change is to think about the relationship between corporatism and charisma. Pioneering sociologist Max Weber famously described authority as charismatic, traditional, or rational legal. *Charisma* works through individual magnetism (think of John F. Kennedy or Winston Churchill); *tradition* depends on established right of rule (the way royalty passes from father to oldest son in some cultures); *rational legal* authority is the basis for the corporation, where authority depends on roles within systems (even a corporate president is limited by regulations and structural constraints). Like democratic leadership in general, all of the synagogues in our study practiced rational legal authority; the rabbis, that is, recognized some degree of corporate boundary setting, if only the normative structure of committees, due process, and board regulations.

Some synagogues abide only loosely by such standards. Others follow them to the letter. It is often imagined that the latter kind of synagogues are too *corporate* to succeed. Are they? Not necessarily. "Nothing can clog an organization like too much red tape, and/or too many stifling layers of management"—institutions with too much corporate density. But in the synagogues we studied, even those with high corporate density managed to overcome bureaucratic excess and were able to use their corporate structure to address systemic dysfunction.

What about *charisma*—can good synagogues depend on corporation-style management, or do they need a charismatic rabbi at the helm? By charisma, we do not mean Weber's model of a pied piper attracting the masses through sheer personal star power. We also mean something other than the traditional Hasidic *tzaddik*, as often as not a charismatic figure but also the traditional inheritor of the family's right to leadership. We have in mind what we call *soft charisma*, which does not come by virtue of a flashy or compelling personality. This is charisma that the rabbis in this study earned by establishing credentials as repositories of Jewish knowledge and by building trusting relationships with lay partners.[19] In addition, they were judged as operating with high moral character, dedicated to their task and to their people, and avoiding Machiavellian political intrigue. In sociological terms, their charisma was *attained*, not *ascribed*. The soft charisma of our study pertains to the degree to which the rabbi as spiritual leader can exercise influence outside of the normative corporate channels.

How effective are corporate mentality on one hand and charisma on the other at handling systemic change? Is one better than the other?

Imagine a corporatism scale ranging from 1 to 5, where 1 is low and 5 is high. A clear 1 is Temple Micah where committees were so weak that, except for the finance committee, Rabbi Danny Zemel was able to dissolve them all virtually overnight. "I hated going to committee meetings and I discovered that everybody else pretty much hated going to committee meetings," Danny explains.

> For sure, nobody misses the social action committee and we have a lot more social action than we ever had with the committee. Instead, anybody that has an idea, I empower them to go ahead and do the idea. It doesn't have to go through a committee. There is no committee thinking

of things to do; the entire congregation is thinking of things to do all the time. And we use the Internet very effectively to advertise a new initiative. If you want to do this, get involved.

With little corporate structure, Danny's soft charisma becomes paramount. "I became," he says, "virtually a committee of one." Congregant David Wentworth agrees, "In virtually everything that happens, Danny is involved in some way."

At the other end of the spectrum was Congregation Beth Am, whose rabbis were perceived as no less wise, learned, and able than colleagues elsewhere, but who functioned within the system. Rabbi Rick Block had come to his task with unusual rabbinic background: a business past that enabled him to work knowledgeably and effectively with committees. A determined personality, he fit well in Congregation Beth Am's corporate culture, with teams of people working in what came to be called task forces. Long-term member Mel Kronick remembers that Rick arrived during Eddie Reynolds's tenure as president. Eddie had "brought into the congregation a lot of collaborative, institutionalized ways of running committees and strategic focus groups." Concern eventually arose, says Mel, that "the congregation was becoming too corporate. It wasn't just Eddie. Rick [too] was more of an executive; he was organized; and the way he managed his time!" The culture took, nonetheless. Janet Marder, who succeeded Rick in 1999 and remains in place today, had by her own testimony "seen a lot of congregations" and was "impressed by the organizational culture here."

With this growing corporate structure came membership expansion. The lure of Silicon Valley and the influx of Russian Jewish emigres propelled the membership upward, straining the competence of the system. "Good things were happening in various programs, but no one was looking at how they fit together," says Rabbi Josh Zweiback. "One educator would change the date of a program, and the other educator didn't know it. The various budgets came in separately, and only the budget committee would see it. There was no coordination." To address these issues lay leaders brought in a consultant who worked with the staff to coordinate the different programs and bring efficiency to the system. Daryl Messinger, a former president, notes, "The process of working out the rules was not easy, but it's really changed the efficiency of the place. There are rules for everything, the minutes changed, they adopted new rules about conducting meetings. It was quite a transformation."

Approaching Congregation Beth Am on the corporate scale are Temple Israel, Congregation Agudath Israel, and Westchester Reform, where change also occurred through channels. But, says Rabbi Jacobs at Westchester Reform, "We're trying to dismantle some of the structures of synagogue corporate life [like] the annual meeting. Why do synagogues have to have an annual meeting? We are not shareholders of Johnson & Johnson who have an annual meeting and report, 'Here's the profit, here's the good news.'"

Beth Shalom is somewhere in the middle—committees met, but Rabbi Amy Wallk Katz was able to avoid attending them, explaining, "I know what I think, and it would drive me crazy if the process were debated." The pivotal role of Rabbi Allen positioned Beth Jacob close to Temple Micah.

Beth Elohim began as a corporate entity, but like congregations at the low end of the scale, it dismantled its structure in a virtual revolution from within. When she was asked to participate in transforming Beth Elohim, Terry Rosenberg recalls, "The deal breaker would have been being told that I would have to join the adult education committee or work through it in some way. If that had happened, I would have walked away." But she didn't have to; Harold Kotler, the molder of the revolution, saw to that. He did retain his executive committee but made sure it "didn't think about little Johnny and sniffling Ellen." Instead, we "talked about the big picture, stayed in the helicopter."

Westchester Reform is poised between corporatism and charisma. High corporate culture fairly screams out from President
Bill Blumstein's recollection of the time Rabbi Jacobs approached
him about joining the ECE. The temple's executive committee
endorsed it and created a task force of forty to fifty people representing the synagogue's entire constituency! But high rabbinic
charisma comes through, too, when Bill recalls that the whole
thing began because "Rick had a vision of where he would like
the temple to go." Angela Warnick Buchdahl concurs: "There's a
culture here that is largely due to Rick."

We think synagogues can change with either high or low corporate scores. We are not sure they can do so without the soft
charisma of rabbinic authenticity. Beth Elohim, however, gives us
pause. There, change was led by lay people who, in effect, toppled
their rabbi in a coup d'état and then brought on another rabbi
who supported the revolution. Could change have been sustained
without him? Could laypeople have run an ever-transformative
synagogue without a softly charismatic rabbi? It is hard to say, but
we think they could. Along with the rabbi, Beth Elohim enjoyed a
cantor of significant stature and then hired two remarkable educators prepared to challenge current structures. The lay support
would have been in place in any event. We would have to say that
none of the synagogues in our study changed without a rabbinic
charismatic presence, but with the right personnel and lay support, they might have.

Cultural Transformation

Harold Kotler spoke for many in our sample when he astutely reflects, "You have all these ideas, but does it become culture?" So
we asked too, "Are the innovations we observed passing fancies
or deep-rooted cultural change?" We do not expect synagogues
to abandon their story, but is the new chapter they are writing a

significant enough twist to alter their synagogue's ultimate fate? Or will it remain just another instance of functional tweaking— greeters in the lobby, say, or an extra learning group and a sung *mi sheberakh* at services? If any of these innovations, desirable in themselves, is mistaken for the *essence* of model synagogues instead of *symptoms* of something deeper, transformation will have failed. So what did we find in our synagogues? Did the culture actually change?

We cannot say that all of our congregations have managed such thoroughgoing reforms. Beth Jacob is perhaps the least transformed, because it saw nothing to transform in the first place. From the outset, it was proud of its independence, content with its offerings, and certain of its vision: "It's an egalitarian, traditional, conservative, synagogue that's built on torah, *avodah*, and g'*milut chasadim*," says Louis Newman.

Beth Shalom seems also to have stopped short of actual cultural change, but for a different reason. Respondents rarely mentioned overall change as a goal: energies were directed only toward one specific aspect of shul life—as its self-proclaimed name Tefillah 2000 indicates. But even the changes there may not all prove lasting, since the congregation may not have secured the ongoing clergy attention required to sustain them. To be sure, some liberalization has crept into the sanctuary service, but the alternative service is no longer growing. As of this writing, Rabbis Katz and Cohen have announced that they are leaving, and the cantor seems more or less content with what is. Equally significant (though we may be wrong here—only time will tell), with the death of Jeanette Wishna, who directed the change team, there may be no laypeople prepared to shepherd change through time, regardless of the rabbis and cantors who come and go.

We can make this important observation: change must have at least the senior rabbis on board. Indeed, it is usually led by them, for more than anyone else it is they who are trained to envision in a Jewish mold and to provide authentic language with which to tell the synagogue story. But synagogues belong to their members, not the professionals. Momentary change becomes cultural transformation only when enough committed laypeople continue the new way of thinking beyond the lifetime of the rabbi who initiates it.

Congregation Beth Am is such a synagogue, as we can readily see by the fact that the principles adopted under Rabbi Block continue under Rabbi Marder, with the addition of a prayer initiative. Not only had the culture changed but respondents also overwhelmingly knew that it had. We found this recognition also in the other synagogues where change promises to be long lasting. The synagogue's altered course will continue because the new culture itself includes a commitment to retain it. *Transformation changes culture, but once changed, culture preserves transformation.*

A major sign of cultural change is the spread of the new way of thinking beyond any single aspect of synagogue life. Transformative change, we said above, must be pervasive. Temple Israel points to its Riverway Project, its invigorated early Friday night service, and its social justice organizing—all good signs that the synagogue is doing things differently. Temple Micah is tiny by comparison, but there too cultural change has allowed the synagogue to shift attention from prayer (its first initiative) to learning (its new center of attention) and to alter the very infrastructure of the synagogue besides—moving from committees to Internet connectivity, for example, and empowering any individual member to introduce ideas and make them into a reality. Beth Elohim and Westchester Reform too are virtually unrecognizable from what they were. They began with prayer or learning, but like Temple Israel and Temple Micah, they discussed changes in one or the other as examples of new cultural thinking overall, not as ends in themselves.

From the Conservative congregations surveyed, we can single out Congregation Agudath Israel as exemplifying such cultural change—but with a caveat: It carefully avoided changing its highly prized Shabbat morning service. Rabbi Morris Allen's Beth Jacob also remained wary of altering services. But whereas Rabbi Allen was content with the shul's overall direction, Rabbi Silverstein decided to develop a far more actively caring congregation—what S2K called "the healing track." "Even before S2K came along," he explains, he had "about 325 regulars." Still, the healing track of S2K "pushed us" to the point where "on a typical Shabbes we'll have about seventy-five to one hundred coming up with names to receive a prayer for healing." The caring committee eventually expanded to include forty to fifty people, tending to shut-ins, driving people to chemotherapy appointments, and seeing to the disabled. And the accent on healing has permeated other aspects of synagogue life: a meditation service has been developed, for example, and the manner in which "the front line" greets and treats strangers has been rethought. As with all the congregations we studied, it is too early to tell for sure, but one would expect that Congregation Agudath Israel will be thinking differently beyond its current leadership. By our criteria, it is a transformative success.

A truism in change management circles is a mathematical equation that expresses the probability of change as a function of (1) overcoming resistance and (2) having at least a modicum of other factors present: $R < D \times V \times S \times F \times B$.[20] Resistance must be less than the product of dissatisfaction, vision, support systems, first steps, and the belief that change is possible.

FIGURE 6.1 The Change Formula

$$R < D \times V \times S \times F \times B$$

RESISTANCE	<	DISSATISFACTION	x	A compelling VISION	x	Strength of SUPPORT	x	Demonstrates that at least FIRST STEPS	x	BELIEF
to change		with the present state		of the future		systems		are possible		that successful change is possible

Everything depends on the power of resistance, and resistance to change in synagogues is enormously high. Lay leaders are likely to have reached their position because they like the system the way it is. Rabbis and professional teams come and go, but they all have been trained in seminaries that are generally content with congregations we have called functional. Nor do national synagogue organizations challenge their congregations very much: they too are functional, not visionary. Hence the importance of this simple equation, which reminds congregations about the basic elements that go into change: *Dissatisfaction* with the status quo, a *Vision* of doing things differently, *Support* systems in place, the satisfaction of having taken *First Steps*, and the overall *Belief* that change is possible. Ideally they should all be present in large measure; if any of them is tiny, change is less likely, although it may still occur if the others are present in sufficient degree. But anything multiplied by zero is zero; so if any of the factors is truly zero, the product is zero, too; the change team will eventually get worn down, and resistance will triumph.

Despite a great deal of talk about living in a postdenominational world, we found that Reform and Conservative congregations do not altogether share cultures—even transformed ones. Rather than predict a blurring of the two movements, then, we expect each one to continue staking out its own proud place on the Jewish spectrum. Conservative Jews belong to shuls; Reform Jews, temples or synagogues. Both emphasize social justice, but for Conservative Jews it is a part of doing *mitzvot*, a word Reform Jews rarely mention. Both speak the language of personalism and aesthetics, but for one it is good *davening*, for the other it is meaningful *worship*. Reform gadflies use the language of brokenness: they have had it with what is; they feel a moral urgency to make things over; they can hardly wait to change the entire thing. Conservative Jews feel less urgency.

In any case, for synagogues of all denominations or of no denomination at all, it takes a *transformation of culture* to sustain change beyond a momentary rush of excitement. Of the many syn-agogues (well over a hundred) with whom S2K and ECE worked, most never got to that very important tipping point, and it is not even clear yet that all the congregations studied here have done so, although plainly some have. We have studied very different congre-gations. But their cultural renewal shares some key ingredients. We can call them the Ten Commandments for Synagogue Cultures. Synagogues that become visionary demonstrate cultures of:

1. Excellence: They do not settle for mediocrity.
2. Risk: They encourage experimentation and understand failures as opportunities to do things better next time.
3. Reflectivity: Everything is constantly pondered and delib-erated upon.
4. Optimism: People believe in themselves and in their ability to do the right thing.
5. Mutuality: Boundaries are porous; roles change freely; people mix and mingle across lay-clergy divides; everyone learns from everyone; no one stands on ceremony.
6. Honor: People support one another, credit each other, show up for each other.
7. Transparency: People work truthfully and trustingly.
8. Compassion: The desire for excellence is mediated by and channeled into concern for others.
9. Meaningfulness: Success is gauged by meaningful experi-ence that links people horizontally to one another and ver-tically to a sense of the transcendent.
10. Joy: People have fun; meetings are as rewarding as the events that they plan. Transformation becomes a fun-filled way of life, not a once-in-a-lifetime chore to get beyond.

CHAPTER 7

Transformation in Theory: Thinking about Change

Over the past two decades, federations, denominations, and foundations have initiated or funded a variety of change projects, both national and local, aimed at synagogue transformation. What have these projects accomplished? Though no systemic, long-range evaluations of these initiatives have been undertaken, Larry, co-principal investigator of Synagogue 2000 (S2K), and Isa, founding director and now senior consultant to Experiment in Congregational Education (ECE), have come to similar conclusions, albeit based on anecdotal evidence. We estimate that roughly a third of the congregations involved in ECE and S2K moved significantly along the continuum from functional to visionary. They were able to institute and sustain wide-ranging changes and, to a greater or lesser extent, were able to alter the congregational culture to become more visionary. Another third made changes that were additive rather than transformational, yielding some new programs while leaving the congregation's culture unaltered in fundamental ways. The final third either made no changes at all or were unable to sustain the initial changes, so that today no trace of their participation in either S2K or ECE is detectable.

There are, of course, a myriad of reasons why a change initiative might not succeed in a particular congregation. The change formula discussed at the end of chapter 6 encapsulates some of these reasons. The equation posits that change always has a cost. That cost can be outweighed, however, if there is a modicum of dissatisfaction with the current situation, if leaders have a vision of a better future, if they have concrete first steps with which to get started, and if they enjoy or garner systemic support of others within the synagogue.

This formula reflects not only the experiences of organizational development specialists in the world of business but also our own research and experience. But it raises as many questions as it answers: What factors make *some* synagogue leaders perceive the cost of change as prohibitive, while others, faced with the same set of changes, see the cost as reasonable? What factors contribute to a sense of creative dissatisfaction rather than despair? What enables leaders to forge a collective vision? What gives people the confidence that they *can* make changes? When do first steps pave the way for deeper change, rather than simply taking pressure off the system and shoring up the status quo? How is it that some synagogues achieve wide-ranging support from boards, committees, and synagogue professionals while others do not?

To answer these questions, we need to go beyond empirical research to theories that can place our data in a larger context, linking them with findings of others in different fields. A full survey of relevant theories is beyond the scope of a single chapter, but we can at least begin a conversation about the theoretical underpinnings of synagogue change. We will focus on three sets of theories in an effort to answer three questions:

First, can a closer look at different *types* of congregations help us understand under what circumstances the move from functional to visionary is made easier or more difficult? To answer this question we will look to the work of Penny Edgell Becker, a sociologist of religion. Offering a slight modification of Becker's typology of congregations, we will argue that one type meets many of the criteria of the visionary congregation. We will also explore the potential for change in synagogues that fall into the other categories.

A second question is, what is the role of change projects in helping congregations move from functional to visionary? To address this question, we will look to organizational theorists Lee Bolman and Terrance Deal's "four frames" approach to thinking about organizations.

Finally, what is the role of individuals in the change process? Drawing on the theories of Robert Kegan and Ronald Heifetz, we will argue that the lay and professional leaders of visionary congregations share a number of key characteristics.

One caveat: We need to be cautious before jumping to conclusions about the applicability of these theories to the world of synagogues. Though we agree in principle with social theorist Kurt Lewin's quip that "there is nothing more practical than a good theory," only time, discussion, and debate will tell how well these theories apply to the field of synagogue change.

A Typology of Congregations

Penny Edgell Becker, a sociologist of religion at the University of Minnesota, studied all of the Christian and Jewish congregations (including twenty-one churches and two synagogues) in three contiguous suburbs of Chicago—Oak Park, River Forest, and Forest Park. At each congregation, she observed services and meetings and studied mission statements, annual reports, brochures, written histories, and sermons. She also interviewed key professional and lay leaders. Though these congregations all held worship services and sponsored various social, charitable, and educational programs, Becker found some important differences between them, over and above the obvious differences in denomination and size. To make sense of these variations, Becker devised a fourfold typology of congregations, which she labeled: "House of Worship," "Leader," "Family," and "Community." These are described in her 1999 book *Congregations in Conflict*.

Houses of Worship are congregations whose mission is narrowly defined, focusing primarily on worship, religious education, and the celebration of life-cycle rituals. What congregants value most is having "a place to worship and to express or explore their belief in God."[1] Few expect to do much socializing at their congregation; they drive in for worship and leave soon after the service ends, finding their friends elsewhere. Nor do congregants look to the congregation to take a public stand or serve as a forum for discussing social issues. The Houses of Worship in Becker's study are "smoothly administered, using the formal decision-making routines and bodies that the denominational guidelines spell out."[2] They take pride in having well-run religious schools for children and in the clergy's adept performance of life-cycle rituals.

Leader Congregations tend to be large and have a significant public presence in the town or denomination or both. Each holds well-publicized positions on certain religious or social issues, positions that have been set by historical precedent or articulated by the clergy. People join a Leader Congregation because they espouse these views and want to be in the forefront of efforts to promote them. Like Houses of Worship, Leader Congregations are not particularly interested in fostering intimacy or personal connections among their members. To them, community is achieved when congregants adhere to a common doctrine or are devoted to a common cause. While Leader Congregations have no trouble recruiting distinguished and accomplished congregants to serve on boards and committees, these lay leaders have a relatively limited role; the clergy are clearly in charge. One of the two synagogues in Becker's study fell into this category.

Family Congregations tend to be small and intimate, with people bound together informally. There is no need to create *chavurot* or sponsor new member get-togethers because congregants make it their business to know of important events in one another's lives and feel responsible for supporting one another in times of crisis. Becker describes the Family Congregation as follows: "The most common adjectives people used to describe their congregation were 'warm,' 'caring,' and 'friendly.' . . . This closeness seems to occur without a great deal of discussion or conscious effort. People refer to the congregation as a family, but there is no elaborated discourse on what it means to be a family."[3] However, this feeling of togetherness comes at a price—debates on substantive issues are either avoided altogether or reduced to personal conflicts; for example, Family Congregations are most likely to report conflict with a member of the clergy and to experience clergy turnover.

In contrast to the congregations in these three categories, six of the congregations, including the other synagogue, in Becker's study were distinguished by their conscious efforts to create a sense of community. These *Community Congregations* are both inward and outward looking, attempting to create a warm, supportive place for their members while also challenging them spiritually and morally.

These congregations do not assume that connections among their members will arise naturally and spontaneously. Mindful that their members are diverse, highly mobile, and very busy, these congregations foster a sense of community by forming small fellowship groups and encouraging people to plug in to a range of organized activities.

Another way Community Congregations differ is that they seek to create a sense of shared meaning through active engagement with their faith tradition and with one another. They see religion as something to be grappled with and figured out rather than simply received and accepted. Congregants expect to be part of this exploration rather than having the decision dictated to them by the clergy. One pastor goes so far as to say, "It does not matter *what* decision the congregation makes, as long as the *process* is open and inclusive."[4]

Like Leader Congregations, and unlike the other two types, Community Congregations see their role as going beyond nurturing faith to taking moral and political stands informed by faith.

Unlike Leader Congregations, however, where the denomination or
the clergy sets the social and political agenda, these congregations
try to balance engagement in issues with maintaining community.
As a result, they tend to steer clear of more politically charged issues and tend toward social action rather than social justice.

Adapting Becker's Typology to Synagogues

Becker's typology, which is based on a single study that has not
been replicated, should be viewed as heuristic and instructive
rather than definitive. She herself speculates that different types
of congregations might be found in a different region. If such a
study were to be conducted today, one might expect to find at least
two new models, given the growth of megachurches and emergent churches since Becker conducted her research. Despite these
limitations, we find the typology very helpful in thinking about
synagogue change, though it does require some adjustments to
better reflect the position of Jews in America and the realities of
synagogue life.

Judaism is more than a religion; it is also an ethnicity and, at
least historically, a nationality. Though this is changing today as
America becomes more diverse, Jews in the twentieth century
were keenly aware of their status as members of a minority. For
most Jews, the synagogue was not primarily a place to *pray* but a
place to belong. The first residents of a new postwar suburb studied by Herbert Gans founded a synagogue to show their children
they had a place to go on Saturday that was every bit as impressive as the church their Christian neighbors attended on Sunday.[5]
Today the synagogue is seen primarily as a place to celebrate life-
cycle events, as evidenced by the fact that so many Jews drop out
after their youngest child passes the bar or bat mitzvah milestone.

The name House of Worship, therefore, is not apt for many
synagogues where life-cycle events, rather than worship, are
paramount. We propose as a substitute the term "Center of

Celebrations," reflecting the reason congregants join this type of synagogue.

CENTERS OF CELEBRATIONS

The *Center of Celebrations* is similar to Becker's House of Worship in that it is more a gathering place for individuals than a community or a polity. Congregants come in with specific needs that are met by the school or the clergy. Parents in the religious school are not looking to meet other parents. Attendees at the High Holidays don't expect to know too many of their fellow worshipers.

The Center of Celebrations is the most functional, and least visionary, of the four types. It is a fee-for-service operation, most of whose members expect to be passive, resisting invitations to become more active. Its regular Shabbat attendees are not necessarily connected to its small number of adult learners, and neither of these groups is likely to be connected to the large population of religious school children and parents.

One of the synagogues in the first S2K cohort, *Beit Chagigah* (a pseudonym that means "House of Celebration"), fits the mold of a Center of Celebrations perfectly. It is a Reform congregation with more than nine hundred member units and four hundred children in its preschool but, by one estimate, "only six adult learners." Other than *b'nei mitzvah*, the synagogue has no services on Shabbat morning. A variety of special Friday nights, such as "Boy Scout Shabbat," bring in an average of two hundred worshipers, few of them regulars. The cantor estimates that barely a quarter of board members attend services regularly. Although having a child of preschool age is one of the nodal moments referred to in chapter 6, a past president at Beit Chagigah voiced his skepticism about the potential for involving preschool parents: "I'm not sure there is anything that could be done to transform [the preschool parents] into viewing the temple as a second home, because they have a whole set of family and work commitments and the like. [They] tend to see the temple as a service instead of a community."

The leaders of Beit Chagigah speak about it as *haimish* (home-like, in Yiddish), but as one active member points out, they may be confusing informality with warmth. For example, people bring their own dinner on Friday nights but do not necessarily socialize with congregants who are not in their immediate circle.

With most congregants viewing the synagogue as a service center, it should come as no surprise that Beit Chagigah is very segmented. The rabbis, cantor, and educators carry out their functions separately. In a 2006 interview, the cantor acknowledged both the "loneliness" and the empowerment of being "able to carve my own path."

LEADERS

Becker's description of the Leader Congregation applies equally to a certain type of synagogue, particularly in the Reform movement, though Conservative Leader Congregations exist as well. These synagogues have distinguished-looking buildings in very visible locations; in some cities they are even called "*The* Temple," as though there are no others (which may have been true when they were founded). Their rabbis have a large public presence; they are quoted in newspapers, appear before the city council, and speak at large denominational gatherings. The members of Leader Synagogues identify with the synagogue's illustrious history and with their rabbis who took courageous stances during the civil rights era or the Vietnam War. The commitment to social justice is very important in the Leader Synagogue; in some synagogues this translates into maintaining a homeless shelter or a soup kitchen, while in others it has been reduced to an annual mitzvah day.

Though they invoke the term *excellence* quite often and may have well-known cantors and educators, Leader Synagogues are not necessarily excellent when it comes to worship or religious education. Like Centers of Celebrations, they tend to be functional rather than visionary, largely because of their members' passivity. Members of these congregations don't equate their rabbi's activism or scholarly achievement with a synagogue-wide commitment to social justice or learning. For example, they expect the rabbi to visit the sick but don't see this as a mitzvah that applies to themselves.

A synagogue that fits this profile, *Beit K'nesset Gadol* (Grand Synagogue, another pseudonym), participated in one of the early cohorts of the ECE. Asked what he valued at this synagogue, a past president who was the head of the ECE task force responded that he valued its standing and long history in the community. When people in the community "think of the center of Judaism in [this city], most of them do not think of Federation, they think of [our synagogue]. It's on the main drag. . . . They notice our spot, and people know us."

The executive director described members' leadership in the wider community: "We have a long proud history here of being involved in the community. . . . A former mayor is a member . . . and we have some of the leading philanthropists in our congregation." He spoke with pride of the synagogue's involvement in the civil rights movement, noting that even those who were not personally involved felt as though they were, through the rabbi.

> Leadership in the area of social change and social justice has always been part and parcel of what we're all about. During the time of [a longtime rabbi], he was very active in the civil rights movement. Congregants didn't necessarily have to. . . . *Those who, for whatever reason, chose not to be [active], because they were busy with their lives or livelihood, could always say, "I'm a member of [the synagogue] where [name of the rabbi] is." So vicariously they were very much part of the civil rights movement* (emphasis added).

The executive director lamented that the synagogue was not "warmer and more caring." He explained, "We always talked about temple family and that we want to be welcoming, but it's hard to do that when you're a large congregation." However he spoke with greater passion, and at greater length, about the congregation's need to maintain a position of leadership in the community: "There is a lot of competition out there in the Jewish community, whether it's the Jewish Community Center, the Jewish Federation, another synagogue . . . and it's not that I don't want those people to be strong and offer what their communities need to offer. I just hope that the temple doesn't lose its leadership position."

LOCAL SHULS

Paying homage to the *shtibls* (small synagogues) of an earlier era, we have renamed Becker's Family Congregation the "Local Shul" to convey these synagogues' informality and small size, in contrast to the more institutional and formal feel of the others. The name *shul* should not be taken to mean that this type of synagogue is found only in the Orthodox and Conservative movements. In 2007, 56 percent of synagogues affiliated with the Union for Reform Judaism had few than 250 member units. (In the Conservative movement, 37 percent had fewer than 200 member units and 28 percent had between 200 and 399 member units.)[6] Many of these are located in areas with small Jewish populations and don't have full-time clergy. Though not all of these synagogues are Local Shuls, many undoubtedly are.

We found only two studies of this type of congregation because many are located in small towns; those in larger cities tend to have a much lower profile and thus don't attract the attention of researchers. Samuel Heilman's *Synagogue Life* is an ethnography of a modern Orthodox synagogue in a large urban area, in which "members have embraced the collectivity. . . turning it into something akin to a large extended family which uses the shul as

the locus of its assembly. . . . One is not surprised to be called sud-
denly to come to shul for a minyan, a class, a meeting, or some
other assembly."[7]

Susan Shevitz studied a Conservative synagogue of 165 member units located in a small Midwestern city (population about
100,000) with a total Jewish population of 1,800.[8] Two teenagers'
description of this Local Shul echoes Becker: "It's this amazing
thing we hadn't had [in other synagogues we were in]. . . . When
someone is not here, everyone knows. Like if Miriam [wasn't]
here yesterday, everyone's like, 'Where's Miriam?' . . . We all really
are a big family here. . . . I am so comfortable with everyone."

The family-like sense of responsibility is what members of
both of these shuls value most. But in an effort to maintain *shalom
bayit* (household harmony), procedures that would contribute to
organizational health and excellence are ignored or avoided. For
example, in the shul Shevitz studied, neither the rabbi nor the educator observes, evaluates, or supervises the congregant-teachers;
when the shul sends these teachers to a workshop, they are not
asked to share what they have learned with other teachers, as if
fearing to impose on them unduly.

Heilman notes that the shul he studied avoids public argu-
ments at all costs:

> The eruption of a quarrel between two or more members brings about
> rapid attentiveness, awesome in its totality. Suddenly, all eyes are on the
> combatants, and other involvement halts. . . . Under this social spotlight
> some people move to end the fight, cajoling, ordering and convincing
> the disputants to stop, while the rest of the congregation maintains its
> silent attention in an unspoken pressure which demands armistice.[9]

Suppression of all argumentation is not necessarily healthy for an
organization, which can learn and grow from disputes, providing they do not become bitter. In this shul even *makhloket l'shem
shamayim* (argumentation for the sake of heaven) is frowned

upon as too fraught with the possibility of fracturing the community. This attitude can dissuade potential lay leaders who are new to the community from joining the board, leaving the board under the long-term control of a small group of insiders.

While the shuls studied by Heilman and Shevitz share many of the characteristics of the visionary congregation, our S2K and ECE experience suggests that a significant number of Local Shuls are not only far from visionary, they are not even particularly functional. Because they are so tightly controlled by a small group bound by rigid conventions about how the synagogue is run, they can be quite resistant to change.

K'HILLOT

Becker calls her fourth category *Community*, but this seems too broad a name for our fourth type of synagogue, because community is a value that all Jews aspire to, at least in theory. Our tradition tells us that "all Jews are responsible for one another," and we refer to ourselves as the "American Jewish community," despite the fact that most of us will never meet face to face. We have chosen the term *K'hillah*, which means "face-to-face community," for this type of synagogue, connoting a group of people who feel a sense of belonging and responsibility to one another. Though members of a K'hillah may be drawn from many different neighborhoods, these synagogues, like Becker's Community Congregations, make a conscious effort to connect congregants with one another. They sponsor coffees and classes for new members; they have official greeters at services; they encourage congregants to join chavurot; and so on.

All eight of the visionary synagogues in our study fall into this category. Community is an overriding value for them. Asked about the most important goal of the educational program at Temple Beth Elohim in Wellesley, educator Alison Kur responded without missing a beat, "creating community. . . . We work hard to help faculty understand that it's not all about the content. The content is important, but the community building is also really critically important. . . . If we're going to have a feeling of warmth and welcoming and family, we have to dedicate some serious time to helping kids know each other." Congregants at Beth Elohim feel the sense of community in powerful ways. Firkins Reed recalled that when her father died "the Caring Community team wrapped around my family—visiting, bringing gifts and food, sitting shiva. They held us in a very powerful way. . . . The temple becomes the family around you when your own family isn't here."

In Mendota Heights, Minnesota, Beth Jacob Congregation's effort at hospitality and inclusion led to creating a formal process for matching people so that "no one ever lacks for a place to go for seder or any holiday meal;" in addition, they have begun to explore ways to better involve children with special needs.

K'hillot are different from Local Shuls because they don't assume that community will happen spontaneously; they sense a need to create community through their programs, such as *Shabbaton* at Congregation Beth Am in Northern California and Sharing Shabbat at Westchester Reform in New York. Likewise, in Boston, Temple Israel's *Ohel Tzedek* connects people in very deliberate ways, beginning with the basic building block, which is one-on-one conversation, and from there networking with congregation leaders and members to learn what members care about and to get them involved. For Martha Chason-Sokol of Temple Israel, involvement in Ohel Tzedek, the synagogue's social justice project, has been "life changing." Before Ohel Tzedek, she says, "I was here as a teacher, but I didn't ever really become a member of the community, because I wasn't getting to know the parents. . . . I was a member, but I wasn't really getting involved with any people at the temple."

The K'hillah differs from the other three types of synagogues in its democratic, transparent approach to all aspects of synagogue life. Temple Beth Elohim's Joel Sisenwine is very deliberate in countering the notion that money speaks at TBE: "It wasn't true, but that was [people's] perception. The key is that the community needs buy-in on any change process, and I just had to convince people that this was not a manipulative transition process or a power grab."

Ric Rudman of Congregation Beth Am recalls a crisis about plans for a new building that "a group of well-meaning members . . . developed in a vacuum." When the congregation balked, the board and staff stepped in to work out a new process that involved members from the beginning and at every step along the way. "By the time we got to the final vote everyone was saying, 'Enough— we know what you're doing, and we like it.'"

K'hillot differ from Becker's Community Congregations in one important respect—they are much less eclectic in their style of worship. In Community Congregations, Becker writes, "the most important thing is that the services and classes meet members' needs, not that they pass on a specific doctrine or ritual tradition. The emphasis is on lay involvement, self expression, and creativity."[10]

FIGURE 7.1 Four Types of Synagogues

TYPE OF SYNAGOGUE	DEFINING CHARACTERISTICS
Center of Celebrations	Minimalist expectations Congregants join looking for religious education and celebration of life cycle rituals
Leader	Large size Prominence in city and/or denomination, usually through clergy Commitment to social justice Community is thought of as devotion to a common cause Governed by the senior rabbi and a small group of lay leaders
Local Shul	Organic sense of belonging Not self-conscious about decision making Small (and often insular) group of lay leaders
K'hillah	Conscious attempts to create community through eclectic worship and programming Values participation Deliberation and transparency in governance Easier to gain commitment to social action, rather than social justice

This is less likely to happen in K'hillot because Hebrew and a fixed liturgy are central to Jewish prayer. While congregants might have some say in selecting music, the liturgy itself is either decided by the clergy or negotiated painstakingly in the ritual committee; once set, it changes very slowly if at all. But the synagogues we saw do attempt to provide variety in alternatives: parallel minyanim or change of service style depending on which Friday of the month it happens to be.

A table summarizing the four types of synagogues is on page 210.[11]

Different Types of Congregations, Different Readiness for Change

We are now in a position to begin answering the first question posed in this chapter: Why are some congregations more success-ful than others in moving from functional to visionary? Our hy-pothesis is that the closer a synagogue comes to being a K'hillah, the more open it will be to change and the more likely it will be to become visionary. To some extent, this is a result of how both K'hillot and visionary congregations are defined. By definition, K'hillot have larger ambitions than Centers of Celebrations. Un-like Leaders, K'hillot are more concerned with creating com-munity for their congregants than with their external role in the movement or the city. Unlike Local Shuls, in which community occurs unselfconsciously, K'hillot realize they have to work at cre-ating community. Creating community is a first step to becom-ing a sacred community. And *working* at creating community often, though not always, requires participation, reflection, and an innovative disposition, three of the hallmarks of a visionary congregation.

What does it take for a synagogue that is not a K'hillah to trans-form itself from functional to visionary? In this section we tell the stories of three synagogues: a Leader Synagogue whose efforts at transformation were stymied; another Leader whose efforts were partially successful; and a Center of Celebrations, the fruits of whose efforts to change did not ripen for fifteen years.

Beit K'nesset Gadol joined the ECE because of its Leader aspirations. The synagogue's ECE adviser commented, "Being part of ECE was another way to differentiate this congregation from others." The synagogue's educator, in fact, had serious reservations. The congregation functioned in a compartmentalized way and the educator "knew this was going to fall on me," but the senior rabbi "twisted my arm."

Despite this, the ECE task force got off to a good start. The leadership team took its responsibilities very seriously, meeting on a weekly basis and incorporating text study into those meetings. An early success claimed by the task force was moving Friday night services to an earlier time, allowing people to eat Shabbat dinner afterwards. In the beginning, the lay leaders felt a sense of partnership with the rabbi; in the words of the task force chair, "ECE fit in because [the rabbi] began to make changes; . . . he would just be part of any sort of actions that we were considering." But halfway through the three-year process, the rabbi lost interest and, in the words of the educator, "it just fizzled." The partnership between the rabbi and the others did not last, and none of the changes endured. Today, other than the earlier Friday night service, there is no trace of the ECE's presence at Beit K'nesset Gadol.

Beit Kavod (Proud Synagogue, also a pseudonym) resembles Beit K'nesset Gadol in its distinguished history, landmark building, and prominence in both its city and its movement. However, the two have a number of differences. First, Beit Kavod has built a suburban branch in an effort to locate the synagogue close to the majority of its congregants. Second, its rabbi is mindful of the need to create a greater sense of community: "We have to work harder because people inherently have less and less of a sense of community. Now we don't just have to compete to be a place of community for them; we have to teach our younger people especially what community even *is*."

Beit Kavod joined the ECE because it wanted to deepen its adult learning and become more reflective in its leadership practices. In weighing the decision to join, the rabbi recognized, "You know, we feel like we're doing pretty well and are pretty healthy; we just want to get a deeper and better and more deliberate sense of ourselves." By identifying this as their aim for getting involved in ECE, the rabbi largely set the agenda for what was to come and limited the overall impact of ECE on the congregation.

In the beginning, the staff continued to chart the synagogue's direction, and the rabbi dominated the process. The synagogue's ECE adviser recalls, "There was very little expected of laypeople in terms of making things happen. At the task force meetings, and even at the leadership team meetings, [the rabbi] came in late, and then he would walk in on a conversation and then add his two cents without knowing what had been discussed; and he didn't get how he could use his role differently."

Yet members of the leadership team began to find their voice, which the adviser credits to text study. "I think that at the individual level, there was Jewish growth. It was very exciting. . . . There were some women for whom [text study] was really, really foreign. And by the end of three years, they really did feel very empowered." Ultimately, however, this sense of empowerment did not translate into truly shared leadership. The ECE adviser continues, "The rabbi had already decided that he wanted to do some worship transformation. . . . What he wanted to have happen is what happened. Now it came in under the guise of ECE. . . . I don't even think he was that subtle in making it even appear that it was coming from [lay leaders]."

While the senior rabbi continues to be, in the words of the long-time member, "a workaholic and a control freak," he has "surrounded himself with more reflective people than he had before." When the educator left, they brought in an educator "who is this incredible reflective person. . . . [Now] they just don't hop from program to program. They really do put a lot of energy into being reflective." Thus, Beit Kavod moved partially along the continuum from function to vision, becoming more reflective, but not significantly more participatory in its leadership.

Finally, we have the example of the belated but no less significant transformation of Beit Chagigah, the Center of Celebrations discussed earlier. Beit Chagigah entered into S2K with great ambivalence. The cantor and a number of lay leaders were enthusiastic and hopeful, while the senior rabbi was only intermittently interested. Though many of the individual members of the S2K task force were highly reflective, their meetings, at times, got stuck on details of the service—such as a long debate about whether or not to revert to the old tradition of turning to face the door at the end of the Friday night prayer *L'cha Dodi*—rather than larger issues of how to conduct worship. As a result of its participation in S2K, Beit Chagigah redesigned the sanctuary to make it warmer and more welcoming, but the service itself changed little. Despite the great emphasis S2K placed on having greeters, the synagogue was unable to recruit congregants to fulfill this function.

But about fifteen years after the S2K experience, Beit Chagigah's senior rabbi retired. Members of the S2K leadership team were active in the search for his replacement and open about sharing their hopes for the congregation. With change as a mandate, they worked closely with the cantor to make the worship service more engaging and participatory. When an opportunity arose to participate in RE-IMAGINE, a subsequent and separate ECE project focusing on rethinking the religious school, the new rabbi responded quickly. Within a year, the synagogue had created a family school similar to Congregation Beth Am's Shabbaton and Westchester Reform Temple's Sharing Shabbat (see chapter 4). As of this writing, they are working to create another alternative model as well. Small but symbolic efforts to build a sense of community abound. For example, the RE-IMAGINE task force made T-shirts for everyone, and the new rabbi makes a point of wearing this T-shirt to meetings.

Although three examples cannot prove a point, they lend credence to our overall argument: Unlike the K'hillot in our study, in which change was led by a partnership of professional and lay leaders (or, in one instance, by the lay leadership alone), leaders and Centers of Celebrations, by virtue of the passivity of their members, cannot change unless the senior rabbi is fully invested in the process. But while a rabbi can create new programs and change the format of old ones, she cannot on her own change the synagogue's culture from functional to visionary. That kind of change requires a participatory community. While it may not be the only path, we would argue that becoming a K'hillah is a stepping-stone to becoming visionary. Greater reflection, a greater sense of participation, and a greater self-consciousness about creating community, all hallmarks of the K'hillah, pave the way for innovations, which in turn can lead to meaningful engagement, a holistic ethos, and, ultimately, a culture committed to a sacred purpose. Not all K'hillot are visionary, but if one is a Leader or a Center of Celebrations, becoming a K'hillah may be a necessary step toward becoming visionary.[12]

On page 216 is the same table that appeared above but with two additional columns highlighting (1) factors that by definition lead the synagogue to be more functional or more visionary and (2) factors that might promote change.

The Role of the Change Initiatives

To better understand the fit, or lack of fit, between change initiative and congregation type, we look to a metatheory of organizational development. In their book *Reframing Organizations*, Lee Bolman and Terrence Deal synthesize a vast array of organizational theories and interventions by assigning each to one of

FIGURE 7.2 Synagogue Types and the Factors that Promote Change

TYPE OF SYNAGOGUE	DEFINING CHARACTERISTICS	TENDENCY TOWARDS FUNCTION VS. VISION	FACTORS THAT MIGHT PROMOTE CHANGE
Center of Celebrations	Minimalist expectations Congregants join looking for religious education and celebration of life cycle rituals	Functional Segmentation Does little to alter the consumerist orientation of congregants	Changes introduced unilaterally by the clergy
Leader	Large size Prominence in city and/ or denomination, usually through clergy Commitment to social justice Community is thought of as devotion to a common cause Governed by the senior rabbi and a small group of lay leaders	Passivity of congregants Visionary, to the extent that the top leadership is committed to a sacred purpose	Changes introduced unilaterally by the clergy
Local Shul	Organic sense of belonging Not self-conscious about decision making Small (and often insular) group of lay leaders	Holistic by nature May not be reflective Resistance to innovation	Appealing to the core group of insiders by giving them power- ful experiences of engagement
K'hillah	Conscious attempts to create community through eclectic worship and programming Values participation Deliberation and transpar- ency in governance Easier to gain commitment to social action, rather than social justice	Participatory Tends to be reflective and open to change	Expressed interest in creating community amid diversity

four frames: structural, human resource, political, and symbolic and cultural. [13]

The *structural frame* deals primarily with roles and responsibilities. Is the division of labor appropriate to the organization's goals? Are lines of authority clear? Synagogue change, from a structural perspective, might include restructuring the religious school so that parents attend along with children or congregants rotate in and out as teachers. It might involve altering the composition of the board, substituting ad hoc committees for standing ones, or making some other change in governance. It might mean instituting new programs for new populations or expanding the options for worship. The strength of this frame is its logic and its straightforward approach; its weakness is that it assumes people will always act rationally.

The *human resource frame* focuses on the needs of individuals and the extent to which the organization attends to them. Are the lines of communication open? Do people feel supported? Included? Heard? Empowered? How does the synagogue communicate with congregants? Does the professional staff work together as a team? This frame directs would-be change agents to look beyond the logical case for change to the perceptions and feelings of those who will be affected by it. It suggests that change either be adapted or explained in a way that can bring people along. The strength of this frame is that it reminds us that change affects real people with real emotions; its limitation is that open communication and teamwork are usually insufficient to motivate people to change.

The *political frame* concentrates on the distribution of resources and the conflict that results from different constituencies vying for power and influence. Synagogue resources include not only its finances but also such things as access to the clergy, getting preferred places and times for events one is planning, and the status attached to various leadership positions. This frame focuses our attention on different constituencies and their intersecting or competing interests or both. What alliances are formed and how stable are they? To what extent is it possible to arrive at a compromise? What do key lay and professional leaders have to gain, and what do they have to lose, by adhering to the status quo or by changing the way they lead? This frame is helpful in sensitizing us to potential conflicts when attempting to change a synagogue. We cannot rely exclusively on this frame, of course, because reducing every situation to a calculus of underlying self-interest discounts the power of ideas and the complexity of human behavior.

The *symbolic and cultural frame* calls our attention to the way in which members of an organization can be motivated, not by rational concerns (as stressed by the structural frame), or by attention to their needs (as stressed by the human resource frame), or even by self-interest (as stressed by the political frame), but by the values embodied in symbols and rituals. Synagogues, in particular, are repositories of symbols and rituals, some ancient and sacred, others more recent and merely conventional. What early experiences have shaped the synagogue's rituals? What stories are told repeatedly, and what values do they represent? What new symbols, stories, or ceremonies might be utilized to reorient the organization's culture? Any change requires explanation and interpretation and may be resisted because of the congregation's self-perception. For example, changing the design of a sanctuary to be more energy efficient or more participatory can be quite controversial because of the history and sense of grandeur that sanctuaries represent. This frame reminds us that change affects people on a profound, often unconscious level, so care must be taken to honor the congregation's culture and unstated norms.

Bolman and Deal argue that working effectively within an organization requires facility with all four frames. Taken together, the four present a more rounded and nuanced picture of organizational life. To develop the capacity for this four-frame understanding, one needs to be aware of the frame(s) one uses most commonly and endeavor to use the others. This analytic perspective enables us to look critically at the change initiatives in which the synagogues in our study participated.

ME'AH—A STRUCTURAL APPROACH

The purest exemplar of a structural approach is found in *Me'ah*, Boston's adult literacy program, which served as a catalyst for change at Temple Beth Elohim. The logic behind Me'ah was very simple: offer people an opportunity to study for two years in a high level program and they will become more deeply connected to Jewish life. This change initiative had a symbolic dimension as well. Recall CJP Director Barry Shrage's impassioned appeal to people's educational ideal and the way he "embarrassed them," according to Terry Rosenberg, by pointing out that their Jewish education lagged far behind their secular level of learning. In addition, Me'ah, at least at the outset, was highly selective and by invitation only, so the prestige of being chosen injected an important political element into the mix. But overall, the structural frame dominated.

ECE: A STRUCTURAL APPROACH WITH ADDED ELEMENTS

ECE, designed by educators to make educational change, also took a structural approach, but like all the change initiatives we studied, it included elements of all four frames. It had a stated goal (transforming synagogues into congregations of learners) and a highly structured process through which this goal was to be achieved. The process, which was an expanded form of strategic planning, offered synagogue leaders detailed instructions for visioning exercises, text study, focus groups termed *community conversations*, and the writing of a formal vision statement. By the end of the third year, congregations were expected to introduce new programs or restructure existing ones in line with the new vision.

Leading this process was a task force, based on Edgar Schein's notion that a new entity, which he terms a "parallel learning environment," would have the best chance to innovate.[14] By bringing together the most reflective representatives of various constituent groups, and freeing them from the ongoing need to maintain existing programs, the task force, it was hoped, could articulate a far-reaching vision and devise credible methods of implementation.

To this structural base, ECE added elements such as small groups and community conversations that addressed the human resource dimension. Interactive text study was the major symbolic element in the ECE. Every task force meeting devoted twenty to forty-five minutes to text study so that people could experience directly the power of discussing classical texts in small groups.

Every ECE task force contained individuals who felt empowered by this experience and went on to pursue learning after the project ended. In some congregations text study became a fixture of many committee and board meetings.

The ECE took the political frame into account by advising synagogues to construct their task forces from the full gamut of potential constituents—from lifelong learners to non-Jewish spouses; from empty nesters to young adults and even high school students; from the congregation president to a new, uninvolved member. But the shortcomings in its approach to the political frame became apparent when, for example, standing committees resented the ECE's encroachment into their turf or when rabbis insisted that adult learning remain under their control.

Each ECE congregation had an adviser who was available to work with the synagogue for twenty days a year. In some cases the adviser was able to intervene and negotiate a compromise or get key players back on board; in other cases, the adviser was stymied. Constituents who favored innovation were strengthened when foundation or federation grants were available. This would suggest that an adviser or assistance in fund-raising, or both, might be the most effective tools that a change initiative can offer in an effort to promote change through the political frame.

S2K—A SYMBOLIC AND
HUMAN RELATIONS APPROACH

In contrast to ECE, S2K drew largely on the cultural-symbolic and human resource approaches. From the outset, S2K outlined a journey along six dimensions, summarized by the acronym PISGAH—prayer, institutional change, study, good deeds, ambience (the synagogue environment), and healing. The term *Pisgah*, meaning "summit" in Hebrew, also had symbolic value, resonant of the summit on which Moses stood as he viewed the promised land.

Though S2K was organized around a task force and had a curriculum for prayer and another for healing, participants report that their most powerful memories of the S2K experience came from the retreats that were held for participating congregations. At these retreats, gifted cantors, rabbis, and artists led what S2K considered exemplary forms of worship. Though some of these innovations were resisted by a few Conservative participants and many of the cantors, they had a powerful effect on most participants, inspiring and motivating them in a way that merely talking about worship could not.

For synagogues in the healing track, S2K provided, in the words of Rabbi Paula Mack Drill at Congregation Agudath Israel, "language and a culture that . . . rippled through the shul." This affected people's perception of the kind of community they wanted to become: "It was a subtle change in language and the way we saw each other and this whole idea that we don't ultimately want to have a caring committee, but we want to be a caring community."

To this symbolic and cultural frame, S2K added an important human resource component. Like ECE, S2K asked each congregation to form a task force. Though the task force was given a curriculum to follow during the first year, at least as important was the directive that task force meetings include a shared meal, an experience of prayer together, and an opening check-in so that members could share their personal concerns. During the second year, the S2K process was organized around journey groups in which text study and personal exploration were fused.

But S2K was much less structured than ECE; its curriculum consisted of a series of short essays as well as group exercises, but was designed to allow synagogues a great deal of flexibility in which of these to use and how to use them. The same open-endedness marked the format of the journey groups that congregations were encouraged to convene. This was in keeping with S2K's notion that the project was about changing culture, not programs. There are pros and cons to this approach. On the positive side, local creativity and initiative were encouraged. On the negative side, planning task force and journey group meetings from scratch was labor intensive; in some congregations, leaders of these groups succumbed to burnout.

Like ECE, S2K did not attend to the political dimension as much as it might have. The constituency most resistant to change, cantors and some rabbis, could easily sabotage the process, and sometimes did. Wealthier synagogues were able to work around this problem by hiring additional cantors and cantorial soloists; and in some situations, recalcitrant cantors or rabbis were encouraged to resign. But when the resistant clergy member had strong backing among congregants, conflict was inevitable, slowing or stopping the momentum for change altogether. Similarly, in cases where funding or an active cadre of volunteers was available for healing services and efforts to organize a caring community, the impetus for change in that area was strengthened; in other cases, the overburdened professional staff found it difficult to maintain the new programs.

NEW KID ON THE BLOCK— CONGREGATION-BASED COMMUNITY ORGANIZING

Congregation-Based Community Organizing (CBCO), the newest of the synagogue change initiatives, began at Boston's Temple Israel in 1998 and was introduced into other synagogues in our study beginning in 2005. Often called relational organizing, its primary approach is through the human resource frame. Rather than a task force (like ECE and S2K) or a program (like Me'ah), its basic building blocks are the one-on-one conversation and the house meeting. Through dozens or, preferably, hundreds of conversations, congregants strengthen their community by sharing their deepest concerns with one another.

Though the ultimate goal of CBCO is political change through legislation and public policy, the primary energy behind CBCO comes from the connections formed by congregants. When they share their fears and aspirations, the result is a thick web of interconnectedness and mutual obligation; though they might be concerned with different social issues, they are able to call on one another for support. Along the way, a strong community is built that goes beyond specific issues.

To this basic human-resource approach, CBCO adds a strong symbolic-cultural component. Participants are encouraged to couch their concerns in terms of stories; these stories are repeated at public actions that aim to hold elected officials accountable and influence public opinion.

Congregants and staff members whose primary way of thinking is through the structural frame are often unable to grasp how individual conversations will lead to large social changes; they find CBCO puzzling and frustrating, at least at first. Problems arise from the political frame, as well. Resistance is sometimes strongest in the social action committee, which tends to be more oriented toward concrete *social action* projects than broad *social justice* matters.

Matching the Congregation to the Change Initiative

Utilizing these four frames, we can now offer possible explanations for why S2K and ECE were most successful in synagogues that were K'hillot. These change projects relied on the willingness of synagogue leaders to enter into a process in which either the steps were not fully elaborated (as in S2K) or the end point not fully articulated (as in ECE). Congregants who had gone through strategic planning or similar processes in their workplace or in volunteer settings were comfortable with ECE's structural approach;

they could reassure fellow task force members that their patience would pay off. They were also able to gently "correct" professionals who either were not sufficiently involved or were overly controlling. Congregants who were therapists became natural leaders in S2K's journey groups and check-ins, modeling how a human resource approach could change the tenor of a meeting and bring people together. In both projects, congregants and professionals who were already comfortable with new forms of worship (in S2K) or learning (in ECE) served as guides and interpreters for those who found these experiences to be foreign. While too few synagogues have gone through CBCO to draw any firm conclusions, the critical role of one-on-one conversations leads us to posit that this approach is most likely to succeed when both key congregants and professionals lead from the human resource frame.

If key leaders preferred the political frame to the structural and human resource frames, and if they used their political influence to undermine the new culture of worship or learning, neither ECE nor S2K worked well. In some cases it was a mismatch between key lay leaders and project. At least as often, however, the problem went deeper: either the senior rabbi or the culture of the congregation— and often both— resisted the open-ended exploration that the two projects required, because by doing so they risked losing power.

In cases where the political frame dominates, congregations might need to look for other approaches. Since in both Centers of Celebrations and Leader Synagogues senior members of the clergy have a great deal of power, it might prove more effective to experiment with programs aimed directly at the synagogue leadership, as STAR (Synagogue Transformation and Renewal) has done and as the Institute for Jewish Spirituality does in its own way. Since congregants of both synagogue types have minimal expectations about their involvement, programs like Me'ah and the Florence Melton Adult Mini-School, services like "Friday Night Live," or large-scale events like *Limud* might be good first steps. Until a critical mass of congregants experiences firsthand what it means to become engaged, there may not be a core group of leaders willing to invest in processes like S2K, ECE, and CBCO.

Another possible approach might be to hire an independent change consultant who would work directly with a small cadre of lay and professional leaders. A skilled consultant could help identify potential lay leaders who would be strong partners in any change effort (we will have more to say about the characteristics of these leaders in the next section). In addition, the consultant can help the leadership become more reflective, holding a mirror to current practices and modeling how to examine and evaluate them.[15]

Intervening in Local Shuls may be more difficult. Their small size is not a problem in itself, as it actually promotes a sense of community. But too often small size means a paucity of lay leaders, ceding control of the congregation to an insular group that may resist efforts at reflection and change.

Raising and Sustaining a New Kind of Synagogue Leader

Up to this point, we have taken a sociological perspective, utilizing organizational theories to understand the culture of the synagogue. We have argued that ECE and S2K's methods were a good match for the synagogues in our study because these synagogues were all K'hillot with reflective and inclusive cultures. At Leader Synagogues or Centers of Celebrations, change was stymied by a mismatch between the synagogue culture and the change initiative.

But the story of synagogue change is not entirely a story of organizational culture; it is also the story of individuals. We therefore turn our attention now to the role of individuals in transforming their synagogues from functional to visionary. In chapter 6, we suggested that these individuals were often at nodal moments in their professional or personal lives, moments that made them particularly open to moving the synagogue in a more visionary direction. But being at these nodal moments was not sufficient.

Everyone passes through a variety of nodal moments throughout their life, but relatively few channel the energy of these heightened moments into productive organizational change. What distinguished the individuals who did? When the change initiative succeeded, there was a fortuitous synergy between these initiatives and the synagogues' lay and professional leaders. To deepen our understanding of this synergy, we look to theories of leadership.

What kind of individual is captivated by the ideal of a visionary congregation and of embracing the reflective practices that transformation requires? These individuals are what Robert Kegan calls "self-authoring."[16] Or, to use the language of Ronald Heifetz, they are able to distinguish between leadership and authority. [17]

We begin with the work of Ronald Heifetz, a professor at Harvard's Kennedy School of Government who studies the connection between leadership and public policy. Heifetz distinguishes between two kinds of work-related challenges, the technical and the adaptive. Technical challenges are routine, well defined, and have reliable solutions. Emergency medicine, for example, is filled with technical challenges, such as treating a severe burn or recovery from cardiac arrest. Emergency rooms have standard procedures for dealing with these situations, procedures that are quite effective when followed faithfully. In technical challenges like these, the leader must have explicit authority. It would be counterproductive for an intern or a family member, for example, to challenge the procedures of the doctor in charge; one authority is needed to direct and control all activity.

Increasingly, however, the challenges organizations face are what Heifetz calls *adaptive* rather than technical. In adaptive challenges, the problem may not be clearly defined and the solution may not be obvious. Many patients come to the hospital with conditions that are not easily diagnosed, often complicated by chronic social problems, such as homelessness or drug abuse, that defy simple solutions. These adaptive challenges cannot be met by a centrally controlled, strict chain of command. The problem may not be fully understood; a range of possible solutions may be proposed; different circumstances might call for varied approaches; and a team approach may be required, with different players exerting leadership at various points in time.

A halakhically based synagogue faces challenges that are largely technical: What time should Kabbalat Shabbat (the Friday night service) begin? At sundown. What is the correct *nusach* (melody) for a certain holiday? Ask the cantor. Is a certain food permissible? Look for the *hekhsher* (rabbinic certification). But the liberal synagogue, whose members are not bound by halakha, faces many adaptive challenges: What type of service will maximize congregants' engagement? How much traditional liturgy should be included? What should be the mix of contemporary melodies and traditional nusach? Given the severe time constraints of the religious school, what is most important to teach? These questions cannot be answered by a single expert. They require study and deliberation; and congregants, along with the clergy, have a role to play in these deliberations.

In adaptive situations, Heifetz argues, leadership and authority are no longer identical. The history of social movements is filled with examples of people who led without authority, from Elizabeth Cady Stanton to Martin Luther King Jr. to Al Gore, *after* he served as vice president. Complex institutions, in particular, require leadership from people at every level, not just the top. Heifetz writes, "Rather than define leadership either as a position of authority in a social structure or as a personal set of characteristics, we may find it a great deal more useful to define leadership as an *activity*. This allows for leadership from multiple positions in a social structure. . . . It also allows for the use of a variety of abilities depending on the demands of the culture and situation."[18]

With regard to synagogue life, two assumptions prevail: first, that the senior rabbi leads by virtue of his or her position; and second, that the more charismatic the rabbi, the stronger his or her leadership. It is certainly true that senior rabbis set the tone for their synagogues, either championing or inhibiting change. In our study, however, a number of congregants, not rabbis, played a key role in transforming the congregation.

One example is Beth Smith, at Congregation Beth Shalom in suburban Kansas City, whom we have already encountered in chapters 3 and 6. Realizing how uninspiring the services at her congregation were to her, she imagined that they must be even less inspiring to a younger generation. "So I got together a few people and said, 'What is it we can do to design a service that will be interesting to young people?'"

Beth's group joined forces with two other congregants, Linda Salvay and Devra Lerner, musicians who had attended *Hava Nashira* (Let's Sing), an annual institute for Jewish song leaders at the Olin-Sang-Ruby Union Institute in Wisconsin. Services at Hava Nashira, Linda recalls, "were so engaging and musical, so uplifting and transforming, and I thought, 'There's got to be a way to bring some of this back to my own congregation.'" Devra notes that none of this could have happened without the blessing of the senior rabbi, Alan Cohen: "Rabbi Cohen is somebody who is open to letting people try to reach God in their own way and not threatened by having an egalitarian Orthodox minyan going on at the same time he's doing a service in the main sanctuary. So, his openness and encouragement through the whole process was critical."

But Rabbi Cohen alone would not have managed change. He got there through working with Beth Smith, Linda Salvay, and Devra Lerner, all of them laypeople intent on transforming worship at Beth Shalom. They exemplify Ronald Heifetz's contention that in today's complex world, leadership should be defined as an *activity*, not as a role.

Congregation Beth Am in Los Altos, California, provides another example of leadership as activity, not position. The impetus for Congregation Beth Am's first education task force came at a 1990 board retreat.[19] In exploring the congregation's future direction, someone asked, "When are we going to do something about our kids' education?" Someone else replied, "What's wrong with our kids' education?" An intense discussion ensued, much of it couched in the language of Thomas Peters and Robert Waterman's book, *In Search of Excellence,* virtually required reading in Silicon Valley in those days.[20] A consensus emerged that the education at Congregation Beth Am's religious school was not excellent. The question then arose—why should congregants settle for anything less than excellence? What would it take to make Congregation Beth Am's educational offerings excellent? Rabbi Rick Block and the congregation president could have easily cut off this discussion. Instead, because of their open and responsive attitude, they created a task force to revitalize the religious school.

This type of participatory leadership continues to this day. In 2001, Ric Rudman, then president of the congregation, and Jim Heeger, who was in line to be his successor, identified two major concerns about Congregation Beth Am's functioning. The first was that the professional staff, which had had significant turnover, including at the level of the senior rabbi, was not working well as a team; the second, that some administrative procedures were inefficient and off-putting. Said Rudman, "They were poor because no one had ever paid attention to them."

Had they felt bound by conventional lines of authority, Ric and Jim might have assumed that these issues were matters best left to the professional staff. Instead, they asserted their leadership by proposing to the new senior rabbi, Janet Marder, that a process consultant be hired to work on these issues. They raised half of the money to pay the consultant and Janet paid the other half from her discretionary fund. By all accounts, the consultant was very effective in her work at Congregation Beth Am. Daryl Messinger, a former president and volunteer coordinator of Shabbaton at the time, recalls:

> The process of working [things out] was not easy but it's really changed the efficiency of the place. They adopted new rules about conducting

meetings, taking minutes, and maintaining the congregational calendar. It helped people make decisions, opened much better lines of communication, and led to a different level of commitment of people to be there for one another. It was quite a transformation.

Yet a third example of leadership as an activity comes from Rabbi Jonah Pesner of Temple Israel, who tells of a turning point in his understanding of social justice. In honor of the synagogue's 150th birthday, Jonah came up with the idea of hanging a giant poster of a thermometer in the lobby, with the goal of accumulating 1,500 "mitzvah points" for activities like working in a soup kitchen. Concerned that Jonah was creating a top-down social action *program* that might undercut the grassroots social justice initiative Ohel Tzedek, Fran Godine, a lay leader, arranged for a lunch with Jonah and the synagogue's organizer to, as Jonah put it, "get some feedback" on this idea. He recalls what happened at that lunch: "So I tell her the plan and she said, 'And how will that help you wrestle with a meaningful sense of justice?' And I started to cry. I literally started to cry because . . . I realized I just wanted to be in the safe place of programs, of bureaucracy, knowing what it would look like."

Rather than deferring to Jonah as the rabbi responsible for social justice, Fran exerted her leadership in a quiet and gentle way, creating a situation in which he got feedback he could truly hear and accept. For his part, Jonah chose to listen rather than stand on his credentials as rabbi; he now tells the tale himself as an instance of his growth into a nationally recognized leader in synagogue organizing.

Encouraging Leadership from "Below"

As the examples of Ric Rudman, Beth Smith, Fran Godine, and others indicate, congregants often have ideas that carry an implicit critique of purely functional synagogues. Many of them are used to exercising leadership in their professional or volunteer work but do not step forward to exert the same leadership in synagogues. Why not? We see three possibilities:

- First, beyond good ideas, leadership requires a sense of self and a sense of responsibility that Robert Kegan calls "self-authoring."
- Second, potential leaders may have competing commitments.
- Third, potential leaders are often stymied by those in official positions of authority.

ENCOURAGING LEADERS TO BE SELF-AUTHORING

Robert Kegan, a professor of education at Harvard, is a life-span developmental psychologist. For three decades he has studied and written about the way adults learn to live, and even thrive, in a complex society with many adaptive, to use Heifetz's term, challenges. What enables some individuals to assert their leadership, while others remain timid or even disgruntled followers? Kegan holds that it is not lack of interest or courage that stands in the way but rather the capacity to view oneself as self-authoring. As individuals gain this capacity, they "shift away from being 'made up by' the values and expectations of one's 'surround' (family, friends, community, culture) . . . [and develop] an internal authority that makes choices about these external values and expectations according to one's own self-authored belief system. One goes from being psychologically 'written by' the socializing press to 'writing upon' it."[21]

The self-authoring individual is able to

- be the inventor or owner of [his or her] work (rather than see it as owned and created by the employer)
- be self-initiating, self-correcting, self-evaluating (rather than have an apprenticing or imitating relationship to what we do). . .

- conceive of the organization from the "outside in," as a whole . . . (rather than see the rest of the organization and its parts only from the perspective of our own part, from the "inside out")
- resist our tendencies to make "right" or "true" that which is merely familiar; and "wrong" or "false" that which is only strange.[22]

Kegan has found that this capacity doesn't usually develop until the third or fourth decade of a person's life and that many people never develop it. Moreover, this ability doesn't develop all at once and is not applied equally to all aspects of one's life. Thus, one can be self-authoring in one's career but not in one's volunteer work. This helps to explain why so many hard-hitting business people seem to suspend their critical faculties when they serve on the board of a nonprofit organization.

In a synagogue setting, it may be particularly difficult for congregants to be self-authoring. Based on Hebrew and Aramaic texts, and brimming with exacting and somewhat esoteric rituals, Judaism can seem remote and daunting to those who were not immersed in a traditional setting as children and do not engage in intensive study as adults. The laity are easily intimidated by members of the clergy, even when the clergy do not appear threatening.

Change projects like S2K and ECE helped task force members feel more comfortable with Judaism and approach their leadership roles more confidently. Diane Schuster studied the reactions of ECE task force members to text study in the very beginning of the process.[23] She found that the majority of the group (nine of eleven)—all of whom had been invited to join the task force because the synagogue leadership saw them as potential change agents—believed that they were deficient and even inauthentic as Jews. When asked about their experience beginning text study, these otherwise highly capable adults described feelings of hesitance, insecurity, and self-doubt. For example, in recalling the first study session, a thirty-eight-year-old psychologist described feeling "inadequate and kind of inept" and worrying about being "in uncharted territory," which could be "an alienating thing." Another member was worried about being "intimidated in front of the rabbi and feeling like a third-grade student with a teacher who knows a lot more than I do."

By the fourth task-force meeting, Schuster's respondents had become comfortable and appreciative of the learning and the insights they gained into both the tradition and themselves. Key to this process was interactive learning in *chevruta* (study pairs) or small groups, which opened up an avenue for greater participation, creating a more genuine and profound sense of community: "It was a diverse group and there was almost instant camaraderie. Nobody tried to take control of the meeting. They were run very democratically. Everybody had a chance to speak."[24] No longer was the rabbi or educator the central figure in the discussion. The lesson was clear: Jewish learning is for everyone, everyone has a contribution to make, and a variety of viewpoints is welcome. In the words of another respondent, "It was interesting to hear the interpretations . . . [of] different people coming with different backgrounds."[25]

What chevruta text study was to this ECE team, Congregation-Based Community Organizing was for Lisa Vinakoor, a public school teacher in her thirties at Temple Israel. She had been designated to confront a senator at a citywide gathering. With some tutoring from the synagogue's organizer, she felt sufficiently self-authored to speak with authority. Afterwards, she and the organizer had a one-on-one conversation:

I spent the whole time raving about Fran [Godine] and Jonah [Pesner]. I had put them up on this huge pedestal. And he turned to me and said, "Do you think you could be a leader like them?" And I said, "Oh, my God. No one has ever asked me that before. I don't even know. I'm just this really angry teacher." . . . And I probably looked at him like a deer in headlights. And he really agitated me in his very smart way. . . . I always felt like he held up the mirror and asked, "Who do you want to be? Do you want to be part of making change, or do you want to just put other people up on a pedestal and complain all day about teaching?"

The organizer, Meir Lakein, gave Lisa books to read, met with her regularly, and urged her to be more strategic and intentional: "He really agitated me out of my old ways." Eventually, Lisa herself became a community organizer.

Clergy members too became more self-authoring as a result of the change process. Cantor Evan Kent of Temple Isaiah in Los Angeles, and a participant in the first S2K cohort, credits his S2K experience with giving him the insight that "cantors are really cultural directors."

> [It] came from sitting with my colleagues and listening to them decry that someone was using the wrong *chatimah* (end of a blessing). And I was thinking, "Oh, my God. It was the wrong chatimah, and it was the wrong nusach. But were you moved at the end of the service?" I'm not saying let's be ignorant or cavalier. But let's understand what we're doing here. How it is we are trying to affect lives. I think ultimately that's what is important. I think you can be liturgically correct, liturgically profound and also change people.

SURFACING AND HARMONIZING COMPETING COMMITMENTS

Competing commitments are another reason why individuals may fail to engage fully in synagogue leadership. Resistance to change is not always a result of opposition or inertia. These competing commitments can create "a kind of personal immunity to change."[26]

Imagine, for example, a congregant who has visited another synagogue, witnessing worship that she considers more engaging and dynamic than her own. Imagine, further, that this congregant has had experience changing the corporate culture in her workplace. At the synagogue, however, she might hesitate to speak out in front of the rabbi and the cantor because of their powerful presence when they visited her mother in the hospital or officiated at her son's bar mitzvah.

To take another example, imagine a father who volunteers in various capacities at his children's public school and has learned a great deal about promoting multiple intelligences in the classroom. He sees a number of ways that the theory of multiple intelligences might be applied in the religious school. Yet he doesn't want to criticize the teacher who has been so loving to his children, so he holds back.

Finally, imagine the assistant rabbi with new ideas about adult learning. She senses that these ideas would be welcomed. She also senses, however, that implementing these ideas would most likely fall to her, and she already feels overworked. Without fully acknowledging the conflict, she keeps her thoughts to herself.

Kegan and Lahey claim that this web of competing commitments is all too often buried beneath the surface. The only way to uncover them, they argue, is reflection: "We need leaders who are able both to start processes of learning and to diagnose and disturb already existing processes that prevent learning and change, the active, ongoing immune systems at work in every individual and organization."[27]

ENCOURAGING A NEW TYPE OF LEADERSHIP

The third reason potential leaders fail to contribute their many gifts to synagogue life brings us back to the culture of the congregation. Too often, these leaders' contribution is ignored, or even sabotaged, by those in positions of authority, such as the professional staff, the board, or members of standing committees. The clergy may, for example, pay lip service to congregant-led *bikkur cholim* (visiting the sick) but routinely neglect to pass along to the committee the names of those who are ill. The board may be offended that a task force has usurped its power by writing a new vision statement and keeps the statement under wraps. A religious school committee may be perfectly happy planning bake sales and resist all efforts to become involved in a curriculum review.

Hebrew Union College Professor Sam Joseph has served as a consultant to both ECE and S2K congregations. He laments how little rabbis understand that sharing leadership with their staff and empowering their congregation are essential "for a congregation to be vibrant and healthy—which means a healthy and vibrant rabbinate for themselves." Rick Jacobs at Westchester Reform Temple agrees. For him, empowering the lay leaders at Westchester Reform was the "biggest takeaway from the ECE." He contrasts the perspective he developed with that of some of his rabbinic colleagues:

> My rabbi friends would come to CCAR [conferences] and . . . they'd say, "You have to do this with the *balebatim* (lay leaders)? Couldn't you figure out better what the education needs of the temple are without these laypeople getting involved and adding their two cents?" And my answer is, I honestly think if the rabbis and cantors and educators were left alone to do all of this, it wouldn't have been nearly as effective as it was. So it wasn't just an act of being nice, like "Let's let the laypeople pretend like they're leading the synagogue." . . . The reality is that the folks added not just a veneer, they added substance and they really helped us stay on track and focus.

Given the natural proclivity of authorities to protect their turf, it is all the more remarkable that Temple Israel's board turned to those involved in Ohel Tzedek to guide them through the board restructuring, reducing it from one hundred to twenty-five members. At first the congregation president devised a plan "behind closed doors," notes Jessica Greenfield, a young board member involved in Ohel Tzedek. But when faced with what she described as a "mutiny," he realized that he had to proceed in a "relational" way, and asked Jessica to lead this process. "An immense amount of time" was spent talking to one another. "We never would have been able to form the compromise that we did if it weren't for those relationships." When the plan was approved, Jessica modeled the kind of tsimtsum (contraction) that would be demanded of the majority of the board by stepping down herself.

The Never-Ending Journey

The journey from functional to visionary is long and arduous. Along the path are any number of recalcitrant players: congregants wedded to a certain kind of worship and unwilling to make changes that would make it more meaningful for a younger generation; professionals who hold onto long-standing routines, despite their increasing lack of effectiveness; congregants who resist any attempt to participate more regularly or to be part of a community; leaders who cling to power. But there are also professionals who discover new meaning in their work; congregants who realize that they love text study, worship, visiting the sick, or working for social justice; congregants who are fulfilled in the process of creating a stronger synagogue; and congregants who are amazed to find they have a talent for leadership.

On the winding road from function to vision, a synagogue can encounter obstacles that seem, at least for a time, insurmountable. Congregation Beth Shalom, for example, found itself unable to transform learning as it had transformed worship. Powerful programs that are life-changing sometimes run their course, like the journey groups and healing services at Congregation Agudath Israel. Parents who have become regular Shabbat-goers for a decade can, like many at Westchester Reform, get out of the habit after their youngest child graduates from Sharing Shabbat.

But then congregations can get unstuck, as well. As we write this, Westchester Reform is attempting to create a different kind of Shabbat minyan, one that will appeal to the graduates of Sharing Shabbat. Congregation Beth Am too is trying to create a new minyan for the Shabbat regulars. When the recalcitrant senior rabbi at a synagogue not in this study retired, the new rabbi quickly moved to sign the synagogue up for ECE and the cantor felt reenergized.

Synagogue transformation and personal transformation go hand in hand. As personal development ebbs and flows, so does organizational development.

CHAPTER 8

Transformation in Perspective: Looking Back and Looking Forward

This research project began as a limited study of synagogue intervention projects. Using Experiment in Congregational Education (ECE) and Synagogue 2000 (S2K) as our two paradigms, but including an independent model as well, we wanted to know if the synagogues that had engaged in interventions had really changed. If so, to what extent? And how did the interventions help the process along? We sought not only to look back but also to look ahead: back on the historical record of synagogue life between 1995 when the interventions began and ahead to the possible fate of other interventions that might be proposed as synagogues move further into the twenty-first century.

It soon became apparent, however, that a lot more was at stake than just an analysis of synagogue change projects. Our work became a window onto the very future of synagogues. The projects had emerged, after all, out of widespread suspicion that synagogues were not living up to their potential. On the positive side of things, synagogue intervention projects multiplied, as did conferences devoted to strengthening synagogues in one way or another. On the negative side, the very increase of those projects and conferences demonstrated just how real these synagogue maladies were, reaching deeper, perhaps, than anyone had suggested.

In 2005 a report that emerged from a conference hosted at Boston's Hebrew College began with the worry that "the reality of the synagogue in America does not even begin to approach its potential . . . only about 1/2 of the 50 percent of Jews who claim synagogue affiliation actually attend on at least a once a month basis." (In fact, the numbers are probably a lot less.) To be sure, the author indicated that even secular Jews remain open to the experience of the spiritual, and "many such Jews are ripe for synagogue engagement, but only once the synagogue has been redefined and reconfigured so as to reach out to the unaffiliated and enable their reentry into Jewish life." The implicit message was that synagogues still required "redefinition and reconfiguration," because they were neither "reaching out" nor "enabling Jewish life" very well.[1] Two years later, a team of synagogue consultants concurred. Despite their overall positive prescription for what synagogues might become, they expressed concern after five years in the field that "so few synagogues appear truly healthy. Rabbis and lay leaders are too often ill prepared for the reality of running the complex organization that is the modern synagogue. What makes matters worse is that they, as well as the national organizations, are often in denial of this reality, setting aside little time and scant resources to improve or repair the situation."[2]

At the same time, research into the post baby-boomer generation investigated the dynamics and characteristics of alternative minyanim that had also developed since the mid-1990s and had begun to attract significant numbers of Jews in their twenties and thirties.[3] As recently as December 7, 2008, Joshua Avedon, formerly of Synagogue 3000 (S3K) but now a cofounder of Jumpstart, an organization dedicated to the growth of emergent synagogues and minyanim, posted an entry on S3K's Synablog that charged:

The view from 30,000 feet is one of institutional religious Judaism, where membership in synagogues (at least in the non-Orthodox world) is both aging and diminishing. These synagogues are frequently failing to attract 20- and 30-somethings, which means their lifeline to the future

is starting to fray. But the view from the street is that the growth of independent minyans and new spiritual communities is exploding, and is
largely fed by that same demographic that is missing from many synagogues. If the mainstream Jewish community doesn't get hip to what
is driving the new start-ups soon, a whole parallel universe of Jewish
communal life might just rise up and make the old structures irrelevant.

Elsewhere too, the malaise regarding synagogues had spread. At
the very least, the growing advocacy of postdenominationalism
was eating away at movement loyalties. In the spring of 2008, Hebrew College and Synagogue 3000 cosponsored a conversation on
the need to outfit rabbis more successfully for synagogue leadership in the changing spiritual environment. In that same year, and
the year after, the downward economic spiral initiated by the collapse of the subprime housing market caused further synagogue
retrenchment and added doubts about the value of synagogue
membership—doubts that were especially disturbing because
they arose as a moment of crisit when synagogues should have
been more, not less, important than ever.

Given all this uncertainty, our book has become a de facto sociological referendum on the synagogue's future.[4] Are synagogues
here to stay? If so, as what? As minimally invasive institutions that
barely touch, let alone engage, the lives of contemporary men and
women? Or as dynamic organizations responding to the social
and individual crises in which people naturally find themselves as
they search for moorings in a rapidly changing world?

Some synagogues are just plain dysfunctional: they cannot
hold rabbis; they are forever in the throes of their own ongoing
civil wars; or they otherwise display repetitive systemic fractures
that make their continued existence a defiance of reason. Our
study set such dysfunctional synagogues aside; whatever future
the American Jewish community has, they are not it. Instead, we
took the best of the highly functioning synagogues that needed to
adapt if they were to meet the changing sociological reality. These
are synagogues that somehow intuited the need for dramatic

reconsideration of their identity and function. If even *they* could not free themselves from the bondage of institutional habit, would synagogues in general have a future worth considering? Would they just disappear? Would it matter if they did? If, however, it could be shown that good synagogues have the potential to become great, to move, in the terms of this study, from *functional* to *visionary*, American Jews might properly hope for a brave new world where synagogues might change lives and really matter to their members and to others.

The value of our study, therefore, transcends the stories of eight congregations. Yes, we do chart the way that synagogues transform their cultures, but even more we demonstrate the exciting possibility that synagogues can generate Jewish communal identity rather than remain marginal to it. If there is one lesson that we learned, it is that visionary congregations can matter a great deal to Jews and to Jewry.

Sacred Community, Sacred Choices, Sacred Strategies

By saying that the purpose of a synagogue is to matter, we mean to focus on more than meeting members' needs. Indeed, functional congregations already do that—that is the definition of functional. The problem is that their members see their needs as rather instrumental. They adjust to what the synagogue is perceived as being able to do, rather than challenge synagogues to define their needs at a higher level of perception. If one equates the needs of synagogue-going Jews as obtaining bar and bat mitzvah celebration, opening their doors for the requisite ceremonial hours on High Holy Days, and the like, even dysfunctional synagogues count as semi-successes. If one expands those needs to include a more sophisticated array of services (educational, ritual, and communal), functional synagogues manage that. But if one takes seriously the "needs" mandated by Jewish tradition, one has an altogether different set of criteria, first among them being that synagogues embody the ancient term for "Jewish congregation," *k'hillah k'doshah,* or "sacred community."

Sacred communities do more than offer adult education courses; they become congregations of learners. More than having mitzvah days, they have mitzvah doers. Congregants not only attend services but they also have a prayer life of their own. Can synagogues become these things? Our study shows they can—if they choose to.

Sacred communities make sacred choices. "I have put before you life and death; blessing and curse," the Torah says, "Choose life . . . by loving the Eternal your God, heeding God's commands" (Deut. 30:19–20). Congregations continually confront this Jewish demand: to choose life—which is to say, to be consequential, spiritual, caring, and compassionate to their core; to organize themselves holistically, not programmatically; to worry more about what they are than what they offer; and to deep-root Jewish values in a culture where excellence drives everything that happens. This study calls these congregations *visionary.*

A common axiom is that no matter how unlikely, if something exists it must indeed be possible. So too with synagogues. The very fact that there exist congregations that have moved along the path from functional to visionary demonstrates that others can as well. That takes leadership, of course, and this book has charted some of the capacities of leaders who are organizationally adept and spiritually grounded. Though rabbis are central to this leadership, they are by no means its sole owners. What John F. Kennedy said of the United States applies equally for synagogues: "One person can make a difference, and everyone should try."[5] Opportunity does not just knock, it also summons; and it summons us all.

As scholars, we seek to contribute to the academic understanding of how congregations differ and how they change. But as Jews who care about what we are studying, we make no apologies for our values: given the evidence that visionary congregations are possible, we seek more of them, a vast network of visionary synagogues at the core of Jewish communities everywhere. Toward that end, we have offered identifiable lessons for change. These lessons can inform and, we hope, inspire movement from *functional* to *visionary*—not simply meeting minimalist expectations of congregants seeking a "product" but shaping communities of inspired and inspiring vision. Functional and visionary are the names we give to the two extremes on a spectrum—no congregation is entirely one or the other. What matters is the congregation's valence and direction. Are congregations stuck or are they advancing toward the visionary? We believe every synagogue can learn enough from our research to at least embark on the visionary path.

First and foremost, such congregations need a rough idea of what *visionary* is, and toward that end we have provided six dimensions, or scales. No synagogue is likely to be wholly functional or visionary. The determining factors are the speed and quality of movement in the right direction.

THE SIX PRINCIPLES

At their very core, visionary congregations aspire to exemplify *sacred purpose* as their overarching and inspiring mission. They contrast sharply with consumerist-oriented institutions that, their rhetoric notwithstanding, operate on a fee-for-service basis, providing congregants with bar and bat mitzvahs, weddings, funerals, and High Holiday seats in return for membership dues and occasional contributions.

Visionary congregations operate *holistically*—their various components work synergistically and in concert, rather than as segmented units with little relationship or connection with one another.

Visionary communities energize broad-based and passionate participation of congregants—as worshipers, learners, caregivers, community builders, activists, and decision makers. They contrast with congregations that depend almost exclusively on the clergy, a hired professional team, and a small inner core of devotees. In short, a visionary community's culture has no such thing as ob-server status. People are *participatory*, rather than passive.

Visionary congregations do not just go through the motions. They excel at delivering *meaningful* experiences, through moving and engaging worship, life-relevant Jewish learning, and nurtur-ing relationships as the basis for caregiving and world-repairing.

Leaders of these congregations exhibit an *innovative disposi-tion*. They welcome novelty, take risks, and overcome the deep-seated resistance and attachment to routine that are endemic to functional congregations.

Finally, leaders in visionary congregations are marked by *re-flectiveness*. They constantly observe, think, consult, evaluate, and adjust.

PRESENT HOLISTICALLY, AND HERE AND THERE

As one would expect from a holistic emphasis, these principles apply throughout the very fabric of congregational life, not just here and there. But they are evident "here and there" as well, for in the end the synagogue is made up of "heres and theres." The principles, that is, show up in each and every discrete domain of congregational endeavor, the most obvious ones being the areas that we studied:

Prayer

We have ample anecdotal evidence that many Jews find worship less than inspiring. It is frequently experienced as routine, bor-ing, incomprehensible, unwelcoming, meaningless, and devoid of the sacred.

But worship need not be that way. We observed congregational prayer that was engaging, welcoming, meaningful, spiritual, sa-cred, and inspiring. When the service leaders reflect, rather than lead services by rote, they can blend familiar liturgical staples with stimulating innovation. They artfully employ the power of music and make the service accessible to participants by adapting the service, on one hand, and educating the participants, on the other. They redesign space, provide alternatives, and accent feelings of connection, community, and intimacy.

To be sure, Conservative and Reform congregations go about worship change differently, but both display our six principles of visionary communities. They are suffused with the sense of the *sacred*; they connect the act of prayer with a *holistic* vision of the synagogue, Judaism, and the larger society; they are marked by high rates of congregational *participation*. They deliver personal *meaning*; they balance *innovation* with regularity; and they derive from *conscious, intentional,* and *reflective* leadership.

Learning

In functional synagogues, congregational education focuses heavily on the young and culminates in bar and bat mitzvah training. Despite the preponderance of time and energy expended on this childhood education, synagogues ascribe low status to it, zone it off from other synagogue activities, and inure congregants to low expectations. By contrast, visionary congregations extend learning beyond the religious school classroom to the congregation as a whole. Jewish learning is *ubiquitous*: It occurs during services, within board and committee meetings, in connection with social justice activities, and while caring for those in need. Leaders and congregants alike view Jewish learning as intrinsically important and of premium value—not a means to something else but an *end unto itself.* Jewish learning becomes a *prestigious* activity attracting everyone, even those with position and status, all of whom engage in Jewish learning *lishmah* (for its own sake). Their doing so elevates learning in the congregational culture to the point where learning even becomes a *prerequisite to leadership.* The standard for what constitutes adequate Jewish knowledge rises. Most critically, Jewish learning becomes exquisitely *meaningful*: it enriches life, speaks to ultimate life concerns, and connects the learner to local congregational peers and to the transcendent community of Jews linked metaphysically to one another over time and space.

The sheer diversity of congregational personalities, backgrounds, capabilities, and interests means that Jewish learning can deliver personal meaning only insofar as it allows for a measure of *personalization*. As with the worship services, Jewish learning in visionary congregations features a *multiplicity of options*.

Often it is the congregation's lay leaders who take the first steps in transforming learning. Congregants who become increasingly dissatisfied with the state of Jewish learning begin to engage in their own Jewish learning and to coalesce around conversations designed to better what the congregation offers. They provide clergy and educators with the mandate, motivation, and support to undertake educational innovations.

Caring Communities

To a greater or lesser extent, all functional congregations care for members who are in need: mourners, the sick, and victims of other forms of distress. Externally, they care for the larger society by what they call social justice work or social action. Both *g'milut chasadim* (acts of loving-kindness) and *tikkun olam* (repair of the world) express Jewishly grounded care for others.

But functional congregations undertake these tasks in compartmentalized or segmented fashion. They are more likely farmed out to committees and scheduled for designated times (a mitzvah day). Few occur organically as outgrowths of the social fabric that knits the congregation's members into a community. And fewer still connect their "caring community" with a broader ethos of social justice.

By contrast, caring in visionary communities permeates the congregation. There arises a *culture of loving-kindness and an ethos of social justice,* not as abstractions but as part and parcel of the way members of the community relate to one another. Calling it a *culture* and not just a *value* denotes caring as the way

the congregation does business, not how the social action committee programs a set of activities.

This caring culture is intrinsically suffused with spirituality,
for caring is a *sacred* act, embedded in other equally sacred acts:
the congregation's life of prayer and learning. Good davening and
learning strengthen the relationships that promote caring. Worship brings the community together to celebrate joyous occasions
and to coalesce around challenging ones; learning connects Jewish
tradition to the lives of people in need. Conversely, caring behavior intensifies the impact of effective worship and learning. *Social*
purpose becomes *sacred* purpose.

The transformation of communities from functional places
with segmented and episodic acts of care to visionary congregations with an integrated and grounded ethos of caring occurs
only with *intentionality*. Since its necessary prerequisite is *strong
sacred relationships* among members, visionary congregations
provide the venue for *personal, meaningful, and sustained conversations*. Examples include small groups like S2K's Jewish journey
groups, and Congregation-Based Community Organizing's one-
on-ones. These begin as supplements to recurring interactions
around *social events* like the kiddush or *oneg Shabbat* but grow
to include structured *community conversations*, where people
think, reflect, and engage in significant discourse on communally
important matters. As these meetings become natural, just the
sort of thing the congregation does, so too does a sense of the
sacred and appreciation for prayer and study that supports the
community's endeavor. Spirituality, learning, and caring operate
synergistically, strengthening one another. Weakness in any one
undermines the others.

Change

Accomplishing all this means change—not additive change, which
is easy, but transformative change, which is not. The work of
transformation never ends, partly because people, communities,

and context are constantly in flux, and partly because human beings are innately curious and naturally experimental. At some point, change becomes routinized as *culture*, what the congregation cannot imagine *not* doing.

Change starts with people who emerge as leaders, rabbis and well-positioned laypeople who may find themselves at nodal moments in their lives—personally or professionally. Looking for new directions, they risk thinking differently. Their position permits them to ask hard questions and challenge congregational assumptions. In that regard, they are *gadflies* who communicate *discontent* and *ambition*—unhappiness with what is and a vision of what might be. *Rabbis* are especially crucial to the process, since they head up congregational activity, and without their active engagement, matters recede in importance on the communal agenda. Rabbis cannot succeed on their own, but through their position and status they can, if they like, become effective obstructionists, just by inaction and inattention.

Leaders establish *teams* that engage in a *process* of discovery, as a formalized task force or some other means to foster congregational conversations. The very thing that draws the team together, however—commitment to a cause, even to the point of considering themselves an elite—can be their downfall, since the faster they progress, the more likely it will be that they leave the rest of the congregation behind. At that point, the board and standing committees will raise objections to what the team is doing. So teams require regularized *support* from other congregational bodies and from the external change project that brings know-how and experience to the task. Eventually, the team articulates a *vision* that board and congregation applaud. It experiments with *low-hanging fruit* to test the vision and to signal to fellow congregants that the tortuous process in which everyone is at least implicitly engaged is well worthwhile.

At some point the teams discover that *process is as important as product.* One improves worship by modeling heartfelt prayer oneself; one transforms learning by engaging in one's own study; and community grows as community is experienced. Congregations are never transformed, only *transforming*.

Postscript for Our Time

In good economic times, people are apt to be too busy enjoying themselves to pay much attention to problems brewing far below the surface. When the economy falters, however, these underlying issues erupt like social volcanoes, making their victims wring their hands in despair at having failed to attend to them before. Our study began in the proverbial seven years of plenty; it is being published in the seven years of famine. We cannot help but look back upon our findings to see how they can help us, especially now, as synagogues reshape their mandate for the future. We began this chapter citing the public record on synagogues. We end with a comparative note from the sociological literature on churches. Synagogues and churches are not unalike, after all. They are both part of the same American spiritual landscape.

Even in 1997, with the stock market beginning its march to an all-time high and America far away from today's economic downturn, sociologist Robert Wuthnow noted a brewing fiscal crisis in churches. "I have been a lifelong participant in churches," Wuthnow began, "and somewhat reluctant to write critically about the churches because there were many good things to say and because there was so much else to criticize in the wider culture. But I am convinced now that I can no longer write responsibly about American religion without raising a critical voice."[6] What gave him pause was the realization that even in good economic times, mainstream congregations were beginning to contend with rising salaries, aging plants, and falling revenue. Yet in the end, his critique was not based on economics. "What makes the present crisis more serious," he concluded "is that it is also a spiritual crisis. . . . Fund raisers cannot fix it." The spiritual side of the problem, Wuthnow continued, "lies in a fundamental unwilling-ness on the part of clergy to confront the teachings within their own confessional heritage."[7] Overemphasizing fiscal issues might even backfire, since 30 percent of the people Wuthnow studied said "they would actually give less money if their churches talked more about finances than they do now."[8] What people wanted to hear was religion's spiritual lessons.

What goes for churches goes for synagogues too. Whatever fi-nancial impact the current environment has on synagogue bud-gets, and whatever fiscal lessons all of us learn once the economy turns around, we can ill afford to ignore the implicit spiritual cri-sis while addressing the explicit financial one. When Wuthnow speaks of each church's "confessional heritage," he means the guid-ance, hope, and insight each denomination has to offer men and women who navigate life's eddies in expectation of that guidance, hope, and insight—not just programs to keep them busy. Using the terms of our study, we can say that synagogues that provide such guidance, hope, and insight are visionary, not functional.

To be sure, Wuthnow seems at first to fault the clergy, but clergy are only part of a much larger system. They cannot teach what people cannot hear; and people cannot hear what is eclipsed by the static of business as usual. Too many synagogues remain mired there —that's the bad news, and it is very bad. But the good news is very good. More and more synagogues have undertaken transformation; and our study demonstrates that transformation is really possible, not as a final state of being but as a culture of on-going risk, experimentation, and excellence, with attention paid to what really matters in Judaism: prayer, learning, good deeds, and a sense of sacred community.

We dedicate this book to the wonderful congregations who showed us what is possible; to the many more we could have stud-ied but did not; and to the others who will read this book and, we pray, be moved to join the ranks of synagogues that are visionary.

Study Participants

• • •

The interviews for this study were conducted in 2004 at Congregation Beth Am, Los Altos Hills, California, and in 2006 in the remaining congregations. Each interview lasted between one and two hours. The questionnaire we used as a guide appears in appendix B. As we prepared the manuscript for publication we contacted all the interviewees that were quoted, giving them an opportunity, if they wished, to polish up their prose or add a clarifying point.

We would like to thank the following staff members and congregants for giving so generously of their time:

BETH JACOB CONGREGATION
MENDOTA HEIGHTS, MINNESOTA

Rabbi Morris Allen
Stuart Bear
Merril Biel
Michael Blumfield
Suzanne Bring
Ricky Calvin
Susie Drazen
Arielle Ehrlich

Harold Gillman
Laura Honan
Sean Hursten
Jeanine Lange
Louis Newman
Randi Roth
Nina Samuels
Mark Savin
Roseanne Zaidenweber

CONGREGATION AGUDATH ISRAEL
CALDWELL, NEW JERSEY

Claire Axelrod
Randi Kleiman Brokman
Renee Buckler
Cantor Joel Caplan
Rabbi Paula Mack Drill
Irene Edelstein
Rabbi Helaine Ettinger
Karen Frank
Alan Gerberg
Dr. Charles Goldberg
Joyce Musnikow Harris
Andrea Kessler
Abby Landau
Amy Lipsey
Debbie Rabner
Rabbi Alan Silverstein
Rabbi Rebecca Sirbu
Tom Speisman
Susan Werk

CONGREGATION BETH AM
LOS ALTOS HILLS, CALIFORNIA

Amy Asin
Ann DeHovitz
Ina Bauman
Jim Heeger
Teddi Kalb
Mel Kronick
Linda Kurz
Lisa Langer
Rabbi Janet Marder
Daryl Messinger
Eddie Reynolds
Ric Rudman
Susan Wolfe
Rabbi Josh Zweiback

CONGREGATION BETH SHALOM
OVERLAND PARK, KANSAS

Rabbi Alan Cohen
Paul Flam
Kay Grossman
Rabbi Amy Wallk Katz
Joel Krichiver
Devra Lerner
Kay and Jeff Roitman
Linda Salvay
Inge Silverman
Sarah Small
Beth Smith
Josh Sosland
Jeanette Wishna

TEMPLE BETH ELOHIM
WELLESLEY, MASSACHUSETTS

Judy Avnery
Nancy Belsky
Rabbi Sharon Clevenger
Carol Clingan
Marjorie Frieman
Gloria Fox
Michael Gilman
Amy Gorin
Debbie Gottbetter
Ronnie Haas
Rachel Happel
Harold Kotler
Alison Kur
Jack Price
Firkins Reed
David Rokoff
Terry Rosenberg
Rabbi Joel Sisenwine
Jeff Stonberg
Cantor Jodi Sufrin
David Treitsch
Rabbi Alan Ullman

TEMPLE ISRAEL, BOSTON, MASSACHUSETTS

Martha Chason-Sokol
Rabbi Ronne Friedman
Dr. Marshall Ganz
Dale Golden
Steven Goldman
Tanya Goldwyn
Jessica Greenfield

Orit Kent
Idit Klein
Meir Lakein
Lesley Litman
Macey Miller
Rabbi Jeremy Morrison
Susan Moser
Jenny Oser
Leslie Ostrow
Rabbi Jonah Pesner
Karen Victor
Lisa Vinikoor
Rabbi Elaine Zecher

TEMPLE MICAH, WASHINGTON, D.C.

Pearl Bailes
Debra Beland
Peg Blechman
Ted Bornstein
Betsy Broder
Larry Cooley
Matt Cutler
Jodi Enda
Peggy Halpern
Judy Hurvitz
Jan Greenberg
Teddy Klaus
Brenda Levenson
Karen Mark
Marty Prosky
Don and Lynn Rothberg
Dr. Josh Seidman
Celia Shapiro
Amy Shilo

Ellen Sommer
Cantorial Soloist Meryl Weiner
David Wentworth
Rabbi Danny Zemel

WESTCHESTER REFORM TEMPLE
SCARSDALE, NEW YORK

Nancy Alderman
Rabbi Jonathan Blake
Sue Bloom
Bill Blumstein
Rabbi and Cantor Angela Warnick Buchdahl
Wendy Cohen
Cantor Ellen Dreskin
Judy Grosz
Liz Gruber
Sharon Halper
John and Marcy Harris
Rabbi Rick Jacobs
Sherry King
Jerry Koch
Sorel Loeb
Lisa Messinger
Nancy Michaels
Bob Miller
Margie Miller
Jane Nussbaum
Debbie Radov
Karen Segall
Peter Wang

Interview Protocol

$\bullet \; \bullet \; \bullet$

INTRODUCTION

We are conducting research for a book about synagogue transformation. We are interested in exploring the following question: How and why do congregations undertake, implement, and sustain change processes? We are grounding our research in interviews and fieldwork at eight congregations across the country, and we appreciate your help and generosity in sharing recollections of your congregation's change process. We will begin with some introductory questions before moving on to your account of the change process and concluding with some more general impressions of the congregation in the wake of the process. Please be as specific as possible with your answers. Thank you in advance for your cooperation and candor.

INTRODUCTORY QUESTIONS
(CONGREGANTS AND LAY LEADERS)

1. What is your name?
2. How old are you?
3. What do you do professionally?
4. How long have you lived in [this city]?
5. How long have you been a member of [congregation name]?

6. How did you decide to join a congregation?
7. Why did you join *this* congregation [as opposed to another one]?
8. What aspects of congregational life do you value most?

INTRODUCTORY QUESTIONS (PROFESSIONAL LEADERSHIP)

1. What is your name?
2. What is your position at the congregation?
3. How long have you held this position?
4. What drew you to this line of work?
5. What drew you to this congregation?
6. What is your vision for your congregation?
7. What drew you to undertake this change process?
8. What or who were your "aces in the hole"?

QUESTIONS ABOUT THE INTERVENTION PROCESS

1. Please take us back to the beginning of the process and walk us through.
2. When and how did you first hear about this process?
3. How did you get involved in it?
4. Why did you get involved?
5. Had you been involved in congregational leadership prior to this?
6. What was your role in the process?
7. How was the process structured?
    a. Did it involve learning? If so, what texts were central in the process?
    b. Did it involve worship or other spiritual elements?
    c. Did it involved meetings or conversations? If so, what kinds and how were they organized?
8. Where did this process begin for you?
9. What were the first noticeable effects / "low hanging fruit"?

    a. Where were the first effects felt?

    b. What did you do that led to these effects?

10. Were there setbacks / stumbles / mistakes?

    a. What were they?

    b. How did you address them?

11. Was there a moment where you realized "this is working"?

12. Was there vocabulary or terminology that became important to the congregation?

13. What were the moments of resistance to this process?

    a. Where did resistance come from?

14. Were there secondary effects to your work?

    a. Where did you notice them?

15. How was information about the process circulated or shared within the congregation?

16. What role did the professional leadership / clergy play in the process?

17. Who else was involved in this process?

18. How was the process managed?

    a. By whom? (Professionals? Lay leaders? Others?)

19. How long did you remain active in the process?

    a. What constituted your contributions?

20. Why did you stay involved?

IMPRESSIONS AND CONCLUSIONS

1. When is the congregation at its best?

2. How do you think this process changed the congregation?

3. How do you think this process changed you?

    a. Changed your place in the congregation?

4. How has this process changed the congregation's leadership?

5. What did you learn about the congregation through this process?

6. Where do you notice its most long-lasting / deepest effects?

7. Where does change still need to happen?

8. What is next for your congregation?

Notes

◆ ◆ ◆

Chapter 1: Snapshots of Visionary

1. Before the 1980s, Orthodoxy was the default affiliation of many Jews who claimed to be Orthodox because their parents had been. By the 1980s, however, Orthodoxy successfully redefined itself as "Orthodox in practice," resulting in a shriking number who might be termed "Orthodox by default" or "inertial Orthodox."

2. We include in this category those who identify as Conservative, Reform, and Reconstructionist as well as members of Jewish Renewal and unaffiliated synagogues and independent minyanim.

3. These are the local shuls described in chapter 7.

4. Lawrence A. Hoffman, *Rethinking Synagogues: A New Vocabulary for Congregational Life* (Woodstock, VT: Jewish Lights Publishing, 2007, www.jewishlights.com).

5. Isa Aron, *Becoming a Congregation of Learners: Learning as a Key to Revitalizing Congregational Life* (Woodstock, VT: Jewish Lights Publishing, 2000).

6. Diana Butler Bass, *Christianity for the Rest of Us: How the Neighborhood Church Is Transforming the Faith* (San Fransisco: HarperOne, 2006).

7. The study was conducted under the auspices of the now defunct Council for Initiatives in Jewish Education (CIJE); these projects ranged from large and ambitious national efforts like the Experiment in Congregational Education (ECE) and Synagogue 2000 (S2K) to local ones that worked with only a few congregations and had more limited goals.

8. To see how Jim Collins, management consultant and researcher, would tackle this problem, see his monograph *Good to Great and the Social Sectors* (Boulder, CO: Jim Collins, 2005).

9. The type of practice the congregation encouraged varied by denomination and by synagogue.

10. Community building and social justice are discussed together in chapter 6.

CHAPTER 2: A PORTRAIT OF "VISIONARY"

1. Reform synagogues often refer to themselves as *temples*; their Conservative counterparts formally use the term *synagogue*, and informally speak of *shul*; Reconstructionist congregations use a wide range of nomenclature. *Congregation*, though not necessarily the preferred option for any denomination, is widely understood and acceptable by all denominations. In this book *synagogue* and *congregation* are used interchangeably.

2. Hoffman, *Rethinking Synagogues*, 143.

3. Aron, *Becoming a Congregation of Learners*.

4. Hoffman, *Rethinking Synagogues*, 210.

5. These remarks were made at a focus group convened at the congregation.

6. Herbert Gans, "Park Forest: Birth of a Jewish Community," *Commentary*, Vol. II (April 1951), 330–339; "Symbolic ethnicity: The future of ethnic groups and culture in America." *Ethnic and Racial Studies*, 2 (1) (1979), 1–20; "Symbolic ethnicity and symbolic religiosity: Towards a comparison of ethnic and religious acculturation." *Ethnic and Racial Studies*, 17 (4) (1994), 577–592.

7. Will Herberg, *Protestant-Catholic-Jew: An Essay in American Religious Sociology* (Chicago: University of Chicago Press, 1955, 1960, 1983).

8. Charles S. Liebman, *The Ambivalent American Jew* (Philadelphia: The Jewish Publication Society, 1973).

9. Hoffman, *Rethinking Synagogues*.

10. Charles Silberman, *A Certain People: American Jews and Their Lives Today* (New York: Simon & Schuster, 1985); Riv-Ellen Prell, *Fighting to Become Americans: Assimilation and the Trouble Between Jewish Women and Jewish Men* (Boston: Beacon Press, 2000).

11. Charles Silberman, *A Certain People: American Jews and Their Lives Today* (New York: Simon & Schuster, 1985).

12. Wade Clark Roof, *Spiritual Marketplace: Baby Boomers and the Remaking of American Religion* (Princeton, NJ: Princeton University Press, 2001).

13. B. Joseph Pine II and James H. Gilmore, *The Experience Economy: Work is Theater & Every Business a Stage* (Cambridge: Harvard Business School Press, 1999).

14. Steven M. Cohen and Arnold M. Eisen, *The Jew Within* (Indiana University Press, 2000).

15. Resistance to change is itself a subject of extensive academic research and an equally extensive literature in such fields as organizational development and business administration. See the end of chapter 6 for a brief discussion of this literature and some citations.

16. *Studying Congregations: A New Handbook* (Nashville: Abingdon Press, 1998). Excerpt is from Isa Aron, *Becoming a Congregation of Learners: Learning as a Key to Revitalizing Congregational Life* (Woodstock, VT: Jewish Lights Publishing), 268-69.

17. Nancy Ammerman, *Congregations and Community* (New Brunswick, NJ: Rutgers University Press, 1997), 51.

18. Mark Chaves, *Congregations in America*. (Cambridge: Harvard University Press, 2004).

19. Michael Meyer, *Response to Modernity: A History of the Reform Movement in Judaism* (New York: Oxford University Press, 1988).

20. Jackson Carroll and Wade Clark Roof, *Bridging Divided Worlds: Generational Cultures in Congregations* (Hoboken, NJ: Jossey-Bass, 2002). Used by permission of John Wiley & Sons, Inc.

21. Ibid., 89.

22. Marshall Sklare, *Jewish Identity on the Suburban Frontier: A Study of Group Survival in the Open Society* (Chicago: University of Chicago Press, 1979).

23. Charles S. Liebman and Steven M. Cohen. *Two Worlds of Judaism: The Israeli and American Experience* (New Haven: Yale University Press, 1990), 128.

24. Ibid.

25. Riv-Ellen Prell, *Prayer and Community: The Havurah in American Judaism* (Detroit: Wayne State University Press, 1989); Steven M. Cohen and Arnold M. Eisen, *The Jew Within* (Indiana University Press, 2000); B. Horowitz, "Reframing the study of contemporary American Jewish identity," *Contemporary Jewry* (2002), 1–23.

26. Lisa Grant, Diane Schuster, Meredith Woocher, and Steven M. Cohen, *Journey of the Heart and Mind: Transformative Jewish Learning in Adulthood* (New York: Jewish Theological Seminary Press, 2004), 67.

27. Alan Wolfe, *The Transformation of American Religion: How We Actually Live Our Faith* (Chicago: University of Chicago Press, 2005), 26.

28. Steven M. Cohen, "Members and Motives: Who Joins American Jewish Congregations and Why" (Los Angeles: S3K Synagogue Studies Institute, 2006).

CHAPTER 3: VISIONARY WORSHIP

1. C. Kirk Hadaway, Penny Long Marler, and Mark Chaves, "What the Polls Don't Show: A Closer Look at U.S. Church Attendance," *American Sociological Review* (1993).
2. Dick Hebdige, *Subculture: The Meaning of Style* (London: Methuen and Company, 1979).
3. Hoffman, *Rethinking Synagogues*.
4. Wade Clark Roof, Bruce Greer, and Mary Johnson, *A Generation of Seekers* (San Francisco: Harper San Francisco, 1994).
5. Marshall Sklare, *Conservative Judaism* (Glencoe: Free Press, 1955); Lawrence A. Hoffman, *Beyond the Text* (Bloomington: Indiana University Press, 1987).
6. Jules Harlow, "Revising the Liturgy for Conservative Jews," in *The Changing Face of Christian and Jewish Worship in North America* (Notre Dame, IN: University of Notre Dame Press, 1991), 131.
7. Ted Campbell, *Religion of the Heart* (Columbia: University of South Carolina Press, 2001).
8. Robert N. Bellah, Richard Masden, William M. Sullivan, Ann Swidler, and Steven M. Tipton, *Habits of the Heart* (Berkeley: University of California Press, 1986).
9. Donald E. Miller, *Reinventing American Protestantism* (Berkeley and Los Angeles: University of California Press, 1997).
10. Samuel Adler, "Sacred Music in a Secular Age," *Sacred Sound and Social Change* (1993), 289–299; Lawrence A. Hoffman, "Musical Traditions and Tensions in the American Synagogue," *Music and the Experience of God: Concilium* 222 (1989), 30–38; Gershon Silins, [and response by Lawrence A. Hoffman]. "The Discussion of Music in Lawrence A. Hoffman's *The Art of Public Prayer*." *CCAR Journal* 38:3 (1991), 9–19.
11. Lawrence A. Hoffman, "Musical Traditions and Tensions in the American Synagogue," *Music and the Experience of God: Concilium* 222 (1989), 30–38.
12. Kimon Howland Sargeant, *Seeker Churches* (New Brunswick, NJ: Rutgers University Press, 2000); Lawrence A. Hoffman, *Rethinking Synagogues*.
13. Janet Marder, "Worship That Works," *Reform Judaism* 25:3 (Spring, 1997).

14. Rick Warren, *The Purpose Driven Church: Growth without Compromising Your Message and Mission* (Grand Rapids: Zondervan, 1995), 279.

15. Thomas R Cole, *The Journey of Life* (Cambridge, UK: Cambridge University Press, 1992).

Chapter 4: Visionary Learning

1. David Schoem, *Ethnic Survival in America: An Ethnography of a Jewish Afternoon School* (Atlanta: Scholar's Press, 1989), 71.

2. Susan Shevitz, "Communal Responses to the Teacher Shortage in the North American Supplementary School" in *Studies in Jewish Education*, volume 3, ed. Janet Aviad (Jerusalem: Magnes Press, 1988); Isa Aron and Adrianne Bank, "The Shortage of Supplementary School Teachers: Has the Time for Concerted Action Finally Arrived?" *Journal of Jewish Communal Service*, 63 (1987), 264–71.

3. David Schoem, *Ethnic Survival in America: An Ethnography of a Jewish Afternoon School*, (Atlanta: Scholar's Press, 1989); Samuel Heilman, "Inside the Jewish School" in *What We Know About Jewish Education*, ed. Stuart Kelman (Los Angeles: Torah Aura Productions, 1992).

4. New York Bureau of Jewish Education, *Jewish Supplementary Schooling: An Educational System in Need of Change* (New York: Board of Jewish Education, 1988).

5. Jack Wertheimer, *A Census of Jewish Supplementary Schools in the United States* (New York: Avichai Foundation, 2008). http://www.avichai.org (accessed February, 14, 2009).

6. Jeffrey Kress, "Expectations, Perceptions, and Preconceptions: How Jewish Parents Talk about 'Supplementary' Religious Education" in *Family Matters: Jewish Education in an Age of Choice*, ed. Jack Wertheimer (Waltham, MA: Brandeis University Press, 2007).

7. Susan Shevitz and Debbie Karpel, "Sh'arim Family Educator Initiative: An Interim Report of Programs and Populations" (Boston: Bureau of Jewish Education, 1995).

8. Reprinted by permission of the publisher from *Tinkering toward Utopia: A Century of Public School Reform* by David Tyack and Larry Cuban, pp. 85, Cambridge: Mass.: Harvard University Press, Copyright © 1995 by the President and Fellows of Harvard College.

9. Ibid., 107.

10. Michelle Lynn-Sachs, *Inside Sunday School: Cultural and Religious Logics at Work at the Intersection of Religion and Education* (Unpublished doctoral dissertation, NYU, 2007).

11. Nancy Tatom Ammerman, *Pillars of Faith: American Congregations and Their Partners* (Berkeley: University of California Press, 2005), 20.

12. Stuart Schoenfeld, "Ritual and Role Transition: Adult Bat Mitzvah as a Successful Rite of Passage" (paper presented at the Conference of the Network for Research in Jewish Education. Chicago, June, 1989).

13. Howard Gardner, *Multiple Intelligences* (New York: Basic Books, 1993).

14. All three are large (just under or well over one thousand member units), and all are affiliated with the Reform movement. To some extent, this is a result of the way the sample of congregations was chosen, but it also indicates trends in congregational education. Recall that the synagogues selected for this study either participated in one of the change initiatives of the early 1990s or conducted their own change process. The initiative that focused most directly on learning during that period was the Experiment in Congregational Education (ECE), which worked exclusively with Reform congregations. This offers a partial explanation for the predominance of Reform congregations, because only one of the congregations discussed in this chapter participated in the ECE; the other two initiated changes on their own. So to this we must add a second explanation: Conservative congregations have placed a high priority on day schools and therefore may feel less urgency about transforming their religious schools. Indeed, a large proportion of the children who belong to the three Conservative congregations in our study attend day schools. As to the size of the synagogues discussed in this chapter, it is an inescapable fact that successful synagogue transformation usually takes money. The bigger the congregation, the greater its ability to raise funds for new programs.

15. Aron, *Becoming a Congregation of Learners*, 19.

16. Aron, Isa. *The Self-Renewing Congregation: Organizational Strategies for Revitalizing Synagogue Life* (Woodstock, VT: Jewish Lights Publishing, 2002).

17. Howard Gardner, *Multiple Intelligences* (New York: Basic Books, 1993).

18. John Dewey, *Experience and Education* (New York: Collier Books, 1938/1963).

19. Isa Aron, "The Malaise of Jewish Education," *Tikkun* 4, no. 3, (May/June 1989), 32–34.

20. This was during a year that plans were being drawn up for expanding the synagogue.

21. Steven M. Cohen and Arnold M. Eisen, *The Jew Within: Self, Family and Community in America* (Bloomington: Indiana University Press, 2000), 205.

22. Edgar Schein, *Organizational Culture and Leadership* (San Francisco: Jossey-Bass, 1999).

23. Eddie Reynolds, "Process of the Beth Am Educational Task Force" in *A Congregation of Learners: Transforming the Congregation into a Learning Community,* ed. I. Aron, S. Lee, S. Rossel (New York: UAHC Press, 1995).

24. David Fetterman, *Foundations of Empowerment Evaluation* (Thousand Oaks, CA: Sage Publications, 2001).

25. Central Synagogue in New York City has, for a number of years, employed full-time professional educators to teach in the religious school. When not teaching children, these educators write curriculum and run other programs within the synagogue. While a number of other congregations are attempting to replicate this teaching arrangement, only the most affluent synagogues will be able to raise the necessary funds.

26. Adam Gamoran, et. al., *The Teachers Report* (New York: Council for Initiatives in Jewish Education, 1998), 12.

Chapter 5: Visionary Community

1. At the time of this writing.

2. S2K created journey groups, small groups of congregants with similar personal or professional interests to study Jewish approaches to their common interest. They are patterned after Pastor Rick Warren's cellular church model wherein a large corporate church is made more accessible by providing smaller, more intimate opportunities for congregants to gather, meet, study, and interact with one another.

3. At the time of this writing.

Chapter 6: Transformation in Practice

1, Hoffman, *Rethinking Synagogues.*

2. Diana Butler Bass, *Christianity for the Rest of Us.*

3. Arnold Van Gennep, *The Rites of Passage* (Chicago: University of Chicago, 1960 [1907]); Victor Turner, *The Forest of Symbols* (Ithaca: Cornell University Press, 1967), *The Ritual Process* (Chicago: Aldine Publishing Co., 1969).

4. Daniel J. Levinson, *Seasons of a Man's Life* (New York: Ballantine Books, 1978).

5. Aron, *Becoming a Congregation of Learners.*

6. Hoffman, *Rethinking Synagogues.*

7. Gareth Morgan, *Images of Organization* (Newbury Park, CA: Sage Publications, 1986).

8. Ibid.

9. Charles Taylor, *Sources of the Self* (Cambridge: Harvard University Press, 1989), 28.

10. Will Herberg, *Protestant Catholic Jew* (Chicago: University of Chicago Press, 1955), 89.

11. Robert N Bellah, Richard Masden, William M. Sullivan, Ann Swidler, and Steven M. Tipton, *Habits of the Heart* (Berkeley: University of California Press, 1986).

12. Richard Cimino and Don Lattin, *Shopping for Faith* (San Francisco: Jossey-Bass, 1998).

13. Virginia Postrel, *The Substance of Style* (New York: Harper Collins, 2003).

14. Charles Taylor, *The Ethics of Authenticity* (Cambridge: Harvard University Press, 1991).

15. Jim Herrington, Mike Bonem, and James H. Furr, *Leading Congregational Change* (San Francisco: Jossey-Bass, 2000).

16. Warren, *The Purpose Driven Church.*

17. Anne Wilson Schaef and Diane Fassel, *The Addictive Organization* (San Francisco: HarperSanFrancisco, 1988).

18. Jeffrey A. Krames, *Inside Drucker's Brain* (New York: Penguin Portfolio Books, 2008).

19. Lawrence A. Hoffman, "Rabbinic Spiritual Leadership," *CCAR Journal* (2006).

20. Variants of this can be found in the following: Michael Beer, *Organization Change and Development* (Santa Monica: Goodyear, 1980) and Richard Beckhard and Reuben T. Harris, *Organizational Transitions: Managing Complex Change* (Reading, MA: Addison-Wesley, 1987).

CHAPTER 7: TRANSFORMATION IN THEORY

1. Penny Edgell Becker, *Congregations in Conflict* (Cambridge, UK: Cambridge University), 57. Reprinted with the permission of Cambridge University Press.

2. Ibid., 68.

3. Ibid., 83.

4. Ibid., 119.

5. Herbert Gans, "Park Forest: Birth of a Jewish Community," *Commentary* (April 1951).

6. Susan Shevitz, "The Power of Their Commitments: Lessons for the Jewish Community from a Small Synagogue School in Lincolnville" in *Learning and Community: Jewish Supplementary Schools in the 21st Century*, ed. Jack Wertheimer (Boston: University Press of New England, 2009), 47.

7. Samuel Heilman, *Synagogue Life: A Study in Symbolic Interaction* (New Brunswick, NJ: Transaction Publishers, 1998).

8. Shevitz, "The Power of Their Commitments."

9. Heilman, *Synagogue Life*.

10. Becker, *Congregations in Conflict*.

11. Adapted from Becker, *Congregations in Conflict*.

12. The same might be said for Local Shuls because they are not, as institutions, very deliberate or reflective. But since we had no Local Shuls in our study, we cannot document our suspicion.

13. Lee Bolman and Terrence Deal, *Reframing Organizations: Artistry, Choice, and Leadership*, 3rd edition (San Francisco: Jossey Bass, 2003).

14. Edgar Schein, *Organizational Culture and Leadership* (San Francisco: Jossey Bass, 1999).

15. We are beholden to Rabbi Rachel Timoner, who read and critiqued earlier drafts of this chapter, for this formulation.

16. Reprinted by permission of the publishers from *In Over Our Heads: The Mental Demands of Modern Life* by Robert Kegan, p. 302, Cambridge, Mass,: Harvard University Press, Copyright 1994 © by the President and Fellows of Harvard College; Robert Kegan, "What 'Form' Transforms? A Constructive-Developmental Approach to Transformative Learning" in *Learning as Transformation*, ed. Jack Mezirow and Associates (San Francisco: Jossey-Bass, 2000). Used by permission of John Wiley & Sons, Inc.

17. Reprinted by permission of the publisher from *Leadership without Easy Answers* by Ronald Heifetz, p. 20, Cambridge, Mass,: The Belknap Press of Harvard University Press, Copyright 1994 © by the President and Fellows of Harvard College.

18. Ibid., 20.

19. Richard Block, "A Pilgrim's Progress: Educational Reform and Institutional Transformation at Congregation Beth Am" in *A Congregation of Learners: Transforming the Congregation into a Learning Community*, ed. I. Aron, S. Lee, and S. Rossel (New York: UAHC Press, 1995).

20. Thomas Peters and Robert Waterman, *In Search of Excellence: Lessons from America's Best-Run Corporations* (New York: HarperCollins, 1982).

21. Kegan, "What 'Form' Transforms?"

22. Kegan, *In Over Our Heads*, 302.

23. Diane Schuster, "Perceptions of ECE Text Study," unpublished report commissioned by the Experiment in Congregational Education, 1997.

24. Ibid., 8.

25. Ibid., 12.

26. Robert Kegan and Lisa Lahey, *How the Way We Talk Can Change the Way We Work* (San Francisco: Jossey Bass, 2001). Used by permission of John Wiley & Sons, Inc.

27. Ibid., 234.

CHAPTER 8: TRANSFORMATION IN PERSPECTIVE

1. Zachary I. Heller, *Re-envisioning the Synagogue* (Hollis, NH: Hollis Publishing Co., 2005), xi, xv.

2. Terry Bookman and William Kahn, *This House We Build* (Herndon, VA: The Alban Institute, 2007), 363.

3. Steven M. Cohen, Shawn Landres, Elie Kaunfer, and Michelle Shain, "Emergent Jewish Communities and their Participants: Preliminary Findings from the 2007 National Spiritual Communities Study" (New York: Synagogue 3000 and Mechon Hadar).

4. See also, most recently, Zachary Heller's *Synagogues in a Time of Change* (Herndon: Alban Institute, 2009).

5. Edward Kennedy, "Award Announcement," news release, November 15, 2004, John F. Kennedy Library Foundation; http://www.jfklibrary.org/Education+and+Public+Programs/New+Frontier+Award/Award+Recipients/Wendy+Kopp/Award+Announcement.htm (accessed January 21, 2010).

6. Robert Wuthnow, *The Crisis in the Churches: Spiritual Malaise, Fiscal Woe* (New York: Oxford University Press, 1997), vii. Used with permission of the publisher.

7. Ibid., 5.

8. Ibid., 32.

Annotated Bibliography

• • •

CHANGE

Aron, Isa. *The Self-Renewing Congregation: Organizational Strategies for Revitalizing Synagogue Life.* Woodstock, VT: Jewish Lights Publishing, 2002.

Bolman, Lee G., and Terrence E. Deal. *Reframing Organizations: Artistry, Choice, and Leadership.* 3rd ed. San Francisco: Jossey-Bass, 2003. A foundational book for understanding the dynamics of organizations and, by extension, the dynamics of leadership and change.

Heifetz, Ronald A. *Leadership without Easy Answers.* Cambridge, MA: Harvard University Press, 1994. Heifetz distinguishes *technical* problems, which can be solved through purely technical skill, from *adaptive* situations, whose resolution requires new conceptions that challenge conventional wisdom. Most complex organizational problems are adaptive ones; and these, Heifetz argues, require coordinated input from a diverse group of leaders and stakeholders.

Hoffman, Lawrence A. *Rethinking Synagogues: A New Vocabulary for Congregational Life.* Woodstock, VT: Jewish Lights Publishing, 2007. New ways to conceptualize congregational life, arising out of in-depth work with more than one hundred synagogues. Emphasis is on systemic change with the goal of achieving sacred community.

Kegan, Robert. *In Over Our Heads: The Mental Demands of Modern Life*. Cambridge, MA: Harvard University Press, 1994. Kegan argues that the capacity to be self-authoring is what enables individuals to maximize their potential most fully. This level of consciousness also enables leaders to persevere, and even flourish, in times that pose adaptive challenges to their institutions.

Kegan, Robert, and Lisa Laskow Lahey. *Immunity to Change: How to Overcome It and Unlock the Potential in Yourself and Your Organization*. Cambridge, MA: Harvard Business Press, 2009. Extending the theory put forth in Kegan's 1994 book, *In Over Our Heads*, Kegan and Lahey describe a stage that goes beyond self-authoring, which they term "self-transforming." This capacity, they argue, is critical for leaders of "learning organizations," enabling them to step back from and reflect on the limits of their own ideology, personal authority, or both.

COMMUNITY

Brown, Erica. *Inspired Jewish Leadership: Practical Approaches to Building Strong Communities*. Woodstock, VT: Jewish Lights Publishing , 2008. An engaging argument for focusing on communal leadership as a key point for intervention in building and nourishing communities.

Ganz, Marshall. *Why David Sometimes Wins: Leadership, Organization, and Strategy in the California Farm Worker Movement*. New York: Oxford University Press, 2009. A scholarly treatment of a social movement from one of the leading scholars of social justice movements and community organizing. Although it appears to have little to say about congregations, it has everything to say about the relationship between organizing, community, and action.

Jacobs, Jill. *There Shall Be No Needy: Pursuing Social Justice through Jewish Law and Tradition*. Woodstock, VT: Jewish Lights Publishing, 2009. An impassioned argument for Jewish commitments to social justice, rooted strongly in the textual tradition.

Oldenburg, Ray. *The Great Good Place: Cafes, Coffee Shops, Bookstores, Bars, Hair Salons, and Other Hangouts at the Heart of a Community*. New York: Da Capo Press, 1999. An engaging analysis of the relationship between place and community, and an argument for creating places where communities can come together.

Pierce, Gregory F. *Activism That Makes Sense: Congregations and Community Organization*. Skokie, IL: Acta Publications, 1997. A thoughtful and engaged study of the crucial role congregations play in community organizing. Written largely for Christian congregations, the book contains many important lessons for Jews interested in community organizing.

Putnam, Robert D. *Bowling Alone: The Collapse and Revival of American Community*. New York: Simon and Schuster, 2001. A classic text examining the weakening of communities and the institutions that have long nourished them.

Putnam, Robert D., Lewis Feldstein, and Donald J. Cohen. *Better Together: Restoring the American Community*. New York: Simon and Schuster, 2004. A follow-up to Putnam's *Bowling Alone*, *Better Together* offers prescriptions and strategies for reconstituting community.

CONGREGATIONAL STUDIES

Ammerman, Nancy. *Congregation and Community*. Piscataway, NJ: Rutgers University Press, 1996. A study of how congregations manage to sustain communities, despite the threats of such life-changing events as economic collapse, changing congregational values, and population growth or decline.

Bass, Diana Butler. *Christianity for the Rest of Us*. New York: HarperOne, 2006. An important ethnographic survey of mainline denominational churches that demonstrate vitality; akin to the synagogues surveyed on this book. Chapter 12 gives specific attention to worship.

Bass, Diana Butler. *The Practicing Congregation: Imagining a New Old Church*. Herndon VA: Alban Institute, 2004. A reconceptualization of renewed church culture, emphasizing intentionality; a parallel to the strategies recommended here.

Becker, Penny Edgell. *Congregations in Conflict*. Cambridge, UK: Cambridge University Press, 1999. A ground-breaking study of the structure and culture of twenty-three congregations (twenty-one churches and two synagogues) in Oak Park, Illinois. This book posits a typology of four types of congregations (Houses of Worship, Family Congregations, Leader Congregations, and Community Congregations) that serves as the basis for the typology of synagogues in chapter 7.

Carroll, Jackson W., and Wade Clark Roof. *Bridging Divided Worlds: Generational Cultures in Congregations*. San Francisco: Jossey-Bass, 2002. A treatment of churches going through generational change, and a typology that is applicable to synagogue as well.

Chaves, Mark. *Congregations in America*. Cambridge, MA: Harvard University Press, 2004. An important summary of what we know about congregational life, drawn primarily from analysis of the 1998 National Congregational Study (NCS), but with findings and trends that persist well beyond that.

Cohen, Steven M., and Arnold M. Eisen. *The Jew Within: Self, Family, and Community in America*. Bloomington, IN: University of Indiana Press, 2000. The baby boomer generation of American Jews, reflecting wider social patterns in the United States, crystallized around "The Sovereign Jewish Self" as the central approach to being Jewish. In contrast with their parents' and grandparents' generation, who selected their Jewish lifestyle with a measure of guilt, moderately affiliated American Jews in the latter part of the twentieth century felt free to decide when, where, and how to express their Jewishness—with implications for Judaism and congregational life.

Heilman, Samuel C. *Synagogue Life: A Study in Symbolic Interaction*. New Brunswick, NJ: Transaction Publishers, 1998. Congregations are communities. They provide times and spaces for human interaction, and the interweaving of the public and private, the sacred and not-so-sacred. This exploration of interactions among congregants at an urban modern Orthodox congregation details aspects of social life that can occur in any congregation—and probably do.

Morgan, Gareth. *Images of Organization*. Newbury Park, CA: Sage Publications, 1986. Not a study of congregations per se, but a survey of organizational systems that apply directly to the way churches and synagogues conceptualize and organize themselves.

Prell, Riv-Ellen. *Prayer and Community: The Havurah in American Judaism*. Detroit, MI: Wayne State University Press, 1989. The Havurah (religious fellowship) movement of the late 1960s and early '70s both anticipated and influenced later developments in American Jewish congregational life. Among them: the rise of intentionality of community, the emphasis on text, Jewish feminism, the decline in decorum, the expansion of Hebrew, and the shift to a more collaborative rabbinic leadership style. This ethnographic portrait of a pioneering Havurah explores these and other features of this influential development in American Jewish congregational life.

JEWISH WORSHIP

Hoffman, Lawrence A. *The Art of Public Prayer: Not for Clergy Only*. Woodstock, VT: Skylight Paths, 1999. The most widely used congregational resource for worship renewal in synagogues. Separate chapters handle such issues as music, space, prayer wording, and the way worship nowadays competes for attention on the synagogue agenda.

Hoffman, Lawrence A., and Janet Walton, eds. *Two Liturgical Traditions*. Vol. 3, *Sacred Sound and Social Change*. Notre Dame and London: University of Notre Dame, 1993. Proceedings of a conference exploring changing musical taste in church and synagogue against the backdrop of the radical social change that affects religious life in North America today.

Long, Thomas G. *Beyond the Worship Wars: Building Vital and Faithful Worship*. Herndon, VA: Alban Institute, 2001. A widely used treatment of worship change that goes beyond the purely emotional argumentation that usually characterizes congregational debates on the subject.

LEARNING

Aron, Isa. *Becoming a Congregation of Learners: Learning as a Key to Revitalizing Congregational Life*. Woodstock, VT: Jewish Lights Publishing, 2000. Based on the process devised by the Experiment in Congregational Education (ECE; see eceonline. org), this book provides a step-by-step guide to leading a task force to rethink and restructure learning in a synagogue. Both the theory behind the ECE process as well as the text study handouts and facilitation guides it created are included.

Aron, Isa, Sara Lee, and Seymour Rossel, eds. *A Congregation of Learners: Transforming the Congregation into a Learning Community*. New York: UAHC Press, 1995. A collection of essays on the transformation of learning in synagogues. Included are analyses of congregational learning from the perspectives of sociology and anthropology, and firsthand accounts from the earliest efforts at transformation of synagogue education.

Rosenzweig, Franz. *On Jewish Learning*. New York: Schocken, 1962. This collection of essays, which dates back to the early decades of the twentieth century, provided much of the ideological underpinnings for approaches to adult education in the 1980s and 1990s.

Schoenfeld, Stuart. "Folk Judaism, Elite Judaism and the Role of the Bar Mitzvah in the Development of the Synagogue and Jewish School in America." *Contemporary Jewry* 9 (1988): 67–85. An account of how the Jewish educational establishment of the 1930s and 1940s persuaded synagogues to band together to institute requirements for b'nei mitzvah. This led parents, synagogue leaders, and even some educators to construe the primary purpose of congregational education as preparation for the bar mitzvah and bat mitzvah ceremony.

Wertheimer, Jack, ed. *Learning and Community: Jewish Supplementary Schools in the Twenty-first Century.* Waltham: MA, Brandeis University Press, 2009. Eight essays on supplementary schools that "work," based on qualitative studies of these schools.

About the Authors

◆ ◆ ◆

Isa Aron is professor of Jewish education at the Rhea Hirsch School of Education, Hebrew Union College–Jewish Institute of Religion, and was the founding director of the Experiment in Congregational Education, a project of the RHSOE now in its eighteenth year. She is the author of *Becoming a Congregation of Learners and The Self-Renewing Congregation.*

Steven M. Cohen is research professor of Jewish social policy at Hebrew Union College–Jewish Institute of Religion and director of the Berman Jewish Policy Archive at NYU Wagner. With Arnold M. Eisen he wrote *The Jew Within,* and with Charles Liebman he wrote *Two Worlds of Judaism: The Israeli and American Experiences.* His earlier books include *American Modernity & Jewish Identity* and *American Assimilation or Jewish Revival?*

Lawrence Hoffman is the Barbara and Stephen Friedman Professor of Liturgy, Worship and Ritual, and the co-founder of Synagogue 2000 (now Synagogue 3000). For over thirty years, he has taught classes in liturgy, ritual, theology, and synagogue leadership. He has written or edited over 35 books, including *Rethinking Synagogues: A New Vocabulary for Congregational Life,* which is widely used by congregations of all denominations engaged in transformational change.

Ari Y. Kelman is an assistant professor of American studies at the University of California, Davis. He is the author of *Station Identification: A Cultural History of Yiddish Radio* and co-author of a number of influential studies of contemporary Jewish identity, community, and culture.